D1486737

Object-Oriented Data Warehouse Design

Building a Star Schema

William Giovinazzo

ISBN 0-13-085081-0

Prentice Hall PTR
Upper Saddle River, NJ 07458
www.phptr.com

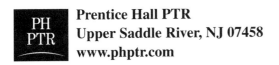

Library of Congress Cataloging-in-Publication Data

```
Giovinazzo, W.A. (William A.)
  Object-oriented data warehouse design: building a star schema / William Giovinazzo.
    p. cm.
  Includes bibliographical references and index.
  ISBN 0-13-085081-0
    1. Data warehousing. 2. Object-oriented programming (Computer science) I. Title.

QA76.9.D37 G56 2000
005.75'85--dc21
                                                                    99-089100
```

Editorial/Production Supervision: *Jan H. Schwartz*
Interior Compositor: *Vanessa Moore*
Acquisitions Editor: *Tim Moore*
Editorial Assistant: *Julie Okulicz*
Marketing Manager: *Bryan Gambrel*
Buyer: *Maura Goldstaub*
Cover Design Director: *Jerry Votta*
Cover Design: *Design Source*

© 2000 Prentice Hall PTR
Prentice-Hall, Inc.
Upper Saddle River, New Jersey 07458

Prentice Hall books are widely used by corporations and government agencies for training, marketing, and resale.
The publisher offers discounts on this book when ordered in bulk quantities.
For more information, contact:
Corporate Sales Department
Prentice Hall PTR
One Lake Street
Upper Saddle River, NJ 07458
Phone: 800-382-3419; Fax: 201-236-7141; E-mail: corpsales@prenhall.com

Product names mentioned herein are the trademarks or registered trademarks of their respective owners.

ArcView® Network Analyst and ArcView® GIS are registered trademarks of ESRI; Informix® is a registered trademark of Informix Corporation; Lotus 123® is a registered trademark of Lotus Development Corporation; Oracle® is a registered trademark of Oracle Corporation; Pentium® is a registered trademark of Intel Corporation; UNIX® is a registered trademark of The Open Group.

Microsoft®, Windows®, Windows NT® and other names of Microsoft products are trademarks or registered trademarks of Microsoft Corporation.

Printed in the United States of America
10 9 8 7 6 5 4 3 2 1

ISBN 0-13-085081-0

Prentice-Hall International (UK) Limited, *London*
Prentice-Hall of Australia Pty. Limited, *Sydney*
Prentice-Hall Canada Inc., *Toronto*
Prentice-Hall Hispanoamericana, S.A., *Mexico*
Prentice-Hall of India Private Limited, *New Delhi*
Prentice-Hall of Japan, Inc., *Tokyo*
Pearson Education Asia Pte. Ltd.
Editora Prentice-Hall do Brasil, Ltda., *Rio de Janeiro*

In Loving Memory

Big Bill Giovinazzo
My Dad, My Hero,

and

Florence Polizzi Giovinazzo,
Whose So Many Sacrifices Were So Little Appreciated.

Contents

Foreword   **xi**

Introduction   **xv**

Chapter 1   **The Data Warehouse**   **1**

1.1   Business Intelligence   2
    1.1.1   The Business of Chess   3
    1.1.2   Business Intelligence   5
1.2   The Data Warehouse   8
    1.2.1   Subject Orientation   12
    1.2.2   Integration   14
    1.2.3   Nonvolatile   18
    1.2.4   Time-Variant Collection of Data   19
    1.2.5   Supporting Management's Decision   20
1.3   Decision Support Systems   21
    1.3.1   Reporting   22
    1.3.2   On-Line Analytical Processing   23

	1.3.3	Data Mining	25
1.4		Summary	30
1.5		Glossary	30

Chapter 2   **Object-Oriented Design**   **35**

2.1		The Development Process	36
	2.1.1	Shortcomings of Waterfall Approach	37
	2.1.2	The Development Spiral	38
	2.1.3	The Advantages of the Development Spiral	41
2.2		Metadata	42
	2.2.1	Types of Metadata	43
	2.2.2	The Central Metadata Repository	45
	2.2.3	Enterprise Data Model	47
2.3		The Objective of Objects	49
	2.3.1	Classes and Superclasses	50
	2.3.2	Aggregations and Behaviors	51
	2.3.3	Modeling Objects	52
	2.3.4	The Advantages of Object Modeling	53
2.4		Summary	55
2.5		Glossary	56

Chapter 3   **Analysis and Design**   **61**

3.1		The Definition Phase	62
	3.1.1	Case Study—Definition Phase	64
3.2		The Analysis Phase	67
	3.2.1	The Interview Process	67
	3.2.2	The Analysis Model	92
3.3		The Design Phase	99
	3.3.1	The Object Model	99
3.4		Summary	124
3.5		Glossary	124

Chapter 4 **The Implementation Model**																	**127**

4.1 Dimensionality																	128
4.2 Dimensionality and Information Systems																	131
    4.2.1 Multidimensional Databases																	133
    4.2.2 Working in Multiple Dimensions																	137
    4.2.3 Multidimensional Database Issues																	143
    4.2.4   Big Brother and the Building Company's Analysis Space 145
4.3 Star Schema																	147
    4.3.1 Working with the Star Schema																	152
    4.3.2   Big Brother and the Building Company's
             Implementation Model																	153
4.4 Summary																	154
4.5 Glossary																	155

Chapter 5   **Dimension Tables—the Nouns of the Data Warehouse 157**

5.1 Dimension-Table Characteristics																	158
5.2 Slowly Changing Dimensions																	160
5.3 Constellations and Conforming Dimensions																	166
5.4 Snowflakes																	170
    5.4.1 Many-to-Many Relationships																	172
    5.4.2 Hierarchies and Aggregations																	173
    5.4.3 Nonanalytical Data																	176
5.5 Dimension of Time																	179
5.6 The Dimensions of BBBC																	181
    5.6.1 Broker Dimension																	182
    5.6.2 Client Dimension																	185
    5.6.3 Commercial Real Estate Company Dimension																	190
    5.6.4 Property Dimension																	196
    5.6.5 Time																	196
5.7 Summary																	203
5.8 Glossary																	203

Chapter 6   **Fact Tables—the Verbs of the Data Warehouse**   **205**

6.1   Fact Tables   206
    6.1.1   Measure By Measure   209
    6.1.2   Precision   211
    6.1.3   Granularity   213
    6.1.4   Additive, Semiadditive, and Nonadditive   215
6.2   Factless Fact Tables   216
6.3   Degenerate Dimensions   218
6.4   Degenerate Facts   218
6.5   Heterogeneous Fact Tables   219
6.6   BBBC Fact Tables   221
6.7   Summary   229
6.8   Glossary   231

Chapter 7   **Implementation Considerations**   **233**

7.1   Parallel Processing   235
    7.1.1   The Perils of Parallelism   235
    7.1.2   The Geometry of Parallelism   236
    7.1.3   The Parallel Nature of the Data Warehouse   241
    7.1.4   Parallel Architectures   246
    7.1.5   Parallel Data Storage   255
    7.1.6   Parallel Databases   263
7.2   Bitmapped Indexing   265
7.3   Star Query Optimization   269
7.4   Summation Tables   271
7.5   Web-Enabled Data Warehousing   275
7.6   The BBBC Data Warehouse   278
7.7   Summary   280
7.8   Glossary   282

Appendix A   **The Spacially Enabled Data Warehouse**   **285**

A.1   Analyzing Patient Needs   291

Appendix B   **Extraction, Transformation, and Loading**   **295**

B.1   The ETL Strategy   296
     B.1.1   ETL Process   300

Appendix C   **Metadata Standards**   **305**

C.1   The Open Information Model   309
C.2   Common Warehouse Metadata   311

Appendix D   **Conventional Wisdom, Tips, Hints,**
                 and General Advice   **315**

Glossary   **327**

Index   **339**

Foreword

In the beginning were applications. Users thought that applications would provide them with information. And insofar as the stated requirements of the applications were concerned, the applications sufficed. But over time the business requirements changed. Keeping the applications in sync with the changing business requirements was a difficult thing to do.

Along the way in trying to keep up with changing requirements, the end users encountered some other limitations to the world of applications. Those limitations were the need for

- integration, and
- historical data.

The applications that the corporation had created or otherwise acquired had no notion of integration. One application thought a customer was one thing. Another application thought a customer was something else. And a third application had yet another interpretation of what a customer was. When it came to the corporate understanding of data, there was—simply stated—no corporate understanding. From a corporate perspective the manager could not answer such basic questions as

- who is a customer?
- what is a product?
- what is a transaction?

In short, the different applications were never designed to work together in an integrated manner.

The second issue was that applications focused inevitably on very current data. Applications could reveal

- how much money a customer had in the bank right now,
- where a shipment was right now,
- what the status of an insurance policy was right now,
- what the quota of a salesperson was right now, and so on.

The applications were designed to keep track of what is going on right now. But when it came to a sense of the need and importance of historical information, the applications treated historical data with no respect at all.

Unfortunately, integration and history represent a very important component of information. And applications simply did not measure up.

The end user's first reaction was to rewrite the applications of yesterday. But this idea quickly fell by the wayside. The end user found that—as far as applications were concerned—the clock could not be turned back. There were simply too many applications, too much undocumented code, too much fragile code, too much complexity to even attempt to roll back the tide of applications.

Thus was born the notion of a data warehouse, an alternative to the dilemma of the end user who needed information but could not impose change on the legacy applications environment.

Like all radical and fresh concepts, the notion of a data warehouse was derided and scorned by the academics and theoreticians. Since the idea of data warehousing had not risen among their ranks, it could not possibly be a valid concept. Today data warehousing is no longer a theory. It is conventional wisdom, and corporations around the world recognize that the road forward leads through the data warehouse.

Data warehousing forms the center of a wide universe. From the corporate data warehouse, with its granular, corporate integrated data, spring many different kinds of decision support activity. The data warehouse forms the basis for such DSS processing as

- data mart, departmental processing,
- simple reporting of corporate information,
- exploration processing,
- data mining,
- operational data stores,
- project warehousing, and so forth.

But data warehousing did not happen all at once. Like a giant jigsaw puzzle, data warehousing has been put together a piece at a time. The world of data warehousing has been led by writers and by practitioners who became writers. These leaders have described from their experience what works and what does not.

Into this realm falls Bill Giovinazzo's book. Its really interesting aspect is that it is

- practical,
- written in language comprehensible to a wide audience, and
- comprehensive.

Based on the reality of data warehousing, Bill Giovinazzo's book is a modern rendition of what you need to know about data warehousing in order to be successful. It strikes a fine balance between theory and practicality. Theories are explained in the cloth of practicality. Rules of thumb and practical realities always have a touch of theory to explain the underlying philosophy.

If you care about success in warehousing, this is the book that belongs on your bookshelf.

W. H. Inmon

Introduction

Why this book? After all, a plethora of books have been written on data warehousing and a number of texts published on star schema design. What does this book offer that is so different?

For an anwser, consider the status of data warehouse projects today. The vast majority of them fail. The percentage of failures may be as high as 70%. These failures, I am convinced, are due not to the inherent nature of data warehousing or decision support, but to the way in which these systems are constructed. We have all heard the stories of analyses with as many as thirty dimensions or dozens of measures. Who could really lay blame for such designs at the feet of the system designer? The fact is that little has been written on the actual design process, despite the flood of ink.

Many books today present schema templates for different industries, assuming that the one schema will pretty much work for any company in that market. One size, however, **does not** fit all. The information needs of every organization are unique as that organization. What does the designer do when the needs of a particular organization deviate from the standard design? How does one derive a design from a set of user needs and desires? These are the questions that this book will answer.

This book presents a software engineering methodology tuned specifically for the design and construction of the data warehouse. Engineering is the application of scientific and mathematical principles to a problem. A methodology is an ordered way of doing things, a procedure. This book presents a procedure for the application of scientific and engineering principles to the construction of the data warehouse. It focuses on the process of how to build something that meets a specific need.

Unfortunately, an awful lot of books have been written about business intelligence. What is unfortunate is that a lot of them are just that, awful. Some texts contain page after page of SQL scripts and descriptions of DBA utilities available in manuals and DBA guides. Others are theoretical edicts that are of little functional value. My goal has been to create something unique, something of real value—a substantive work that gives *data warehouse architects* a practical set of tools—a methodology that they can take and apply to their individual projects—something to turn the 70% failure rate into a 70% success rate.

I have used two examples throughout this book. The first is our *scratch* project, an auto dealership. I will use it throughout to demonstrate different aspects of the methodology or the star schema. The second is our case study, a commercial real estate company. We will use this company to develop our methodology, taking the project from the initial analysis all the way to the implementation model. This company does not represent any one organization but is a composite of many companies in which I have been personally involved.

While the examples in this book focus on the application of business intelligence to marketing, remember that business intelligence can be applied to any business process. Many decision support systems have been implemented to examine processes that are internal and unrelated to *touching* the client.

Finally, I must acknowledge all those kind and wonderful people who have assisted me in preparing this work. First is Jane Boies. She is not only a mentor and guide but also a true and valued friend. Without Jane's help, this book would be something much less than it is. Mike Schmidt, too, has contributed greatly to the quality of this work. I appreciate his patience in keeping me on the right path. I hope to someday be as skilled and knowledgeable as he. I must also thank Bill Inmon. When I first cut my teeth in this industry and read his landmark book *Building the Data Warehouse*, I would never have even dreamed that he would read anything I might write on the subject, much less contribute to it. I am very grateful for his help. Last of all I need to thank Tonoose Dimeo, my oldest and dearest friend, who once described my writing career as "the best collection of rejection notices he has ever read." Thank you. I truly appreciate all of you and what you have done to support this effort.

William Giovinazzo

CHAPTER 1

The Data Warehouse

This book presents an engineering methodology for the design of a data warehouse. The data warehouse is not an end to itself. It is actually part of an overall structure, or more appropriately an infrastructure—Business Intelligence (BI). The BI structure includes the data warehouse or data mart, On-Line Analytical Processing (OLAP), and data mining. Before delving into the depths of data warehouse design, we will examine the BI structure in which it resides.

Figure 1–1 presents the Business Intelligence loop. Data from the outside world flows into this loop through the operational environment. This data contains information about customers, suppliers, competitors, products, and the organization itself. As data enters the warehouse, it is cleansed and transformed to meet certain standards of quality and format of the data within the warehouse. It is then stored in some central repository. This central repository can be either a multidimensional or a relational database. The extraction, cleansing, transformation, and storage of data are the data warehouse/data mart portion of the business intelligence loop. The second section of this chapter will look at the data warehouse in detail.

Decision Support Systems (DSS) are the next step in the loop. Decision Support Systems retrieve the data and present it to the business strategist. DSS actually meets a spectrum of needs extending from simple reporting through OLAP to data mining. While traditionally DSS is viewed as retrieving data from the data warehouse or data mart, many products are now being offered that feed directly off the operational environment. Typically they do this by creating an internal intermediate storage area. We will examine DSS in the third section of this chapter.

Business Intelligence is the entire loop shown in Figure 1–1. BI brings the information stored in the data warehouse and discovered through DSS back into the operational environment. The human element, the business strategist, is integral to this loop. Section 1.1 will examine Business Intelligence more closely as well as its importance to the organization.

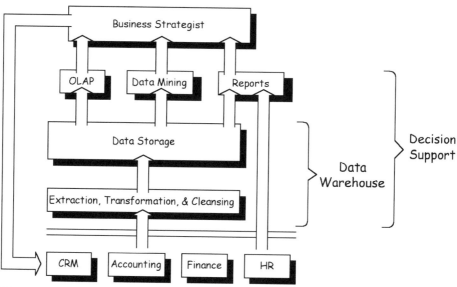

Figure 1–1   Business Intelligence loop.

1.1 Business Intelligence

Any discussion of Business Intelligence must begin with the primary question *why*. What is the purpose of the BI? The justification of any project is the benefit it brings to the organization. What benefits are derived from BI? The answers to these questions lie not in a spreadsheet, but in the context of the organization in which these systems exist. In the not too far distant past one might have argued that BI provided a sustainable competitive advantage. This is no longer the case. There has been such a proliferation of DSS in the past few years that BI could be considered no more of an advantage than an e-mail system or a local area network. It would be more accurate to say that the lack of BI is an enormous competitive disadvantage. The organization without it will be outmaneuvered, outmarketed, and outsold by the competition time and time again.

DSS is a strategic weapon. It is a weapon the organization wields in the marketplace to gain advantage over its opponents. The infrastructure of an organization lacking a data warehouse cannot support the strategic use of the data hidden within its information systems. The thinking of such organizations is doomed to be shallow and reactionary. Organizations with a data warehouse as part of their competitive arsenal will inevitably beat those who lack one.

1.1.1 The Business of Chess

Organisms continually confront the question: *what shall I do next?* The answer differs for the Arctic bear, African lion, and Asian tiger. For each, the answer is part of an overall method of survival based on the context in which the animal exists. Each has adapted its overall survival strategy to its environment. As we shall see, organizations are like these animals. They must continually decide what to do in their environment. The organizations that do more than just survive—those that thrive—do so by employing a strategy.

Modern man is greatly removed from the struggle to survive. Few think strategically. Most people and organizations are *"interrupt driven;"* the most pressing or painful issue of the moment receives the greatest attention. New markets are quickly entered and exited with little or no regard for any strategy other than AFAB (Anything For A Buck). One day the Internet is in vogue, so investments are made in the Internet. The next day the Decision Support market looks like a good place to dump a few boxes, and after a few weeks that market is abandoned. This is hardly strategic thinking.

The classic example of strategic thinking is chess. It demonstrates all the basic characteristics of strategy. The objective is simple and clear: capture your opponent's king. All of your resources are focused on that one key objective. Anything that does not advance this cause is dross. What makes chess interesting, and ultimately all strategic encounters, is the element of conflict. While you are trying to capture your opponent's king, he is trying to capture yours. As one tries to attain a goal, another is trying to prevent him from doing so. The conflict progresses with every move, and the opponents modify their tactics to meet the changing environment. The strategy, however, *should* remain intact.

In applying this to the business world, the mission statement defines the objectives of an organization. The very point of the mission statement is to communicate the purpose and objective of the organization to managers and personnel. The mission statement provides the vision and direction needed to motivate employees toward a common goal. Just as in chess, where the resources focus on capturing the king, the mission statement guides management in mustering resources towards the common objective. In the business world, of course, there is always something that opposes the achievement of that goal.

The environment in both chess and business is far from static. There is a constant change, and strategies adapt to this change. The classic image of a chess match is of two combatants sitting quietly, studying the position of every piece on the board and trying to anticipate their opponent's next move. The chess master prepares by studying the past moves of his or her opponent along with those of past masters. The master uses this data to anticipate his opponent's strategy. Moves that are made reveal strategies, and competing strategies adapt to meet developments.

In the business world the chess master is the *business strategist*, who is any person responsible for defining the strategy of some part of an organization. From department managers to the CEO, each has responsibility for plotting the course in a particular domain. It is a mistake to think of business intelligence in terms only of sales and marketing. Although the examples in this book deal with marketing issues, strategy applies to every decision made by an organization. Business strategists can be found everywhere—in purchasing, on the shop floor, in support, and even in finance.

These levels in the organization differ only in scope. As we shall soon see, this difference drives a difference in their information needs.

The business strategist looks for behaviors in the organization's environment. A behavior is a repeatable response to an external stimulus. What does my opponent do in response to a particular type of sales strategy or market condition? What actions can manufacturing take when the quality of raw materials is marginally acceptable? Although we have used the metaphor of chess and conflict, we look to other behaviors besides those of an organization's opponents. The behaviors the business strategist seeks to understand relate to the nouns of the business environment—the persons, places, and things of the business. Examples of business nouns include customers, prospects, products, sales, geographic regions, and distribution methods. The chess master tries to predict five, ten, fifteen moves out. The business strategist tries to predict the behavior of the business nouns in the next, the next two, or even the next four fiscal periods. As we shall see in the next section of this chapter, this approach has enormous implications in the design and construction of the data warehouse.

In chess, all participants see the entire chessboard. The metaphor starts to break down at this point. There are no surprise attacks in chess, only the failure to anticipate. The business environment is full of unknowns. New products and competitors constantly enter and exit the marketplace, each lacking the courtesy to notify you of its complete plans and intentions. In such an environment, information becomes a precious commodity—a very precious commodity.

The value of accurate and complete business information makes the Information Technology (IT) department a vital partner in the development of any and all corporate strategies. This partnership places a particularly awesome burden on the shoulders of those responsible for the corporate information infrastructure. How can they provide information easily and quickly to perhaps their most important customers, the business strategists?

1.1.2 Business Intelligence

In 1575 the Spanish physician Juan Huarte defined intelligence as the ability to learn, to exercise judgment, and be imaginative. One can extend this definition of intelligence to include the ability to think abstractly, to be able to organize volumes of information and reason. Business intelligence, therefore, implies thinking abstractly about the organization, reasoning about the business, organizing large quantities of information about the business environment. The development of a strategy requires that the business strategist takes a set of facts and creates something new. This is the very essence of business intelligence. The sheer size of most organizations, however, requires the presence of an information infrastructure to facilitate this level of intelligent thought.

Recalling the analogy between organisms and organizations, we see that intelligence within an organism is facilitated by the central nervous system. The central nervous system of an organization is the information infrastructure. Consider the similarities. The central nervous system receives information from the outside world and transmits that information to the brain. The brain processes the information and directs instructions for behavior to the rest of the organism. In the organization, the information infrastructure receives data from the outside world as transactions. Some server receives the transactions and takes appropriate action. If the transaction is a purchase, orders may be filled and customers billed.

The human brain is composed of three distinct concentric layers. The innermost layer is the oldest; it controls the automatic biological functions. These are the things that we do not think about, such as digesting, breathing, or sleeping. Often this innermost layer is referred to as the reptilian brain. The second layer controls the emotions; this is the limbic system. The third layer, the new brain, is where the thinking is done. This is the cerebral cortex. The cerebral cortex carries out such functions as observing, organizing, and responding.

In scanning the business world, we see that organizations have evolved to varying levels. Organizations that have only operational systems are at the lowest rung of the evolutionary ladder; they function only with a reptilian brain. Parts of the organization will signal when there is pain or pleasure. The operational system receives the stimulus and passes it on. For example, when stock levels fall too low, certain parts register hunger, and the organization reacts by ordering more stock. When sales exceed expectations, certain parts register pleasure, and payroll cuts bonus checks. Organizations with purely operational systems are unable to make meaningful information out of the volumes of data locked within these systems.

Some companies have evolved to the level of the limbic system. These companies are often worse off than those at the reptilian level. Limbic companies are continually buffeted by market forces, reacting and overreacting to events in the marketplace. Earnings drop a cent per share, and a hundred people lose their jobs. Six months later a new promising market opens, and a hiring frenzy commences. Organizations in this mode are emotional companies. Strategy cannot exist in this environment. They don't shape their market; rather, the market shapes them. They optimize the stock price—often at the expense of the long-term health of the company. The information systems of these organizations provide some analytical capabilities, but they produce only a snapshot of the current environment. The picture is seen in the context of past or projected future events.

The new brain, the cerebral cortex, is the thinking brain. This is where the capacity to think abstractly exists. It is where reasoning occurs and vast quantities of information are organized into meaningful systems. In the information infrastructure, the data warehouse is the part that transforms volumes of information into something meaningful. Within the warehouse is a detailed history of past experiences. DSS tools allow the strategist to find patterns in these experiences for comparison to the current situation. In this way, the strategist can better predict the future.

So, why does an organization need business intelligence? In order to survive, the organization must develop a strategy. In order to develop a winning strategy, one must be able to anticipate future conditions. Understanding the past is the best way to be able to predict the future. For this reason, information is the meat upon which a strategy feeds. The decision support system is one eye through which the business strategist can look out on the organization's environment and see behaviors amidst the havoc. The next section contrasts the data warehouse with operational systems. Here we shall see why operational systems cannot fulfill the needs of the business strategist.

1.2 The Data Warehouse

The previous section discussed the unique purpose of business intelligence. This section will describe how the data warehouse, the heart of the business intelligence loop, supports this purpose. We will define a data warehouse and identify each of its components. We have observed that the warehouse sits outside the operational environment, receives its data from it, and provides a central repository for strategic information—information that will be used as a basis for business strategy.

The data warehouse, then, is a system sitting apart from the operational environment feeding off it. What exactly does this system consist of, though? The very term *data warehouse* evokes images of large buildings of corrugated metal, where dingy yellow forklifts loaded with crates of information scurry between bare steel girders. To the computer literate, a nebulous vision arises of big computers with petabytes of disk drives, associated with some sort of on-line archive of operational data. In this idealized world, users magically fly through volume upon volume of information, rooting out that one item that will make all the difference.

The situation brings to mind the old story of the blind men and the elephant. One man felt the legs and thought the elephant was like a tree, while another felt the trunk and thought it was like a snake. Finally a third felt the tail and thought it was like a vine. In a similar fashion, each view of the data warehouse grasps some element of the truth while missing the overall picture. It is true that data moves data from the operational environment to the warehouse, but the warehouse is more than an archive. It is also true that the warehouse contains large volumes of data, but the central repository where the data is stored is only part of the overall warehouse. The key to understanding the data warehouse is seeing how the parts interact with one another—a Gestalt, if you will, of the data warehouse. This is clearly a case where the whole is greater than the sum of the parts. Figure 1–2 shows each of these parts and its place in the warehouse.

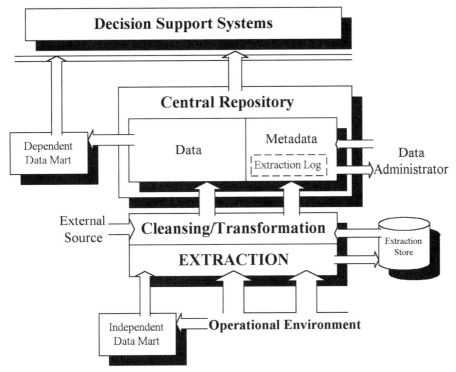

Figure 1–2 Data warehouse.

Let us follow the path that data takes from the operational environment to the business strategist. The following list describes this flow.

1. **Operational Environment**—The operational environment runs the day-to-day activities of the organization. Such systems as order entry and accounts payable and receivable reside within the operational environment. These systems collectively contain the raw data that describes the *current* state of the organization.

2. **Independent Data Mart**—A common misconception is that a data mart is a small data warehouse. The actual difference between them is scope. The data mart focuses on an individual subject area within the organization, the data warehouse on the entire organization. An independent data mart receives data from

external sources and the operational environment, independent of any data warehouse.

3. **Extraction**—The extraction engine retrieves/receives data from the operational environment. The extraction process can occur in a variety of ways. The warehouse can be the passive recipient of data from the operational environment, or it may actively take data from the operational environment. Transportable tables and data replication are examples of alternative techniques for moving data into the warehouse.

4. **Extraction Store**—Data received from the operational environment must be *scrubbed* before it is incorporated into the data warehouse. The extraction store holds the extracted data while it is awaiting transformation and cleansing. One might say that it is the Ellis Island of data warehousing.

5. **Transformation/Cleansing**—*Scrubbing* consists of data transformation and cleansing. Data transformation is the process of converting data from different systems and different formats into one consistent format. Cleansing is the process of removing errors from the data. Refer to Section 1.2.4, "Data Integration," for more information on these processes.

6. **Extraction Log**—As the operational data is integrated into the data warehouse, an extraction log is maintained to record the status of the extraction process. This log is actually part of the data warehouse's metadata and is critical in maintaining data quality. It will serve as input to the Data Administrator to verify the quality of the data integrated into the warehouse.

7. **External Source**—Data originating from outside the organization is also included in the data warehouse. It might comprise stock market reports, demographic data, interest rates, or other economic information. An external source could also provide metadata such as SIC codes.

8. **Data Administrator**—The Data Administrator ensures the quality of the data in the warehouse. It should not be confused with the data**base** administrator. The database administrator is responsible

for the operation of the system that supports the data warehouse. The data administrator is the team member responsible for the quality of the data within the warehouse. One of the responsibilities of the data administrator is to review the extraction log searching for changes in metadata, inaccurate data from the operational environment, or even data errors generated by the operational system. The data administrator will take the necessary corrective actions, such as making changes to metadata repository, correcting erroneous data, or notifying operations of programming errors.

9. **Central Repository**—The central repository is the cornerstone of the data warehouse architecture. This central location stores all the data and metadata for the data warehouse.

10. **Metadata**—This is *data about data*. One way to describe metadata is that it provides the context of the data. It describes what kind of information is stored, where it is stored, how it is encoded, how it relates to other information, where it comes from, and how it is related to the business. Metadata also contains the business rules of the data, in essence the use of the data within the organization.

11. **Data**—The data store contains the raw data of the data warehouse. The central data store can be either a multidimensional database or a relational database system. The structure of this data and how this structure is designed is the focus of this book.

12. **Dependent Data Mart**—Unlike an independent data mart, a dependent data mart relies on the data warehouse as the source of its data.

This description of the warehouse, however, just examines the parts. It does not provide us with a complete picture. Let us take a moment to look at the data warehouse as a complete entity; i.e., let's look at the forest before we start to study the trees. Almost everything written on data warehousing begins with the obligatory and often verbose comparison between the data warehouse and the transaction-oriented operational world. Despite Emerson's disparagement of consistency, we follow this precedent, because contrasting these two environments does clarify some of the most important characteristics of the data warehouse.

W. H. Inmon defines the data warehouse as *"a subject oriented, integrated, nonvolatile, time variant collection of data in support of management's decisions."*[1] I find this definition to be most clarifying, in that it highlights the most vital features of the warehouse. In the next few subsections we will discuss each of these features and how they differ from those of the operational world.

1.2.1 Subject Orientation

Inmon's first characteristic of a data warehouse is *subject orientation*. Section 1.1.2 discusses the nouns of the business and their behaviors. These business nouns are the subjects of the data warehouse. The operational environment focuses its attention on the day-to-day transactions that are part of the normal operation of the business. The data warehouse is concerned with the **things** in the business environment that are driving those transactions. Figure 1–3 shows the difference in data orientation. This difference has far-reaching effects on the entire system.

The transaction-oriented system structures data in a way that optimizes the processing of transactions. These systems typically deal with many users accessing a few records at a time. For reasons too numerous to discuss here, minimizing record and table size improves overall system performance. System architects *normalize* transaction databases to structure the database in an optimal way. Although a complete discussion of normalization is outside the scope of this book, it is sufficient to note that data pertaining to a specific subject is distributed across multiple tables within the database. For example, an employee works in a department that is part of a division. The employee, department, and division information is all related to the subject employee, yet it will be stored in separate tables.

---

1. W. H. Inmon, *Building the Data Warehouse*, Wiley-QED, 1992, 1993.

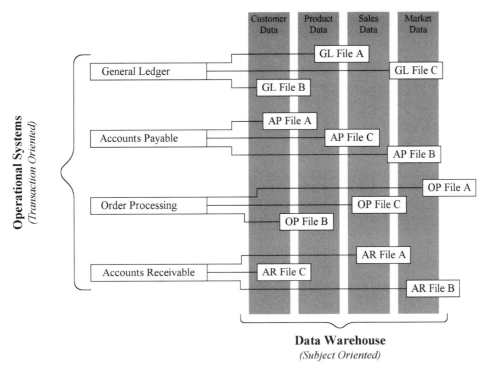

Figure 1–3 Data orientation.

Operational data is distributed across multiple applications as well as tables within an application. A particular subject may be involved in different types of transactions. A customer appearing in the Accounts Receivable system may also be a supplier appearing in the Accounts Payable system. Each of these systems has only part of the customer data. We are back to the blind men and the elephant. Nowhere is there a single consolidated view of the one organization.

Considering the way in which the business strategist uses the data, this structure is very cumbersome. First, the business strategist is interested in the behavior of business subjects. To get a complete picture of any *one* subject the strategist would have to access many tables within many applications. The problem is even more complex. The strategist is not interested in a single occurrence of a subject, an individual customer, but in all occurrences of a subject, all customers. As one can easily see, retrieving this data in real time from many disparate systems would be impractical.

The warehouse, therefore, gathers all of this data together into one place. The structure is such that all the data for a particular subject is contained within one table. In this way, the strategist will be able to retrieve all the data pertaining to a particular subject from one location within the data warehouse. This greatly facilitates the analysis process, as we shall see later. The task of associating subjects with actions to determine behaviors will be much simpler.

1.2.2 Integration

The difference in the orientation of the data drives the need to gather the data together into one place. The warehouse, however, does more than gather the data. In a sense, it derives its data from the operational environment. The operational data is the basis of the warehouse. The integration process forms it into a single cohesive environment. The origin of the data is invisible to the business strategist in this environment. The integration process consists of two tasks, data transformation and data cleansing (Figure 1–4).

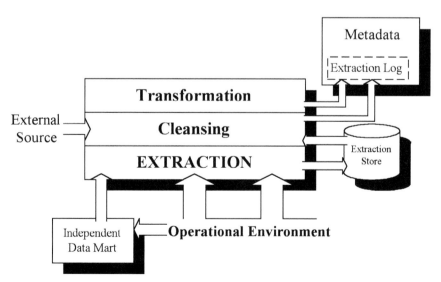

Figure 1–4 Data integration.

1.2.2.1 *Data Cleansing*

Data cleansing is the process of removing errors from the input stream and is part of the integration process. It is perhaps one of the most critical steps in the data warehouse. If the cleansing process is faulty, the **best** thing that can happen is that the business strategist will not trust the data and the warehouse will fail. If that's the best thing, what could be worse? The worst thing is that the warehouse could provide bad information and the strategist could trust it. This could mean the development of a corporate strategy that fails. The stakes are indeed high.

A good cleansing process, however, can improve the quality not only of the data within the warehouse but of the operational environment as well. The extraction log records errors detected in the data cleansing process. The data administrator in turn examines this log to determine the source of the errors. At times, the data administrator will detect errors that originated in the operational environment. Some of these errors could be due to a problem with the application or something as simple as incorrect data entry. In either case, the data administrator should report these errors to those responsible for operational data quality. Some errors will be due to problems with the metadata. Perhaps the cleansing process did not receive a change to the metadata. Perhaps the metadata for the cleansing process was incorrect or incomplete. The data administrator must determine the source of this error and take corrective action. In this way, the data warehouse can be seen as improving the quality of the data throughout the entire organization.

There is some debate as to the appropriate action for the cleansing process to take when detecting errors in the input data stream. Some purists feel the warehouse should not incorporate records with errors. The errors in this case should be reported to the operational environment, where they will be corrected and then resubmitted to the warehouse. Others feel that the records should be corrected whenever possible and incorporated into the warehouse. Errors are still reported to the operational environment, but it is their responsibility to take corrective action. The concern is making sure that the data in the warehouse reflects what is seen in the operational environment. A disagreement between the two environments could lead to a lack of confidence in the warehouse.

The cleansing process cannot detect all errors. Some errors are simple and honest typographical mistakes. Some are more nefarious and will challenge the data administrator. For example, one system required the entry of the client's SIC code for every transaction. The sales reps did not really care and found two or three codes that would be acceptable to the system. They entered these stand-by codes into the transaction system whenever the correct code was not readily available. These codes were then loaded into the data warehouse during the extraction. Errors such as these make it clear that, though many tools are available on the market to assist in cleansing the data as it comes into the warehouse, no software product can get them all.

Data cleansing is the child of the data administrator, an essential player on the data warehouse team. The data administrator must take a proactive role in rooting out errors in the data. While no one component will guarantee the success of a data warehouse, some will ensure its failure. A poor cleansing process or a torpid data administrator is definitely a key to failure.

1.2.2.2 Data Transformation

Rarely does one encounter operational environments where data is consistent between applications. In a world of turnkey systems and best-of-breed heterogeneous environments, it would be more surprising to see data consistency than not. Data transformation addresses this issue. The data transformation process receives the input streams from the different operational systems and transforms them into one consistent format.

The sheer task of defining the inconsistencies between operational systems can be enormous. Table 1–1 demonstrates the different types of integration challenges facing the data warehouse architect. The table shows that as each new source of data is identified, the complexity of the integration process increases. Each system contributing to the data warehouse must be analyzed to understand both the data elements that are of interest and the format of these elements. Once these elements have been selected and defined, an integration process must be defined that will provide consistent data.

Table 1–1   Integration Issues

	Sales Voucher	Purchase Order	Inventory
Description	Customer Name— I.B.M.	Customer Name— IBM	Customer Name— International Business Machines
Encoding	Sex— 1 = Male 2 = Female	Sex— M = Male F = Female	Sex— X = Male Y = Female
Units	Cable Length— Centimeters	Cable Length— Yards	Cable Length— Inches
Format	Key— Character (10)	Key— Integer	Key— pic '999999999'

Table 1–1 presents some basic issues concerning data integration. Let's look at each of these in detail:

1. **Description**—This can be the most heinous of all integration issues. How does one determine that the three names presented in the table represent the same client? The transformation process must take each of these different descriptions and map it to a specific customer name.

2. **Encoding**—There are four types of scales:[2] nominal, ordinal, interval, and ratio. When discussing encoding, we are concerned with a nominal scale. This is the simplest of all four scales. A number or letter is assigned as a label for identification or classification of that object. When integrating this data, map the input scales to the data warehouse scale.

---

2. A scale is defined as any series of items, progressively arranged according to value or magnitude, into which an item can be placed according to its quantification.

3. **<u>Units of Measure</u>**—Integration of units of measure can be deceptive. While it may seem at first that it would be a simple mathematical calculation, issues such as precision must be considered.

4. **<u>Format</u>**—The originating operational systems may store data in a variety of formats. The same data element may be stored as character in one system and numeric in the next. As in the integration of all data elements, consider the ultimate use of the data within the warehouse.

One final note on the transformation process: do not underestimate the task of defining an enterprise data format. It is necessary to get consensus on any format. The unfortunate truth is that when more than one person is involved in a decision, there are politics involved. Surprisingly, data elements can become highly controversial and highly political topics. Forewarned is forearmed. When defining data elements, expect political battles.

1.2.3 Nonvolatile

A major difference between the data warehouse and transaction-oriented operational system is volatility. In the operational environment data is volatile; it changes. In the data warehouse, however, once the data is written, it remains unchanged as long as it is in the warehouse. Figure 1–5 demonstrates the difference between the two system types as it relates to volatility. We begin on Monday. The quantity on hand for product **AXY** is 400 units. This is recorded in the inventory system in record XXX. During the Monday extraction, we store the data in the warehouse in record ZZZ. Tuesday's transactions reduce the quantity on hand to 200. These updates are carried out against the same record XXX in the inventory system. That night during the extraction process the new quantity is extracted and recorded in a completely separate data warehouse record YYY. The previous ZZZ record is not modified.

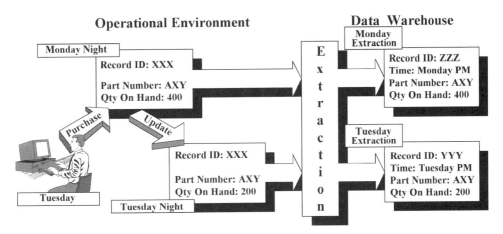

Figure 1–5   Data volatility.

In essence, the nonvolatility of the data warehouse creates a *virtual* read-only database system. No database can literally be a read only. Somehow, at some time, data must be stored in the database. The data warehouse does this in bulk. An extraction adds new records to the database; detail records already in the database are not modified. One challenge of a transaction-processing system is that multiple users attempt to read and write to the same records, causing the database to lock records. This is not a concern in the data warehouse, since users only read the data.

The database engine itself benefits from the nonvolatile nature of the data warehouse. While it is still critical that appropriate backup procedures be in place for the central repository, the database can eliminate many background processes used for recovery. For example, databases generally keep a *redo log*. These logs allow database administrators to return the database to its proper state after instance failure. Since updates are not being made against the data warehouse, there is no need to run this process.

1.2.4 Time-Variant Collection of Data

The nonvolatility of the data within it adds another *dimension* to the data warehouse, that of time. If one were able to extract all the data from the operational systems in one specific moment in time, it would create a snapshot of the state of the organization. The warehouse in essence does this. At specified intervals, the warehouse takes a snapshot of the operational environment. The snapshots stored in the warehouse become frames on a roll of film, and this renders a movie. Time is not a variable for a snapshot; it is static. In a movie, however, time becomes a variable. The film can be run in whatever direction at whatever speed the viewer may wish.

The data warehouse is like the movie described above. The business strategist can view the data across the field of time at whichever level of detail he or she may wish. This allows viewing patterns and trends over time. Time has become one variable that the analysis can manipulate. In short, the data warehouse is time variant.

1.2.5 Supporting Management's Decision

The first section of this chapter discussed the strategic mission of the data warehouse. Calling upon this understanding, we see yet another difference between the data warehouse and the operational environment. The typical operational system is some automation of a manual process. The user community, therefore, is typically involved in the lines of production. As we said earlier, the data warehouse user is the business strategist. The strategist is any individual within an organization responsible for the strategy of any part of the organization. This includes product managers, marketing, department managers, and even CEOs!

It is very important that the actual business strategist interacts with the data. Management can no longer be satisfied to act as the passive recipient of static reports generated by the IT department. The average IT professional lacks the business acumen of the business strategist. When the strategist examines data, he or she will see things that will lead to further inquiries. Some of these keys will be more overt than others; some may even be recognized by a *sixth sense* on the part of the strategist. Static reports will not answer these inquiries, neither can the IT professional be expected to anticipate what questions may be asked. Regardless of the cause, the business strategist must be the main user.

The data warehouse architect must keep this difference in user communities in mind when building the system. It is critical that the system renders the appropriate performance to allow the business strategist to interact with the data in a timely and efficient manner. The user interface must also be designed to allow the business strategist to explore the data within the warehouse. The challenge for the business strategist should be understanding the data, not retrieving the data from the system.

1.3 Decision Support Systems

One could loosely define DSS as the presentation layer of the data warehouse. It is important, however, to emphasize the word *loosely*. When we discuss DSS, we are looking at more than just the presentation of the data within the warehouse. As shown in Figure 1–1, DSS extends from the extraction of the data through the warehouse to the presentation of that data to the business strategist. To classify these tools as mere presentation vehicles would greatly undervalue them. These systems come in a variety of flavors, each meeting different needs within the organization.

Earlier we noted that business strategists exist at every level from the department manger all the way up to the CEO. Each has unique information requirements. The higher one moves up in the organizational structure, the higher the level of data summarization he or she requires on a daily basis. There are different categories of DSS tools to meet the requirements of each of these different levels. Figure 1–6 shows the spectrum of DSS tools.

At the most rudimentary level, one could consider *reporting* to be a certain level of DSS. Comparatively speaking, reporting involves a passive consumption of data. This does not relegate it to the mere production of static green-bar reports; today's reporting systems are much more than that, as we discuss below. The next level of DSS is analytical; this is filled by *OLAP* (On-Line Analytical Processing) tools, which allow the business strategist to interact with the data. *Data mining* extends this interaction to a level of discovery. This is where new behaviors within the data are unearthed and explored.

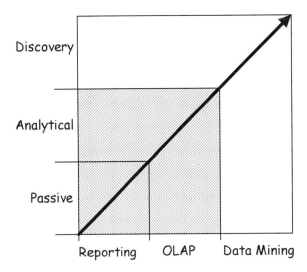

Figure 1–6   DSS spectrum.

1.3.1 Reporting

Though it is often not recognized as a decision support system, reporting fills an important role. As we said earlier, the higher the level of the business strategist in the organization, the higher the level of summarization required. Today most higher levels of management are not interested in *interacting* with data; rather, they are interested in simple *dashboards*—systems that will display leading key indicators of an organization's health. While the rise of younger, more technically astute management to corporate leadership may change this, most corporate leaders today are more than happy to receive simple reports. While *they* may see them as simple reports, however, there is nothing *simple* about reporting.

If an organization's initial foray into DSS is reports based, the data warehouse architect must think beyond simple static green-bar reports and move on to the overall enterprise. Enterprise-class reporting in today's world should simplify the creation, maintenance, and distribution of reports. The enterprise reporting tool should make it as easy as possible to get the data to whoever may require it. For this reason an enterprise reporting tool should have the following capabilities:

1. **Rapid Development**—The tool should have wizardlike capabilities that walk the developer through the creation of the report. The tool should also allow the developer within the development environment to view the report exactly as it will be seen.

2. **Easy Maintenance**—The user should be able to go back to the wizards with which the report was created to make modifications.

3. **Easy Distribution**—The report engine should be able to direct the same report or portion of a report to different media. For example, a portion of a report could be posted to a Web site, another section sent to management via e-mail, and a third sent via standard mail to stockholders.

4. **Internet Enabled**—The reports server should be able to receive request from both Web- and non-Web-based clients.

1.3.2 On-Line Analytical Processing

On-Line Analytical Processing (OLAP) takes the business strategist to new levels in data analysis. With OLAP, the business strategist's analysis interacts with the data contained within the system. It leverages the time-variant characteristics of the data warehouse to allow the strategist to look both back and ahead in time. In looking back, the strategist is able to identify trends that may be hidden in the data. In looking ahead, he can use these trends to forecast future conditions, and he can examine the characteristics of these trends. The strategist can anticipate how changes in these trends will affect the organization's environment.

A variety of OLAP tools have been developed to achieve the objectives described above. Some have been based on a *multidimensional* database specially constructed and tuned for analytical processing. These are sometimes referred to as MOLAP (Multidimensional On-Line Analytical Processing) tools. We will discuss multidimensional systems as well as some of their shortcomings in Chapter 4, "The Implementation Model." Many OLAP tools have taken a ROLAP (Relational On-Line Analytical Processing) approach, where the multidimensional view of the data is implemented on top of some relational engine. OLAP engines that are a combination of the two, or hybrid, are frequently referred to as, you guessed it, HOLAP.

A complete discussion of OLAP could fill a book by itself. We will look here at some high points that provide a general understanding. Figure 1–7 presents a typical OLAP interface. Although it might appear to be a standard spreadsheet with rows and columns, an OLAP tool is much more powerful. OLAP allows the user to present the data in multiple dimensions. In our diagram we are presenting the sales data for auto-sales dealerships, where the dimensions are time, product, and dealership. As we can see, time is spread across the columns, and the rows represent each of the different products. Each *page* will represent a different dealership. At an absolute minimum OLAP must be able to present data in multiple dimensions at one time. Although our simple example shows three dimensions, the OLAP tool should be able to extend the presentation of the data to many more.

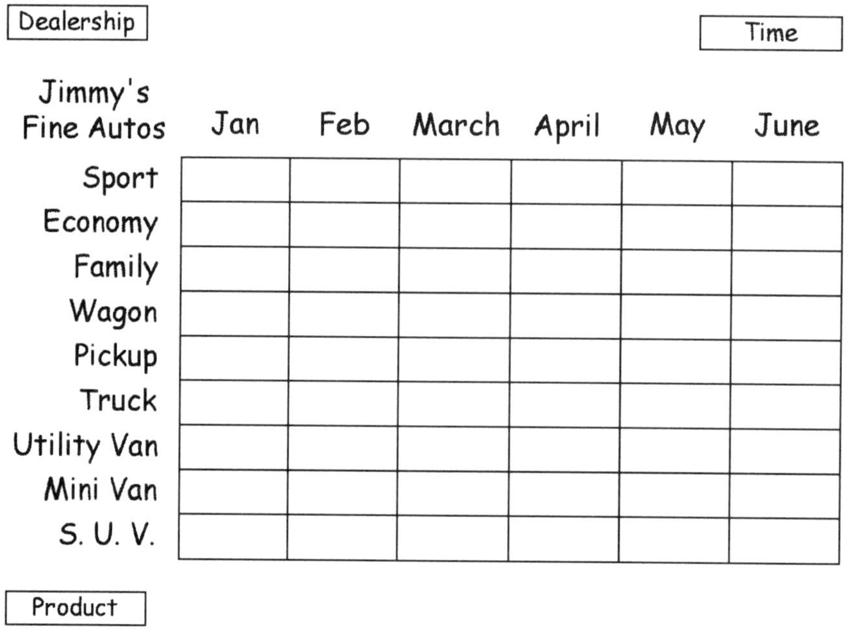

Dealership						
Jimmy's Fine Autos	Jan	Feb	March	April	May	June
Sport						
Economy						
Family						
Wagon						
Pickup						
Truck						
Utility Van						
Mini Van						
S. U. V.						

Time

Product

Figure 1–7   OLAP interface.

The OLAP tool should also allow for the *rotation* of data. A rotation changes the orientation of the display. The dimension that runs across the columns is exchanged with the row data, for example. In the display in Figure 1–7 a rotation would distribute the products across the columns, and each row would represent a month. The key here is that with OLAP this can be done easily through an intuitive interface.

Another important feature of OLAP is the ability to *drill-down* and *roll-up* data. This allows the user to look at data summaries. In our example we have shown data at the dealership level. Each cell in the matrix is the sales of that particular product for that particular dealership. Roll-up will allow the strategist to sum the data of the different dealerships into a single regional sales number for each product. Drill-down is the same operation in reverse; it allows the strategist to look at the detail records of a summary. If we were to present regional sales numbers, a drill-down would allow the user to look at the sales number of the individual dealerships in those regions.

OLAP gives the business strategist the tools necessary to detect trends and analyze their characteristics. This would include the ability to perform *"what if"* analysis. Here the OLAP tool must allow the strategist to build models based on the data and manipulate the variables in the model. The strategist can examine the effects both of particular trends and of changes in those trends.

Again, a thorough treatment of OLAP alone would take an entire book. Here we have presented a basic understanding of OLAP as well as the basic requirements of an OLAP tool.

1.3.3 Data Mining

Not long ago the latest rage was hidden pictures. These were pictures of seemingly random patterns and colors in which, when you looked at them just right, you were able to see a totally hidden picture. The trick was to look at the entire picture at once, and after several hours (and a headache) you were able to see this *hidden picture*. I never could do it; I could never see the hidden picture. The reason is that I am color blind. So I could stare at those things all day and never see anything but a bunch of squiggles and such. Data mining, in a way, is similar to those pictures. The data as a whole seems to be nothing but a collection of random events. Data mining allows us to see the picture hidden within those events.

There are two basic types of data mining: classification and estimation. With classification, objects are segmented into different classes. In a marketing data warehouse perhaps we could look at our customers and prospects and categorize them into desirable and undesirable, based on certain demographic parameters. The second type of data mining is estimation. Estimation attempts to predict or estimate some numerical value based on a subject's characteristics. Perhaps the business strategist is interested in something more than just desirable and undesirable customers. The strategist may be interested in predicting the potential revenue stream from prospects based on the customer demographics. Estimation might be able to say that certain types of prospects and customers can be expected to spend a percentage of their income on this product or that. It is common to use classification and estimation in conjunction with one another. Perhaps the strategist would perform some classification of customers and then perform estimations for each category.

Whether performing a classification or an estimation, the process of data mining is basically the same. We begin with the data or, more appropriately, a subset of the data. This is our test data. The size of the data set depends on the deviation of data characteristics. In other words, if there are relatively few variables whose values do not greatly deviate from one another, then we can test on a small number of records. If the data has many variables with many possible values, then the test data is much larger. As with the data warehouse, the data is cleansed and merged into one database. If we are working directly from a data warehouse, we expect this process to have already been carried out. This does not mean that we assume the data is cleansed and transformed. The data quality must still be verified to ensure accurate results.

We then define the questions to be posed. The strategist must define some goal for the mining process. Perhaps we would like to segment our market by customer demographics or we would like to know the market potential of certain economic groups. In either case we need to specify what we are trying to discover.

Taking the test data, we then construct a model that defines the associations in which we are interested. We have known results in the test data set. We know that certain records represent desirable or undesirable customers, or we know the market potential of a set of clients. The model will look for similarities in the data that have similar results. Once we have built the model, we train it against subsequent test data sets. When we are confident in the model, we train it against the actual data we wish to mine. At times the model will not include some records that should be included or will include records that it should not. In either case there will be some level of inaccuracy in the data model. No model can predict with perfect accuracy, so we should expect some margin of error.

1.3.3.1 Decision Trees

The models themselves can come in a variety of types. One type commonly used is the decision tree, as shown in Figure 1–8. The decision is represented with a box and each alternative with a circle. The branches extending from each node are labeled and assigned a probability. In the figure we have a decision as to whether a company should carry out a marketing campaign or invest the money where there would be a 10% return on the investment.

For each alternative in the tree there are three possible outcomes. If the campaign is executed, there is a 50% chance that sales will increase by $1,000,000, a 40% chance that sales will be constant, and a 10% chance that sales will decrease by $100,000. We multiply the probability of each outcome by the value of that outcome. We then deduct from the sum of these outcomes the cost of the campaign. We do the same with the decision to invest the money, adding the benefit derived from the investment to the sum of the possible outcomes. We see that the decision to execute the campaign has the value of $490,000 and the decision to invest the money has a value of $15,000. While the present example shows two alternatives with three possible outcomes, decision trees can have many alternatives, outcomes, and subsequent decisions.

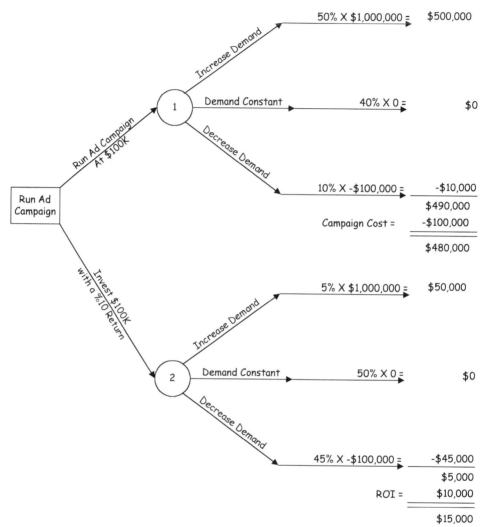

Figure 1–8   Decision tree.

1.3.3.2   *Neural Networks*

A neural network is an interesting approach to data mining. The structure of the model mimics the structure of the human brain. The brain is composed of neurons, each of which could be thought of as a separate processor. The inputs to the neuron are scattered over its dendritic tree. Axons in the brain are the white matter that insulates the neurons. The axon is in a sense an output device for the neuron, where the dendrite is the input. The axon passes the output of one neuron to the dendrite of the next. Each neuron processes the information it receives and passes its results down the line. How this results in human thought is the subject of another book.

The neural network model attempts to perform this same kind of processing. It has a number of nodes, which could be processors in a massively parallel processing system or simply processes in a multiprocessing system. We show this in Figure 1–9. The network receives as input the location, age, gender, and income of the prospect. These are taken in by the neurons, and some algorithm generates an output. These outputs are added in a weighted sum to determine some final result, such as the prospect's being likely to buy or not buy a particular product.

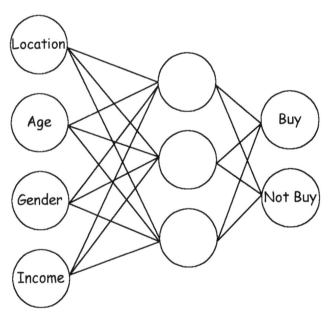

Figure 1–9 Neural network.

1.3.3.3 Genetic Modeling

Genetic modeling is well suited for categorizing. It comes from the concept of survival of the fittest—in this case survival of the model that is

the fittest. We begin by randomly placing the data into the desired categories. The model then evaluates each member of every category, based on
some function that determines fitness. Members that are not well suited to
the class are moved to other categories. The class will continue to alter
itself. Even as it receives new data, it will alter itself to arrive at the best fit.

1.4 Summary

The primary question in the construction of a data warehouse is "why?"
Why build a data warehouse? In order for an organization not just to survive
but to thrive, a strategic plan must guide its actions. The business strategist
defines the strategy in the context of the environment in which the organization competes. In order to do so, the business strategist must have ready
access to reliable, complete information about environmental conditions.

The information infrastructure in many organizations cannot meet the
needs of the business strategist. The BI infrastructure, however, does provide the strategist with the information necessary to detect behaviors within
the business environment. Based on these behaviors, the business strategist
is able to define a successful strategy.

The data warehouse is the heart of BI. It is more than just an archive of
operational data. W. H. Inmon defines the data warehouse as *a subject oriented, integrated, nonvolatile, time variant collection of data in support of
management's decisions."* The data warehouse derives data from the operational environment. As the data is brought into the warehouse, it is transformed into a single cohesive image. From this image the business strategist
through a decision support tool is able to analyze past behaviors, giving
insight into current trends. This enables the strategist to project future conditions.

1.5 Glossary

Business Intelligence Thinking abstractly about an organization, reasoning about the business, organizing large quantities of
information about the business in order to define and execute a
strategy.

BI Business Intelligence.

Business Strategist The primary data warehouse user. Responsible for defining strategy for the organization or some subset of the organization.

Central Repository Storage for the data, metadata, and master data within the warehouse.

Data Administrator Team member responsible for the quality of the data in the data warehouse. The data administrator reviews the extraction log for metadata changes, inaccurate data, or data errors.

Data Cleansing The portion of the data integration process that removes errors from the data being loaded into the data warehouse from the operational environment.

Data Extraction The process of extracting data from the operational environment and loading it into the data warehouse. Data can be pulled from the operational environment where the warehouse proactively retrieves the required data, or pushed from the environment, where the warehouse passively receives data.

Data Integration The process of taking data from the operational environment and consolidating it into the central data repository. The three-step data integration process consists of data extraction, data transformation, and data cleansing.

Data Mart A data warehouse whose scope is limited to a single subject area, such as a department. Data marts come in two flavors. Dependent data marts receive their data from the enterprise data warehouse. Independent data marts receive data directly from the operational environment.

Data Mining The discovery of the information hidden within the data.

Data Transformation The process of converting data from many disparate systems into one standard format.

Data Warehouse "A subject oriented, integrated, nonvolatile, time variant collection of data in support of management's decisions."[3]

Decision Support Systems The presentation of data to support management in making decisions.

DSS Decision Support System.

Extraction Log A record of the status of the extraction process. The extraction log records an exception to the extraction process. This log serves as input to the data administrator to verify the quality of the data loaded into the warehouse.

Extraction Store Temporary storage of operational data as it undergoes transformation and cleansing.

Metadata This is *data about data*. It describes what kind of information is stored, where it is stored, how it is encoded, how it relates to other information, where it comes from, and how it is related to the business. Metadata also describes the business rules of the data, in essence the use of the data within the organization.

Nonvolatile Data Data that remains unchanged. Once the data is written into the data warehouse it is not updated as long as it is within the warehouse.

OLAP On-Line Analytical Processing.

On-Line Analytical Processing The interactive access and display of data in multiple dimensions.

Operational Environment The parts of the organization that support day-to-day functions. These are typically transaction-oriented tactical systems. The functioning of these systems usually entails the automation of some manual process.

---

3. W. H. Inmon, *op. cit.*

Subject Orientation   The structure of the data that groups the information pertaining to a specific subject. Subjects include such things as products, customers, competitors, or employees.

Time Variant   Allowing the time variable to be manipulated by the business strategist.

Object-Oriented Design

$\mathbf{I}$t has been well documented that the majority of data warehouse projects fail. This failure rate is not inherent to the construction of a data warehouse but is due to inadequate engineering methodologies employed by those designing these systems. While the traditional *waterfall* method of system development is generally accepted as not suitable to data warehousing, this cannot justify the wholesale abandonment of engineering and architectural principles. A new method of analysis and design must be defined that conforms to engineering principles while adapting to the unique challenges posed by decision support systems.

The methodology presented in this chapter, the development spiral, overcomes the deficiencies of the waterfall approach. It replaces the rigid traditional approach with a more flexible process tuned to the unique challenges of the decision support environment. The development spiral is based on an object orientation. The focus moves from data and how it is processed to objects and how they behave. This maps well into the very nature of a data warehouse. Where the operational environment optimizes for processing, the data warehouse aligns to subjects. These subjects in the decision support environment are derived from objects in the development spiral.

As we shall discuss later in the chapter, metadata describes data. When the data warehouse architect performs analysis and design, he or she is working with metadata. It is the very substance of these processes. The architect understands the current environment by analyzing metadata and expresses the design of the proposed warehouse in terms of metadata. An object orientation to analysis and design gives the architect a vocabulary to express this metadata in a way consistent with the development spiral.

Section 2.1 presents an overview of the development spiral, contrasting it with the waterfall approach. This section also discusses how the development spiral is more applicable to the construction of a data warehouse. Section 2.2 explores metadata. This section expands the traditional myopic view of metadata to a more complete picture. Finally, Section 2.3 presents object orientation and shows how it is better suited to the needs of the data warehouse architect.

2.1   The Development Process

The traditional software development methodology has been described as a waterfall approach. Figure 2–1 illustrates this approach. The first step establishes a set of requirements that are documented in a requirements specification. An analysis based on this specification defines the environment in which the proposed system is to exist. The design presents a system that meets the requirements specification in the environment described by the analysis. The system is then developed, tested, and accepted by the user. Once accepted, the system is rolled out to the user community.

Any change or addition to the system requirements affects subsequent stages of the waterfall. The further along the project is, the greater the impact of a requirements change. Changes during the analysis or design phase usually have a minor impact. During acceptance testing, however, if the user community discovers a significant requirement has been overlooked, the development team will have to go back and rebuild that portion of the system. This is an expensive mistake. Great care is taken by the software development team, therefore, to make sure they have the requirements properly defined. Once defined, user acceptance is documented and the requirements are frozen. Any changes must be formerly requested by the users and accepted by the development team.

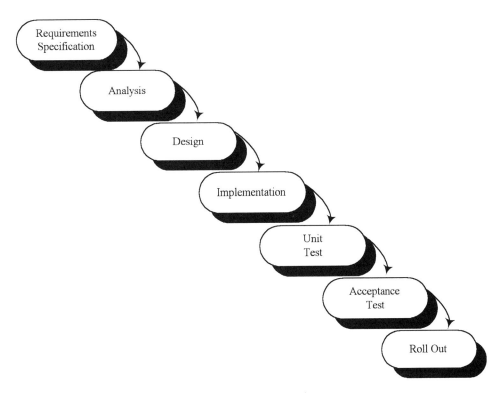

Figure 2–1   Waterfall software development cycle.

2.1.1 Shortcomings of Waterfall Approach

While the waterfall method has served for a decade as an appropriate for the traditional operational environment, it makes several basic assumptions that are untrue in the business intelligence environment. First, the traditional method assumes a static set of specific system requirements. In the business intelligence environment, nothing is static. It is actually desirable for the decision support system requirements to be dynamic and evolving. It would be ludicrous to think that a business strategist could sit with a data warehouse architect and list all of his or her strategic information needs. If a decision support system is delivered to a group of users and there are no changes to that system, it probably means that the users are not using the system. In effect the decision support system has failed.

In a successful business intelligence environment, users will begin to expand their use of the system. They will discover new areas that need exploration. They will think new questions they had not anticipated. If *they* did not know what they were going to ask, chances are that the architect didn't either. The system scope will widen into new subject areas and new types of analyses in order to meet the expanding and growing needs of users.

The waterfall method also assumes that there is a consensus within the user community concerning the system requirements. This is rare in the operational environment, much less in the world of business intelligence. Every department and every group within every department will have its own set of needs and will attempt to drive the design of the system. Anyone having had even the briefest of encounters with corporate politics will confirm this observation. As data marts grow into data warehouses, the architecture must be flexible to meet each of the various needs.

The most critical shortcoming of the waterfall method for business intelligence is a matter of time. The waterfall method assumes that the development team has the time to develop a detailed analysis and design. This is not so in the case of a data warehouse. The data warehouse development team must deliver quality information into the hands of management as soon as possible. Projects that extend past three or four months in their initial implementations should reconsider their scope. It is better to develop something on a smaller scale that will prove the concept to management than to develop an all-encompassing system that will take years.

2.1.2 The Development Spiral

Given these demands, a data warehouse development methodology must have three basic characteristics. First, it must be flexible. The data warehouse construction crew must be able to begin the development process without a detailed definition of every screen and data element in the system. They must not look to have all the answers when construction begins. Second, the crew must be able to construct a system that will meet the diverse and often competing needs of the user community. An enterprise-class system will have to deal with enterprise-class politics. Finally, the development process must be quick and right. The data warehouse construction crew cannot employ the old saw, "Do you want it fast or do you want it right?" It must be both.

To meet the demands of the data warehouse we have replaced the waterfall approach with the Development Spiralas shown in Figure 2–2. The spiral methodology begins modestly and expands outward. One could envision the first few iterations as a proof of concept, forming the foundation of the system and establishing much of the basic system infrastructure. This limits the amount of business functionality built in. With each pass through the spiral, however, new functionality is added, expanding the spiral outward. At the end of each pass through the spiral there is an evaluation phase, when users confer with developers to evaluate not only how well the system is progressing but what functionality should be added in the next iteration.

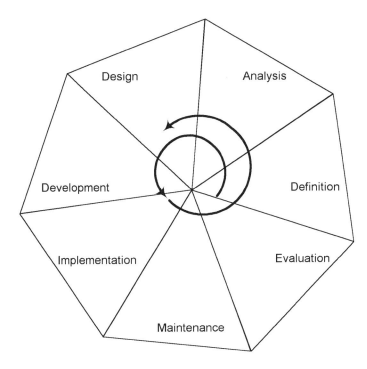

Figure 2–2 Spiral software development.

This book focuses on the first three phases of the development spiral. The actual development, implementation, maintenance and evaluation phases are beyond its scope. Below, however, we list the different phases of the development spiral:

1. **Definition**—This phase describes the objectives and scope of the data warehouse. It is driven by the user community and addresses the needs expressed by those sponsoring the warehouse. The definition is documented in the project statement along with the initial project objectives.

2. **Analysis**—This phase examines in more detail the needs expressed in the definition phase. It also studies and documents the environment in which any proposed solution will reside.

3. **Design**—The design phase is an iterative process within itself. The process begins with a high-level conceptual model, which is refined with each iteration. The ultimate goal is to arrive at an implementation model—a model with enough detail to allow developers to begin.

4. **Development**—The development phase takes the detailed design and makes it into a reality. The data structures are built and the software is written based on the design. The development phase includes both unit and integration testing. This phase is outside the scope of this book.

5. **Implementation**—This phase is also referred to as roll-out. Within this phase, users are trained and the system is deployed.

6. **Maintenance**—This phase is an ongoing process. It continues for the entire life of the system. Again, this phase is outside the scope of this book.

7. **Evaluation**—Within this phase, system sponsors and developers review the initial project statement. What was delivered is compared with what was requested. Another iteration of the process may be initiated, based on the findings within this phase. The evaluation examines not only what was done, but how it was done. The development team within this phase must look for ways to optimize their delivery of future enhancements to the system.

2.1.3 The Advantages of the Development Spiral

This method of expanding the scope benefits all involved in the project. The user community benefits by getting something they can use quickly. The sooner a decision support system is put into the users' hands, the more quickly the organization will begin to benefit from it. The development team benefits by building their credibility with the user community. With each successful delivery the value of the system and the expertise of the development team increase in the eyes of the user community. Finally, the system itself benefits. What the development team learns in an implementation can be applied to subsequent iterations of the development spiral.

The development spiral maps well with our criteria for a data warehouse development methodology. First, the methodology is flexible. By limiting the scope of each iteration and establishing a short time horizon for delivery of each new version of the software, we maintain a high level of maneuverability. Each iteration is evaluated and examined by the user community prior to initiating the next iteration. This keeps them in close communication with the development team. Second, as the spiral expands in scope, additional users are brought into the process to include their needs. In essence the development team divides and conquers the user community. Finally, the process is quick. Each iteration of the development spiral should take no more than three to four months. Users are continually receiving enhanced functionality to the system. While technically the additional functionality may not amount to much in the eyes of the developer, an additional subject area may make a world of difference to the business strategist.

Consider what this means as it relates specifically to the development of the data warehouse. The prescribed method of constructing a data warehouse is to start small. It is usually recommended that the initial scope not exceed a single subject area, in essence a data mart. The system expands into other subject areas only after deployment and results are delivered to the users. Once the business strategist receives the system and starts to use it, he or she will be better able to suggest enhancements.

2.2 Metadata

What is metadata? The standard definition is that it is data about data. While concise, this definition provides little to expand our understanding. *Meta* comes from the Greek meaning beside or after. Applying the prefix *meta-* to an object means it is at a later or a higher stage of development than the base object. It is something that is beyond, transcending, or more comprehensive than the base. In terms of data, metadata is more comprehensive than data. It transcends data in the sense that it goes beyond the individual data item and provides the context in which the data exists. This context provides meaning to the data.

As discussed earlier, this book focuses on the first three phases of the development spiral: definition, analysis, and design. All three phases have one thing in common: metadata. The definition and design phase create metadata, while the analysis phase consumes it. The definition phase provides the context of the overall system. The design phase describes the data elements, the structure of the database, and the processing that can be performed on which data elements. The analysis phase actually attempts to collect the metadata that relates to the issues to be resolved, as described by the project definition.

Metadata is commonly mistaken for mere data-typing information, integer versus floating-point for example. Given the above definition, we see that metadata is much, much more. Consider the number 5,000. What does the number mean? The format—what is mistakenly thought of as metadata—is clearly present. Without a context, however, the number is meaningless. It could mean feet, miles, or money. Even this information is incomplete. Let's say that we are discussing $5,000. Is this the price of a car, the commission earned by selling a car, or the weekly salary of the local paper boy? Such information provides further context for the data. As we consider this context, we internally fill in additional information about the data. In a sense, the additional metadata is inferred. If it is the price of a car, we think *inexpensive (cheap) car*. If it is a commission, we think *nice pay*. If it is the weekly salary of the paper boy, we start to look for a paper route. Even the information that was mentally added to the number is metadata. It is all part of the context.

2.2.1 Types of Metadata

The example above raises an interesting point. If a number is a price, commission, or salary, we have a certain understanding of the context. We fill this in on our own. In the business world, often much of the data's context is left undocumented. It is assumed that the user will understand what is meant. Often system engineers and administrators content themselves with only a partial description of the data—the format. If we truly want to capture the context of the data within a system, be it a data warehouse or an operational system, we need to expand our view. Figure 2–3 presents a mapping of the many different types of metadata that are required for a complete context.

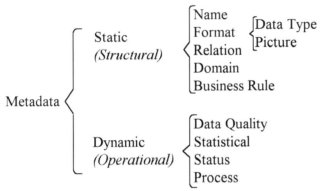

Figure 2–3 Types of metadata.

The following list provides a more complete description of each metadata type:

Static
- <u>Name</u>—Provides the name by which the data element is known to the system. For example: Employee_name, Customer_Name, or Customer_ID.
- <u>Description</u>—Provides a full text description of the data element.
- <u>Format</u>—Provides the data presentation rules.

- Data Type—Defines the data that is stored within the data element. For example: Integer, Floating Point, or Boolean.
- Relation—Defines the relationships between objects within the system. For example: Customers buy product.
- Domain—Provides the domain or range of valid values.
- Business Rules—Provides the rules of the organization that govern the data element.

Dynamic

- Quality—Describes the quality of the data within the system, such as the accuracy, completeness, consistency, and validity of data. An example of quality metadata within the data warehouse is the extraction log discussed in Chapter 1. This log provides statistics on the data loaded into the data warehouse.
- Statistical—Describes usage and administrative characteristics of the system. Maintaining statistics on which data is most frequently accessed or the types of analysis performed on the data could be extremely useful to system developers in enhancing the performance of the system. It is also common to keep statistics on which users are accessing the system, how often, and for how long.
- Status—This category of metadata keeps track of the general health of the system. It is also beneficial to keep a record of backup statistics, such as when was a backup last performed, how long did the backup take, and what errors occurred. It is also helpful to keep track of disk utilization, system failures, Mean Time Between Failures (MTBF), and Mean Time To Repair (MTTR).

Figure 2–3 shows that there are two basic types of metadata: static and dynamic. One can view static metadata as describing the structure that contains the data and dynamic metadata as describing the overall status of that structure. As described earlier, one of the most critical and yet least documented static metadata types is that of the business rules. It is often assumed that these rules are known by the user. With business rules, however, even the most obvious data elements are not always clear. What is a car? What distinguishes one car from another? Looking at two different cars, you could distinguish between car A and B. What if I take parts from car B and use them as replacement parts for car A? How many parts moved from A to B will it take to make A into B? This may look like a ridiculous example, but my cousins at Crash's Auto Parts, a junk yard, would disagree. It is a very real issue. The business rule is simple; the car's serial number is attached to the dashboard under the windshield. The car to which A's dashboard is attached is car A. The business rule is simple, but not necessarily known unless documented.

Obviously, there will be changes to business rules, so one might object to the inclusion of business rules as static metadata. By "statistic," however, we do not mean that the metadata never changes, but simply that it changes less frequently than dynamic metadata. "Dynamic" relates primarily to the state and use of the metadata. Dynamic metadata has an operational flavor. It reflects the changing state of the system. Consider the different types of statistical metadata, such as backup, data usage, space usage, and user access. All of this data is constantly changing.

2.2.2 The Central Metadata Repository

As we can see from this discussion, there is a need for accurate and reliable metadata throughout the entire organization. This need extends from the data warehouse architect all the way through to business strategist. Figure 2–4 shows the different groups that require metadata. Each has its own unique metadata needs.

At first glimpse, one might not consider end users to be interested in metadata. When we consider our definition of metadata—that it provides the context for the data—we see that users are the ultimate consumers of metadata. Metadata, especially in a business intelligence environment, is critical to the end users. When the user is looking at a particular data element, the metadata provides the meaning. The reverse is true as well: when the users know what data they want, the metadata tells them where to find it.

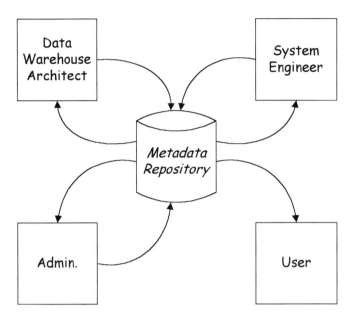

Figure 2–4   Metadata users.

As seen in Figure 2–4, end users are different in that they consume metadata but do not have direct input into the metadata repository. The data warehouse architect, system engineers, and administrators all provide input. Some interactions with the metadata repository are as follows:

- **<u>Data Warehouse Architects</u>** define the basic structure of the system as well as enhancements. This in turn defines most of the metadata.

- **<u>System Engineers</u>** enhance the environment that changes the metadata. For example, a review of data utilization may show that users are consistently asking for certain sets of aggregations. The system engineers may decide to pre-compile these aggregations. The metadata repository is updated to reflect this change.

- **<u>System Administrators</u>** review performance statistics, such as disk and CPU utilization. Administrators modify the environment to improve system performance.

- **<u>Database Administrators</u>** review data utilization statistics and modify the environment to improve performance as well. Database administrators will do such things as build indices or rebuild fragmented tables.

- **<u>Data Administrators</u>** have perhaps the most interesting interaction with the metadata repository. One might even consider them as **owning** the metadata. The data administrator monitors the quality of the data and detects changes in metadata. It is his or her responsibility to maintain the quality of not only the data but the metadata as well. For example, the data administrator reviews the extraction log. This log will detect when the metadata for the operational environment is not synchronized with the data warehouse. The data administrator is responsible for updating the warehouse to allow for proper data loading.

The central metadata repository is critical to the success not only of the data warehouse but also of the entire organization. As such, its scope should extend to the entire enterprise. This enterprise-level view is contained within the enterprise data model. This model is not strictly part of the data warehouse project, but we will address it, because it affects the warehouse.

2.2.3 Enterprise Data Model

The central metadata repository, as discussed in the previous section, contains an enterprisewide view of the data. The repository organizes this metadata into a data model whose scope encompasses the entire organization: the enterprise data model (EDM). It provides, in a sense, a schema or blueprint of the organization's business. In the preceding section we discussed how metadata provides the context for data. When the context encompasses the entire organization, it in essence describes the organization's business. To achieve this end, the EDM is a compilation of metadata from all systems within the organization, as shown in Figure 2–5.

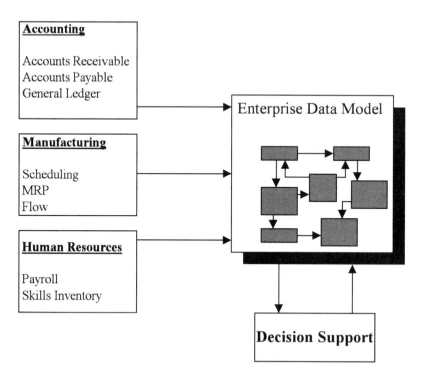

Figure 2–5 Enterprise data model.

Each department provides its own input into the EDM. The departmentments need to provide complete metadata for each system. The data administrator integrates this information into the model. The challenge for any system that spans departments is reaching a consensus. There will be disagreements concerning the data's definition, attributes, and business rules. Virtually all the metadata elements have the potential of becoming hotly contested issues. The only real blessing for the data warehouse architect is that this is the responsibility of the data administrator.

Actually in shifting the responsibility to the data administrator I am half joking, but only half. Strictly speaking, the EDM is not part of the data warehouse project any more than it is for the implementation of any other system. It is often confused as being part of the warehouse because the warehouse is the first system that truly attempts to integrate the data from the disparate operational systems. As shown in the figure, the data ware-house not only contributes to the EDM but receives input from it as well. While in a perfect world new systems would be designed with consistent metadata, in reality this is rarely the case. Most often departments will pur-chase systems from multiple vendors, selecting the best of breed. As of this writing, vendors have not done us the courtesy of providing a standard set of metadata.

The construction of an enterprise data model is not a trivial task. If an EDM exists, then all the better for the data warehouse. The architect can draw most of the metadata for the warehouse from this source. If an EDM does not exist, the data warehouse architect should be warned against grafting its development into the data warehouse project. This will only delay the ultimate delivery of the warehouse, jeopardizing its probability of success.

2.3 The Objective of Objects

The analysis process is meant to provide an understanding of both the requirements of the proposed system and the environment in which that system is to exist. The analysis gathers such information as the required data elements, their type and format, and their business rules. All these were described in the previous section as metadata. The analysis, this compilation of metadata, drives the design of the system. The design describes among other things the required data elements, their type and format, and their business rules. Again, we see metadata. The question facing the data ware-house architect is how to discover and document this metadata in a way that is easily understood. The answer is *objects*.

What is an object? It is simple enough to describe an object as a thing. If we look at the world, objects surround us. This book, a chair, a computer are all objects. These are all things that we can observe through one of our senses. We can see the book or feel the chair. They are tangible entities. If we relate this to business, objects are those things in business that we can see, touch, or hear. In the music business a piece of music is a real object. Objects are not limited to just the tangible world. An object can be a concept. In the business world we have objects such as service. Although we can see the service being carried out, the agreement between the two organizations for that service is a concept.

Given this definition, the analyst can begin to view the organization in terms of objects. What things are both products and the means of production? These are objects. What these objects do is their behavior. We can see how the organization functions when we put the behavior together with the objects.

2.3.1 Classes and Superclasses

In Figure 2–6 we present a variety of different objects. Looking at this diagram, the mind automatically starts to categorize the objects. Someone might see as few as two groups of objects in this diagram: cars and people. Someone else might see as many as five groups: women, men, sports cars, economy cars, and practical cars. Both cases demonstrate the natural tendency to group objects by some common set of characteristics. We can refer to these characteristics as attributes. When we group objects by these attributes we are creating object classes.

Figure 2–6 Objects.

Let's look at the differences in the two examples of classification discussed above. Where the objects are divided into five classes, more attributes are used to differentiate the classes. The people are distinguished not only from the cars but within themselves by their gender. Performance and cost differentiate the cars. One might consider this more refined grouping of objects superior, since it provides more information. Breaking the objects into more classes, however, loses information as well, although it may not be obvious in this simple example. While there are men and women in the more refined grouping, we do not have people. The three classes of cars do not provide us with a class of car objects.

Object modeling provides a solution to this problem. An object class can be created that is not a specific object but a classification of classes. These special classes are referred to as a *superclass*. In our example we have two superclasses: cars and people. Within the cars superclass we have performance cars, practical cars, and economy cars. Within the people superclass we have men and women.

2.3.2 Aggregations and Behaviors

As we shall see in our discussion, objects relate to one another in different ways. Although objects are discrete and separate entities, there are times when one object is composed of others. A book and a library are separate objects, yet the library is composed of books. This is known in the object-oriented world as *aggregation*. Aggregation is a unique relationship between objects, where one set of objects combine to form a new object. If we look at the objects in Figure 2–6 we see that the combination of wheels, an engine, a body, some seats, a transmission, and a steering wheel makes a car. None of these objects in and of themselves are a car, but combined they make a new object. The interesting thing is that the object-oriented world calls this aggregation.

Again, if we apply this to an enterprise we see different types of aggregations. A corporate structure is an aggregation. A company is composed of divisions, and divisions are composed of departments. It is noteworthy that this relationship cannot be recursive. If a company is made up of divisions, the divisions cannot be composed of companies. We shall see later that aggregation of this sort will have a direct impact on the construction of the data warehouse.

Another way objects interact with one another is through stimulation. One object acts on another object. We can see this action as a verb and the objects as nouns. Object A does something that stimulates object B. The object acted upon reacts in some way. When an object reacts to a stimulus, that reaction is referred to as the object's behavior. A behavior, as mentioned in Chapter 1, is a predictable response to a stimulus. One assumes that software objects behave predictably. In our example the people objects drive cars. Cars in turn transport people.

2.3.3 Modeling Objects

Figure 2–7 models all of these concepts. In this diagram the superclasses are represented by the rectangles with rounded corners. The name, attributes, and behaviors are listed in the diagram. The attributes listed in the superclass are passed on to the subclass unless otherwise specified. This is known as inheritance. In the example the superclass of cars has the attributes name, engine size, doors, and price. The superclass also has the behaviors accelerates, stops, and depreciates. These attributes are passed down to the subclass so that each car has them. Each car may have its own specific attributes. Sports cars, for example, have the attribute acceleration rate that applies only to sports cars. Cars of any other type do not have an acceleration rate.

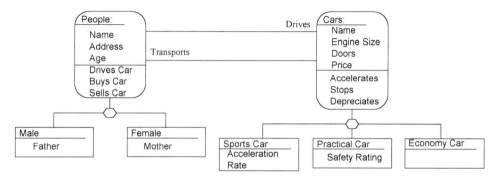

Figure 2–7 Object model.

The figure also demonstrates how to represent the interaction between objects of different types. The action is listed on the line closest to the object of the action. We see that "Drives" is on the line between people and cars next to the cars object. This is read as *"people drive cars."* "Transports" is on the line between cars and people next to the people object. This is read as *"cars transport people."*

A final note: there is a difference between an object and an instance. The figure describes types of objects. These are not specific occurrences of the objects. An instance, on the other hand, is an actual object represented by the type. The people class is a type. Lisa Miller, Jed Perkins, and Tony Runci are examples of people instances.

2.3.4 The Advantages of Object Modeling

The first part of this chapter discussed the shortcomings of the waterfall method and suggested the development spiral as an alternative. The advantages gained by the spiral, however, cannot be realized without the use of an object-oriented approach. While this may seem a strong and debatable statement, consider the expected advantages of the development spiral. The spiral is more flexible, faster, and more adaptable than a traditional waterfall approach. If one were to attempt to marry the development spiral with another analysis method, such as structured analysis and design, much of the flexibility and adaptability would be lost. This, of course, would lead to delays and slow delivery. To understand the importance of the object orientation, let us contrast the two different methodologies.

Figure 2–8 takes a traditional structured approach to the car sales application. If we compare this to Figure 2–6, we see that much of the subject information is lost. The traditional structured approach focuses on the processes, and the metadata is embedded within the design. In Figure 2–6 the different objects within the system are clear: cars and people. This figure also clarifies the relationship between the different objects. Cars are driven, sold, and purchased by people. People are transported by the cars. In the structured approach we do not see any of this information. We see that there are orders, applications, and products, but the objects they represent, along with their attributes, are hidden. The sales process allows someone, presumably a user, to enter orders. These orders are then verified and, after verification, processed. The focus with the traditional approach is the process and not the objects of this processing.

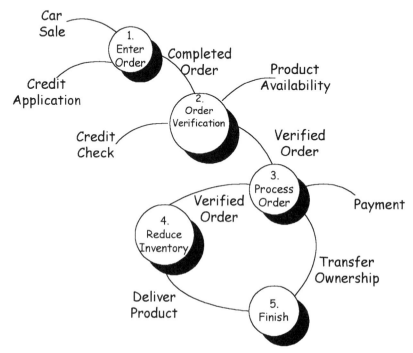

Figure 2–8   Structured design.

One might ask, so what? Why is one methodology preferable to the other? In simply comparing the two diagrams we see that the structured method is not as rich in content as the object-oriented method. While we see the process clearly, we do not see which objects are part of this process or what their attributes are. We miss how these processes cause the different objects or subjects within our area of study to interact with one another.

Although it may seem that we are comparing apples and oranges, remember we are trying to make orange juice, not apple pie. The data warehouse is defined as a "subject-oriented" database. Its purpose is to examine subjects and their behaviors, not the processes that carry out these behaviors. The analysis and design tool employed by the data warehouse architect must facilitate this view of the world. Clearly the traditional process-oriented system design tools do not support this view well. Their focus is on the process, while that of the object tool is on the subjects.

We see that the process view is less flexible than the object view. If there is a change to a behavior or relationship in the object-oriented world, the modifications to the metadata are limited to affected objects. With a process orientation, wherever the object appears the appropriate modifications must be made. This has the effect of limiting the adaptability of the structure. If new objects are to be added to the system, or new behaviors to existing objects, we again face the task of weaving through the processes, searching for changes. In the object-oriented world new objects are grafted into the object model where appropriate.

2.4 Summary

This chapter has introduced the data warehouse software engineering methodology. Where in the past the waterfall development methodology had sufficed for most operational systems, the demands of the data warehouse require a new approach. It must be more flexible, more adaptable, and faster. The solution is the software development spiral. The spiral's first iteration is one of limited scope, expanding outward with each iteration. The initial pass establishes the basic system infrastructure with limited business functionality. As the scope expands with each pass, new functionality is added to the system.

Metadata provides the context of the data within the system. It goes beyond traditional raw data and explains what the data is meant to represent. Metadata has traditionally been thought of as static information pertaining to the structure of the database and the format of the data elements, but it goes far beyond this simple view. Metadata includes the business rules pertaining to the data as well as the state of the system in which the data resides. The first few phases of the development spiral entail the definition of the system's mission, analysis of the requirements and current environment, and the system design. The definition and the design phases generate metadata while the analysis phase consumes it. The analysis and design tools used by the data warehouse architect must, therefore, assist in the collection, documentation, and retrieval of this metadata.

The use of an object-oriented methodology is essential to the application of the development spiral to the data warehouse design. The data warehouse is a subject-oriented database. As such the analysis and design tools employed by the data warehouse architect must facilitate this subject orientation. The object model makes clear the attributes and behaviors of objects as well as the relationships between objects. This is exactly the view in which the data warehouse architect is interested: the objects within the scope of the data warehouse or the data mart and how they behave.

As we shall see in the next chapter, the analysis process begins with high-level object models that are further refined to detailed implementation models. From these implementation models, schemas will be constructed to support multidimensional analysis.

2.5 Glossary

Analysis A detailed methodological examination of the current user environment as well as the user needs expressed in the definition phase of the development spiral.

Behaviors The predicable response of an object in response to stimuli. Behaviors as they relate to software objects are the object's permitted actions.

Central Metadata Repository Contains the EDM. The central metadata repository is accessible to the entire organization and contains all the metadata for the organization.

Definition The phase of the development spiral in which the objective and scope of the project are established. The output of this phase is the mission statement which is a collaboration between the project sponsor and the data warehouse architect.

Design The process of developing a detailed implementation model from which databases may be constructed and software written. The design phase is an iterative process that begins with a high-level conceptual design and is refined with each iteration. The refinement provides additional data on each of the objects.

Detailed Design Model The last model to be developed by the system architect prior to system development. The detailed design model provides all the information necessary for the system engineers to begin work. It takes into consideration all aspects of the actual implementation requirements.

Development The phase of the development spiral that transforms the detailed design model into an actual system. In this phase that database is constructed and software is written and tested.

Development Spiral An iterative object-oriented software engineering methodology. Each iteration of the development spiral expands the scope of the functionality of the system. Initial iterations provide limited business functions to the end user in order to lay the infrastructure upon which future iterations will be based.

Dynamic Metadata Metadata that primarily reflects the overall state of the system. Dynamic metadata is in a constant state of change. Dynamic metadata describes the data quality, usage, and status.

Enterprise Data Model (EDM) A data model whose scope encompasses the entire organization. The Enterprise Data Model receives metadata from all systems within all departments in the organization, combining it into one cohesive model.

Evaluation The final phase of the development spiral, in which the delivered product is examined and assessed as to how well it meets user requirements. The evaluation phase also takes into consideration the development process. The result of the evaluation phase is most critical to the development team. It provides them with a means to improve future iterations of the development spiral.

Implementation The phase of the development spiral in which the product is delivered to the users. This phase is also referred to as roll-out.

Maintenance This phase corrects any problems that are encountered in the use of the product. It continues for the life of the system.

Metadata Metadata describes data, or provides a context for the data. Metadata transcends data in the sense that it goes beyond the data and provides a description of what exists around the data.

Mission Statement Defines the overall objective to be achieved by the project. The mission statement provides the foundation for establishing the scope of the project.

Object Discrete entities that are either tangible or intangible. Objects can be atomic entities that cannot be decomposed into lesser objects. Objects are also aggregations, which are combinations of other objects to form a new object.

Object Aggregation Object aggregation should not be confused with aggregation of data. Object aggregation combines objects to form a new object. For example; a disk drive, memory, terminal, motherboard, CPU, and keyboard are combined to make a computer. The computer is an aggregation.

Object Class A grouping of objects based on a set of common attributes and behaviors.

Object-Oriented Analysis A methodology that views the environment in terms of objects and their associated behaviors.

Object-Oriented Design The expression of a system design in terms of objects and their behaviors.

Object Superclass A object classification that contains classes of objects.

Static Metadata Data that describes data elements. Static data changes less frequently than dynamic metadata and is relatively stable. In addition to describing the format and domain of the data, static metadata also describes the business rules that govern the data elements.

Waterfall Development A methodology that focuses on establishing a set of formally accepted system requirements which are frozen during the development process. The waterfall development methodology is composed of the requirements-specification, analysis, design, implementation, unit-test, acceptance-test, and roll-out phases.

CHAPTER 3

Analysis and Design

In this chapter we deal with the first three phases of the development spiral: definition, analysis, and design. These phases are crucial in that they establish the foundation of the data warehouse. They are the bridge between the user's perceived needs and the manner in which the system meets these needs. If the definition and analysis fail to accurately portray the user's desires and the environment in which the data warehouse is to reside, there is no way for the resulting system to succeed. In like manner, the design must be able to define a structure that successfully integrates into the current information infrastructure while fulfilling the system's purpose.

In this chapter we begin working with models. A model is something with which we can work when we cannot easily work with the actual object. So we could describe a model as a representation of reality. Models are useful in analysis and design for two reasons. First, we include in the model only those attributes that are relevant to the design. This simplification eliminates extraneous information, focusing only on what is critical to the task at hand. The second advantage is that of adaptability. Models can be easily modified. The analysis changes our understanding of the customer needs, and the analysis model changes to reflect that understanding. The design model evolves as we review and enhance the design of warehouse. In this chapter we will create models—representations of the business realities—with which we hope to work. The models we will build are based on objects. By working with objects we will be able to easily modify and adapt the models as we develop our understanding and ultimately our design. Objects will also provide a means to organize the elements of our design, limiting the attributes to what is relevant.

We begin by discussing the definition phase of the development spiral. In this phase we will establish the scope and overall objective of the system. The second phase is the analysis. In this phase we take an in-depth look at both the user's needs and the system's environment, and we encounter the first of our models. The output of the analysis phase is the analysis model. This model will define the major objects within the scope of our data warehouse. The final phase discussed in this chapter is the design phase. Within this phase we fill in the details of the objects discovered in the analysis phase. The output of the design phase is the object model. The object model serves as the basis for the implementation model. We will discuss the implementation model in a later chapter, after discussing multidimensionality and the star schema.

3.1   The Definition Phase

Obviously, before a construction team begins a project, any project, they must first decide what they are going to build. Imagine a team that begins constructing a barn, only to find that the client requested an office building. As ridiculous as this example may be, it is no less preposterous than attempting to construct a data warehouse or data mart without an appropriate mission statement. Using an architect as our example, we see that structures are designed around the needs of the clients. The architect first meets with them to gain an understanding of the construction's purpose. He or she then develops the design from there. The data warehouse architect would do well to follow this methodology. In order to construct a successful data warehouse, the data warehouse architect must **first** develop a clear understanding of the needs and wants of the client.

There must also be an interface between the construction crew and the users, a bidirectional medium of communication that encourages and facilitates a dialog between the two groups. This is the role of the *project spon-sor*. On the one hand the project sponsor communicates the desires and needs for the system to the construction crew. In a sense he or she is the user community's representative within the development team. In this way the sponsor keeps the data warehouse moving in the right direction. The emphasis here is on *keeping the project moving*. The sponsor must also communicate *to* the user community, setting expectations and championing the warehouse. It is critical that he or she believe in the warehouse and be willing to drive its success. This entails assisting the development team in making decisions as well as continually selling the project to upper manage-ment. The project sponsor should be in the lead, pushing for a data ware-house, overcoming political and organizational obstacles.

Given that the role of the project sponsor is to facilitate communica-tion, his or her first task is to collaborate with the data warehouse architect on the definition of the system. This is where the data warehouse architect **begins** to develop an understanding of the user's needs. The definition phase articulates the findings of this phase with the *mission statement*, which is a single statement that defines the purpose of the proposed sys-tem. The following is a list of sample mission statements:

Create a data mart that will provide data to support the analysis of changes in services provided to clients such as services added to or removed from client contracts.

— A services organization

Create a data mart that will provide data to support the analysis of customer demographics such as age, gender, and income for all product lines.

— A direct sales organization

Create a data mart that will provide data to support the analysis of throughput and inventory for all products.

— A manufacturing organization

Create a data mart that will provide data to support the analysis of demand and production capacity.

— A manufacturing organization

Note that the completion of the mission statement starts the clock ticking. Once the user community have defined a direction for the data warehouse, they start waiting. Of all the different types of people in the world who do not like to be kept waiting, users like it the least. The time between the end of the definition phase and delivery of the system, therefore, must be kept as short as possible. The sooner the user is able to start using the system, the greater the probability of success. The inevitable system bugs that may exist will be more tolerated in a system delivered on time than in one that is long awaited.

3.1.1 Case Study—Definition Phase

The case study begins with an introduction of the company. This introduction will provide a brief history of the organization. The second half of this introduction will provide a brief discussion of the mission statement of the data warehouse.

3.1.1.1 *Big Brother & The Building Company*

Shortly after the First World War, Joe Rizzo and his younger brother Tony kicked off their feet the dust of their home town in the frozen hills of northern New York and headed west. They had nothing but the clothes on their back and a dream in their hearts. They didn't know how, but they knew they were going to make it big. They found themselves about as far from home as two young men could be, San Diego. When the Depression hit, Joe and Tony toughed it out until things started to turn around. Joe started dealing in real estate, industrial property at first. Tony became the money man, taking care of the books. Joe did the selling and became known as Big Brother. Everyone knew, though, that Tony made the company run; he was The Building Company. You knew that when you did business with Big Brother and The Building Company, you were going to be taken care of. Joe and Tony would make sure of it.

When the Second World War hit, the big one, so did the fortune of the Rizzo boys. The company quickly expanded, at first throughout sunny California, then north and east. By the close of the fifties, now known throughout the west as Big Brother & The Building Company, it was preeminent in the commercial real estate market. Joe and Tony retired in 1960, selling the company to the Bank Of The Pacific, who changed the name to Pacific Commercial. The influx of funds gave the company the capital it needed to really take off, expanding its geographic coverage as well as its breadth of services. The following is a list of Pacific Commercial's business units and their areas of responsibility:

- Brokerage—The sale and lease of commercial real estate.
- Property Management—Maintenance and oversight of clients' commercial real estate.
- Appraisal—Appraising the value of clients' commercial real estate.
- Realty Advisors—Consults with clients concerning their commercial real estate needs.
- Investments—Consults with clients concerning commercial real estate investments.

In 1986 the Bank Of The Pacific became the object of a hostile takeover, falling victim to corporate raiders. During the ensuing pillage of company assets the new owners sought to divest themselves of the commercial real estate division. The employees purchased the company and reinstated the name Big Brother & The Building Company. A ceremony commemorating the event was held on the site where Joe and Tony Rizzo opened their first office. Although Joe Rizzo had been lost at sea several years early, Tony was able to attend. Since that time the employees and stakeholders in Big Brother & The Building Company have developed a common corporate mission: to assist business in the acquisition, maintenance, and sale of commercial real estate while maintaining the high standards of professionalism, courtesy, and honesty established by the company founders, Joe and Tony Rizzo. When it comes to commercial real estate, Big Brother & the Building Company (BBBC) will take care of you, just like the Rizzo boys did.

3.1.1.2   Mission Statement

The mission statement for the BBBC data warehouse is as follows:

> The BBBC data warehouse is to support the analysis of the various commercial real estate markets in which the organization competes. The system is to provide management with information pertaining to clients, client behavior, BBBC's performance, and the state of each of the commercial real estate markets.

The mission statement identifies the BBBC data warehouse as a marketing data warehouse. The scope of the system is to include all markets in which BBBC competes. The warehouse will need to address not only a nationwide market, but the variety of services offered by BBBC. This means the scope should extend beyond brokerage into investments, property management, realty advisors, and appraisal. In this way, the warehouse will provide BBBC management with a full view of their entire business. The scope of the warehouse, as described by the mission statement, may be too large for the first iteration of the development spiral. The architect needs to consider how to scope the project better to provide the best initial return while maintaining a realistic scope.

The mission statement also defines the objects that are to be included in the data warehouse. The warehouse must contain information that will allow the business strategist to perform analysis on the state of the overall commercial real estate market as well as BBBC's performance in that market. At this point the data warehouse architect should be thinking about the information sources. The operational systems will provide data concerning market activity involving BBBC, but this is only a segment of the market. The warehouse architect must also be concerned with how to gather information on the overall state of the commercial real estate market. The sources will have to be external ones that will report on market activity in which BBBC is not involved.

The definition phase has provided our warehouse architect with some direction. As we proceed into the analysis phase, we recognize several areas that will bear further investigation. First, we will want to look for ways to reduce the scope of the initial phase of the data warehouse. How can we resize the project to provide the greatest return on investment while keeping the scope manageable? Second, we need to look for our data sources. Which systems in the operational environment contain the raw data that we can upload into the warehouse? We answer these questions in the analysis phase of the development spiral.

3.2 The Analysis Phase

Analysis is the second phase in the development spiral. This phase examines in more detail the needs expressed in the definition phase. It also studies and documents the environment in which any proposed solution will reside. If we refer back to our construction analogy, the construction crew now knows what is to be built. We need to construct a beach house, but not all beach houses are the same. We need to talk to the family and see what their expectations are. Do they want a front porch? Do they want the porch enclosed or open? What about the number of bedrooms? These details need to be examined. Once they are understood, the architect documents the requirements and verifies with the user that they are correct. We then need to see the beach. We need to see the soil to determine what kind of foundation to pour and how deep to dig it. We need to look at the zoning ordinances and local building codes. That will describe the environment for the house. The design of the house will have to meet the needs of the user in the context of this environment.

This is the analysis process. Interviewing the individuals involved in the data warehouse gives the warehouse architect an understanding of the requirements for the construction and the environment in which it will reside. Once completed, the architect documents the findings in the *analysis model*. This model is then presented to the user for verification. The following subsections discuss the steps of the analysis process—the user interviews and then the construction of the resulting analysis models.

3.2.1 The Interview Process

In the interview process the data warehouse architect, just like the architect building the beach house, has to understand what is to be built as well as its environment. In the preceding section we noted that the impetus for the data warehouse must come from the user community and that the project sponsor is the spokesperson for that community. This is where the architect begins the analysis. As one might surmise, the dialog between the project-sponsor and the data warehouse architect began while composing the mission statement. During the analysis process the architect starts to dig deeper into the needs expressed by the project sponsor. The sponsor, however, is the starting point for the analysis, not its sole focus. The architect must expand the analysis outward. This is not to denigrate the role of the sponsor. Rather, the sponsor now begins to focus on facilitating communication, acting as a launch point into the user community and helping the architect find the right people to interview for the analysis.

The architect's objective is to gather a complete picture of the needs and the environment. Even the best of project sponsors will not have complete knowledge of the business processes and subjects within the scope of the data warehouse. To gain a complete picture the expansion of scope encompasses management, additional users, and information technology (IT) staff. These additional interviews will assist the warehouse architect in gaining a more complete picture. Interviews with senior management can assist the architect in understanding what is truly expected of the warehouse. Users will provide additional views of the business processes and how they really work. Interviews with IT will give insights into source systems and the quality of data contained within these systems.

In the best of situations the architect completes the picture drawn by the project sponsor. Many situations are less than optimal. The architect must assess the political culture within the organization. What is the attitude toward the data warehouse? Is the IT department accepting of a decision support system? What is the attitude toward the group that is pushing for the warehouse? Does management see a need for business intelligence? Is there a consensus within the organization that this is an important project, or is the project sponsor viewed as some nut off on a crusade? The architect must be politically adept at getting the answers to these questions. In some environments it may be appropriate to just ask. In others it may be necessary to gather this information indirectly.

Another element important to the interview process is the overall direction of the data warehouse project. This is somewhat akin to the political question. The architect must determine with each iteration of the development spiral whether the subject area addressed by the warehouse provides the greatest return on investment of all the possible alternatives. While the project sponsor or the group represented by the sponsor may feel strongly in favor of a particular subject area, interviews with senior management or the user community may discover other areas that could provide greater return on investment. ROI—return on investment—that is the name of this game. ROI is especially critical in the first few iterations of the data warehouse. The goal of the warehouse construction crew should be to demonstrate a high ROI, especially in the first iterations of the development spiral.

In discussing the spiral's beginning iterations we noted that one could almost view them as a proof of concept. The greater the ROI on these initial iterations, the easier the path for subsequent iterations. This is where it gets political. If the area described by the project sponsor provides the best ROI and there is consensus throughout the organization, there is obviously no problem. If, however, the selected area is not the optimal and the user community is behind the sponsor, the architect is faced with the issue of how to change direction without alienating his or her greatest allies. Other problem situations may be where the project sponsor lacks support within the user community and management desires another direction. An analysis of how to deal with each of these situations would fill several books. Suffice it to say at this point that the warehouse architect will exercise the limits of his or her political acumen when dealing with the factions surrounding the construction of the data warehouse.

The interview process is more than just blasting a series of questions at the user. It is an opportunity for the architect to begin a dialog with the different members of the organization. The architect should use this opportunity to both gather and disseminate information. During these initial discussions the interviewers should establish a spirit of openness and teamwork with the interviewee. It is a time in which expectations can be established within the user community. While all of this may seem like motherhood and apple pie, these elements of the analysis process are critical to the success of the warehouse. As such they require some discussion here.

In the following subsections we will discuss the types of questions to ask the respective groups in the organization. We will also discuss the overall objectives in these discussions.

3.2.1.1   *The Project Sponsor*

The objective in interviewing the project sponsor is to develop a more complete vision of the data warehouse. Where the mission statement defined the overall objective, the project-sponsor interview will *drill-down* into a deeper level of detail. The mission statement may have stated that the warehouse is to support management in understanding the sales demographics of various product lines. The warehouse architect must now determine what that means. What details are needed in order to complete the mission described in the mission statement? This is what the architect is trying to determine in this interview.

The three areas where the project sponsor could provide additional information are data, users, and system evaluation. Now that we know the organization is interested in understanding its sales better, we need to know the data that is going into developing this understanding. What are the products and where is the data describing these products? What is the time horizon for this data? Different industries will have different time horizons. Where the auto industry may look at mini-van sales over the past few years, the cosmetics industry may examine lipstick sales of only the past few months. We will also need to understand the user community better. The project sponsor, as a member of this community, will be an excellent resource. The sponsor will be able to describe the typical user profile as well as the user community's expectation for the warehouse. Part of this expectation will include the parameters for determining the success of the data warehouse. No doubt the sponsor will have input into these expectations as well.

The following are the beginnings of a list of questions that might be asked of the project sponsor. The interviewer should add or remove questions from this list as may seem fit, feeling free to paraphrase where appropriate.

- Data-Related Questions
    - Which objects are related to the business needs stated in the mission system?
    - Where does the data concerning these objects currently reside?
    - How far will an analysis look back in time?
    - Is this data available in any existing information systems?
- User-Related Questions
    - Who are the users?
    - How will the users interact with the data warehouse?
    - Will users have their own desktop systems? If so, what is a typical configuration?
    - If they have their own systems, what is the typical software environment?
    - Are these users currently using any analysis type tools?
    - What is a typical analysis for these users? Financial, sales, etc., etc.
    - Do the users expect to receive static hard-copy reports, or will they receive the information dynamically on-line?
- System Evaluation
    - What parameters do you think will determine whether the data warehouse has been a success?
    - What are the top five questions you expect to be able to answer with the data warehouse?

3.2.1.2 *Management*

Interviewing senior management gives the data warehouse architect the opportunity to understand management's expectation of the data warehouse. Management will reveal in these interviews what they perceive as the benefits. This expectation is part of the definition of the data warehouse. The architect is able to incorporate these expectations into the system design. Of equal importance is what the architect communicates to senior management. This is an opportunity to set expectations on the part of management.

Senior management interviews also provide the architect with a reading of the political waters. In these interviews one detects the support or resistance that management might have regarding the warehouse. This will weigh heavily not so much in the design process as in the implementation. In environments where there is a great deal of resistance, it is important for the warehouse to show some return as quickly as possible in the hopes of overcoming this resistance. There is an interesting correlation here. The greater the resistance to the warehouse, the greater the need to deliver a return quickly. However, the greater the resistance, the more difficult it becomes to deliver something quickly. Such is the plight of the data warehouse architect; if it were easy this stuff would come shrink wrapped.

The following are the beginnings of a list of questions that might be asked of senior management. Again, the interviewer should add or remove questions from this list as may seem fit, feeling free to paraphrase where appropriate.

- User Profile
  - Do you have a personal computer or workstation? If so, what programs do you use?
  - Are you comfortable using computer systems?
  - How would you describe yourself when it comes to computer usage? A power user? An intermediate user? A novice? Technologically adverse? *(Ask this with a smile. Don't alienate your users.)*
- System Vision
  - What do you see as the objective of the data warehouse?
  - How do you see it achieving these objectives?
  - What is the most important use you could make of the data warehouse?
  - What information do you need that you are not getting now?
  - Do you see this as something that you will personally use?
- System Evaluation
  - What parameters do you think will determine whether the data warehouse has been a success?
  - What are the top five questions you expect to be able to answer with the data warehouse?

3.2.1.3 Users

There are two groups of users to be interviewed by the warehouse architect: users of the data warehouse and the users of the source systems. The source systems are the operational systems from which the data warehouse draws its information. The purpose of interviewing data warehouse users is twofold. First, the architect is repeating what has been done with senior management—that is, to read their expectations of the data warehouse. What benefits do they expect to derive from the system?

The second purpose is to understand the information the users are currently receiving. The data warehouse architect, like a physician, must ascribe to a Hippocratic oath. Like the physician, the architect is to do no harm. The state of the user should be improved by the data warehouse. The user should have access to better information with the advent of a decision support system, not worse. There may be situations, especially in the first few iterations of the development spiral, when users have no net gain in the information they receive. The reason may be that a particular iteration is establishing a foundation upon which later iterations may build, it is creating an infrastructure. Users, however, must never be left in a position where they have less or poorer-quality information than they had before the implementation of the data warehouse. In short, DO NO HARM!

The following are the beginnings of a list of questions that might be asked of data warehouse users. Again, the interviewer should add or remove questions from this list as may seem fit, feeling free to paraphrase where appropriate.

- Current Sources of Information
    - Are you currently receiving strategic information? If so, what is the source of this information?
    - What is your function within the organization?
    - How do the information systems within the organization currently support what you do?
    - What reports do you receive? In what form are these reports? Electronic? Paper?

- User Profile
    - Do you have a personal computer or workstation? If so, what programs do you use?
    - Are you comfortable with using computer systems?
    - How would you describe yourself when it comes to computer usage? A power user? An intermediate user? A novice? Technologically adverse? *(Ask this with a smile. Do not alienate your users.)*
- System Vision
    - What do you see as the objective of the data warehouse?
    - How do you see it achieving these objectives?
    - What is the most important use you could make of the data warehouse?
    - What information do you need that you are not getting now?
    - Do you see this as something that you will personally use?
    - In every system implementation there are challenges. What do you see as the biggest challenge facing the data warehouse?
- System Evaluation
    - What parameters do you think will determine whether the data warehouse has been a success?
    - What are the top five questions you expect to be able to answer with the data warehouse?

The second group of users to be interviewed by the data warehouse architect are the users of the source systems. The objective in interviewing these users is to gain an insight into the use of the operational systems and the business processes they support. Here the architect is trying to discover information about the data sources. In many cases it may turn out that the users of the decision support system are also users of the operational systems. When possible, it is beneficial to blend both interviews into one. The users can then give their views not only on the decision support system, but on the operational environment as well.

Remember when interviewing this second group of users to look for data-quality issues. For example, in a one data warehouse implementation, senior management was interested in segmenting the customer base by SIC code. During the user interview phase a problem arose concerning this code. As it turns out, data entry did not know the SIC codes of the various clients and would default to some fictitious code that passed the system edits but had nothing to do with the customer's actual business.

- User Profile
  - What is your current function within the organization?
  - Describe what you do? *(At this point give the user free reign of the conversation. The answer to this question will give you insights into the business processes.)*
  - Do you have any issues in the quality of data you receive?
  - Do you know what happens to the data once you have entered it?
  - Once you have entered data into the system, what feedback do you receive? *(This question relates to data quality. If they say they receive no feedback, you may have quality issues.)*
- System Vision *(Optional, depending on the user's possible involvement with the decision support system.)*
  - What do you see as the objective of the data warehouse?
  - How do you see it achieving these objectives?
  - What is the most important use you could make of the data warehouse?
  - What information do you need that you are not getting now?
  - Do you see this as something that you will personally use?
  - In every system implementation there are challenges. What do you see as the biggest challenge facing the data warehouse?
- System Evaluation *(Optional, depending on the user's possible involvement with the decision support system.)*
  - What parameters do you think will determine whether the data warehouse has been a success?
  - What are the top five questions you expect to be able to answer with the data warehouse?

3.2.1.4   Information Technology Staff

The Information Technology Department will have key insights into the current state of the organization's information system as well as any obstacles that may hinder the construction of the warehouse. In short, *they've been there; they've done that.* Whether the architect is from an outside consulting firm or a direct IT employee, a consensus must be built within IT. The architect must meet with the IT staff responsible for the source systems as well as those responsible for any decision support systems. In these interviews establish a dialog; go beyond questions of which operational systems will provide which pieces of data. The architect must understand how well the different groups will work with one another. The support for the warehouse must be gauged. The IT interviews should provide the lay of both the technological and political landscape.

The following are the beginnings of a list of questions that might be asked of data warehouse users. The interviewer should add or remove questions as may seem fit, feeling free to paraphrase where appropriate.

- Current Environment
    - Are any DSS applications currently in use within the organization?
    - What is the level of sophistication of the users?
    - What are the biggest support issues with the users?
    - When interviewing [*specify a group*], they expressed an interest in analyzing [*specify a subject area*]. Which information systems within the organization provide data on this topic?
    - Who are the users of these systems? (*The answer to this question may lead the architect back to the user community to conduct more user interviews.*)
    - Is there current documentation on these systems? May I see it?
    - Is there a data dictionary for these systems? May I see it?
    - Can you give me an overview of these systems?
    - Which of these systems is your responsibility?
    - Who is responsible for the systems that are not yours?
    - What do you see as the biggest challenge in integrating some of these systems with the decision support system?

- System Vision
    - What do you see as the objective of the data warehouse?
    - In every system implementation there are challenges. What challenges do you see with the implementation of the data warehouse?
    - How do you see the data warehouse affecting you?
    - Will you be responsible for any aspect of the warehouse, once it is implemented?
    - This is what I am hearing concerning the mission of the data warehouse. [*Present the mission statement.*] What are your ideas? What do you think?
- System Evaluation
    - What parameters do you think will determine whether the data warehouse has been a success?
    - What are the top five questions you expect to be able to answer with the data warehouse?

3.2.1.5 *Big Brother & The Building Company Interviews*

The following subsections contain the interviews of the different players in the case study. I have not included all the interviews that one would conduct in the analysis phase, but rather a selection of different interviews from different groups to give a flavor of the interview process. I have attempted to include all the main points necessary for the analysis of the BBBC data warehouse's environment.

An Interview with Mike Rochelle, the Product Sponsor. The following is the interview conducted with Mike Rochelle. the product sponsor. Mike's primary role within the organization is Vice President of Brokerage Services. Mike started with BBBC as a data specialist in a remote field office and worked his way into a broker position. After several years of being one of the top performers in his region he was promoted into management. From there he worked his way up the corporate ladder to where he is today. Mike first promoted the idea of the data warehouse because of his own personal experience in the field. As a broker, and later as a manager, he understood the need for strategic information. It was not until he discussed his needs with Peter Andrews, the CIO, that he knew he wanted a data warehouse.

Q: Which objects—that is, things in BBBC business—are related to the business needs stated in the mission statement?

A: *Clients, obviously. We want to center this thing around the client types rather than the property types.*

Q: Why is that?

A: *Traditionally we have looked at the market as industrial, office, and retail property types. We need to change that perspective to a client. For example, a user of retail space has uses for other property types. A large retail company uses retail space. They also use distribution facilities and office space. In the old way of looking at things we would have three different sets of people calling on them. This new perspective has one. Investors are another example. They still want to be looked at as one customer, even though they invest in many different property types.*

Q: What are the client types?

A: *Well, there are investors, RET's, insurance companies, pension funds, capital markets, users of space, and owners of space. Real estate developers would fall into the owners-of-space category; they own the property for a short time and then sell it.*

Q: What are RET's?

A: *Real Estate Investment Trusts.*

Q: What other types of objects?

A: *Property and Brokers—that is, providers of real estate services.*

Q: Where does the data concerning these objects currently reside?

A: *APS, The Available Property System, that is our listing system. Then there is the Transaction Voucher System (TVS). We also work with the National Listing of Properties (NLP).*

Q: What is a listing?

A: *A listing is just a type of notification that a property is available for sale or lease. Just like when you go to sell your house, you list it with some real estate agent, our brokers list commercial real estate. A listing describes the building's particulars and what the property owner is asking.*

Q: Would you mind describing the use of these systems in more detail?

A: *No problem.* [Mike's description of these systems is provided in "Big Brother & The Building Company Analysis Model" on page 98. We will also interview the users of these systems at a later time. These interviews are not included for brevity's sake.]

Q: How far will an analysis look back in time?

A: *Real estate is not a static thing. We need to see trends. So I would think that we should at least go back two years. It would be terrific if we could go back five years. Anything more than that would most probably be cost prohibitive.*

Q: Why is that? Why would it be cost prohibitive?

A: *Five years ago we had much older, more antiquated systems. Getting the data out of those systems will be very difficult.*

Q: Who would use the system?

A: *It is easier to ask who wouldn't use it. Our philosophy would be to open it up to management, staff, clients, real estate professionals. We will need to make it secured. The different classes of people will not necessarily see the same amount of information, but they should all have access. One of the goals is to break down the barriers between people.*

Q: You mean between the different business units?

A: *Within business units!! Sure there are barriers between business units, but we need to break down the barriers within the departments as well.*

Q: In opening this up to clients, are you concerned about the competition getting hold of some of the data?

A: *No, it all depends from where you come. We come from a position of trust. We expect that the data stays with the client. We have to expect that some of the data will get out. But then we're not going to give them, the clients, all the data. Now, that is my personal position, but that is the way I am.*

Q: How do you envision users interacting with the data warehouse?

A: *Browsers and the Internet. The advantages are numerous. I can expand on that if you like.*

Q: Sure, go ahead.

A: *The reason, from my perspective, that most systems are never fully implemented and used is due to training and support. The browser metaphor is intuitive; the use of the browser is pretty well known. Also, we don't have to develop the infrastructure to support the system in our field offices or client sites. The barriers to entry are easier and less expensive than what it was 10 years ago.*

Q: Will each user have their own desktop system? If so, what is a typical configuration?

A: *A minimum of a Pentium processor, probably a thin client type of environment. It isn't necessary to specify an operating system with a browser interface. The browser can run in a Windows or UNIX environment.*

Q: If they have their own system, what is the typical software environment?

A: *Most have been Windows based, but there are some that are UNIX based. Then again the browser environment takes care of that.*

Q: Are these users currently using any analysis-type tools? DSS-type tools?

A: *There really isn't anything in use today. Some folks have played around with some tools, but nothing that is of the magnitude of the data warehouse.*

Q: Do the users expect to receive static hard-copy reports, or will they receive the information dynamically on-line?

A: *They want both.*

Q: What parameters do you think will determine whether the data warehouse has been a success?

A: *That it is used. That it meets the objectives that we have set. That we deliver on time.*

Q: What are the top five questions you expect to be able to answer with the data warehouse?
      1. *What do specific geographic markets look like?*
      2. *What are the trends in specific markets concerning properties?*
      3. *What are the trends in specific markets concerning clients?*
      4. *What are the trends within certain client types?*
      5. *What are the trends within certain property types?*

An Interview with Brian Berry, Chief Financial Officer.   Brian is another BBBC success story. Brian was hired right out of school and worked his way up the ranks. At first, he worked in the Information Technology Department, putting together budgets and assisting IT management with financial analysis. A major restructuring of the IT Department gave Brian his first big break. During that shake-out, Brian handled the department finances. Senior management recognized his talents and moved him to *the 10th floor,* the offices of corporate management. He worked as assistant to the CFO, Ron Grunner. When Ron retired, Brian was moved into his spot. Because of his past experience at IT, Brian has felt relatively comfortable with technology and has always kept in close contact with his friends in IT.

Q: Do you have a personal computer or workstation?

A: *Yes, a Pentium Laptop.*

Q: What programs do you use?

A: *E-mail, Word, PowerPoint, and Lotus 1-2-3. Although the standard is Excel, I've stuck with Lotus. I have a lot of spreadsheets I've built over the years that I don't want to loose. I just translate the files when I share them with other people.*

Q: Are you comfortable with using computer systems?

A: *Somewhat. I am a bit slow on the learning curve because I have so much going on, I don't have time to learn new things. It took me months to getting around to learning how to use a browser, but once I had the time to learn it, I picked it up quick. When it comes time to learn this stuff, I don't want to learn from an IT guy. I want to learn from other users. People who understand what I am doing, who speak my language.*

Q: How would you describe yourself when it comes to computer usage? A power user? An intermediate user? A novice? Technologically adverse?

A: *An intermediate user. I know how to do basic things, and I could get around with out too much help from other people. It is only when something breaks or that I have to learn something new that I go to someone else.*

Q: What do you see as the objective of the data warehouse?

A: *Very simple. the goal is to provide Jim Bean with the ability to know the top 100 clients, the details of those transactions, the type of transactions and all that.*

Q: How do you see it achieving these objectives?

A: *I would assume that the warehouse would be able to build a report on an up-to-the-minute basis, as opposed to calling someone to put some hard-copy report together.*

Q: What is the most important use you could make of the data ware-
    house?

A: *I think it would be useful in trend analysis. It would be helpful if it gave
    us insight not only on where the market has been but where it is going
    based on past performance. Since we are a large firm, we tout being
    able to do this, but we really don't have the information to support us.*

Q: So how do you do it now?

A: *We have the legacy system. The biggest issue with that is garbage-in/gar-
    bage-out. Because the voucher system doesn't require certain fields,
    brokers only put in what they need to put in to get their checks. As a
    result, we don't get a good read on what the market is doing. The data
    warehouse would be good for two things: long-term strategic planning
    and business generation.*

Q: To accomplish that, what information do you need that you aren't get-
    ting now?

A: *I don't know. Once I see the data warehouse I'll get a better image of the
    data that I need.*

Q: Do you see this as something that you will personally use?

A: *Yes, without a doubt. Trend analysis, forecasting where our specific
    markets are going, keeping an eye on interest rates. Interest rates affect
    our clients' ability to get loans. Knowing what the money market is
    going to do will give us an early warning that a market drop-off is com-
    ing. Simply put: If we saw problems in the mortgage banking branch,
    we would know that selling problems are coming down the road. Right
    now all this is done by phone calls. A brokerage manger calls banking
    and asks, "Hey, how is your business going?" The public aspect of the
    data warehouse is also very important. Trend analysis would help us
    when speaking to market analysts. We could not only have better
    answers for what happened, but be able to answer their "what if" type
    questions as well.*

Q: In every system implementation there are challenges. What do you see as the biggest challenge facing the data warehouse?

A: *Data quality. That is it. Without the quality, forget about it. We need to set up some structure in the field offices to make sure they are proactive in putting in the right type of information.*

Q: What parameters do you think will determine whether the data warehouse has been a success?

A: *If we were able to be more proactive in getting business with targeted companies. Instead of being able to do "one-off" transactions where we hope for the best, the data warehouse needs to help us put together a long-term plan and build relationships. Unless we are able to coordinate all the different offices with this system, we remain just a collection of local operations.*

Q: What are the top five questions you expect to be able to answer with the data warehouse?
   1. *Who are our top 10 to 100 clients?*
   2. *Number of transactions by type?*
   3. *Standard variance analysis? What areas are going in the tank and where do we have to put in more resources?*
   4. *Average rent rates by cities and locations around the globe?*
   5. *Competitive information. Where are our competitors strong? Where are we weak?*

An Interview with Jim Bean, the CEO.   Jim Bean, the CEO—throughout the organization he is known simply as Jim. When referring to a statement made or opinion espressed by Jim, there is rarely any confusion as to which Jim it is. To say that he rules with an iron hand would be soft by comparison to the reality. He is a no-nonsense, cut-to-the-chase style of manager. Jim worked his way up through the organization. He is referred to as an Old Sales Guy and considers it a compliment. He was a senior manager when he led the charge of employees to buy back the company. As CEO he is now leading the charge to take BBBC public. The following is the *encounter* with Jim:

Q: Jim, I want to thank you for taking the time to meet with me today. I know how busy you must be.

A: *You're right I am busy. So, let's get to it.*

Q: Do you have a personal computer or workstation?

A: *I have one at my desk.*

Q: What programs do you use?

A: *E-mail, occasionally. Most of the time I have Katie [Jim's secretary] print off my e-mail and whatever else I need from the system. Sometimes I look at some spreadsheets that Berry sends me. That kind of thing.*

Q: Are you comfortable using computer systems?

A: *I can see how it is helpful to most people. Frankly, I don't have time to play with that stuff. I've got a company to run. That's why I have Katie, she can print out anything I need to see. On occasion I'll use it, but it is not my primary tool.*

Q: What do you see as the objective of the data warehouse?

A: *Wait a second, isn't that why we pay you? Aren't you supposed to tell me what the objective is for this thing?*

Q: True. What I am trying to discover is what you hope to get out of the system.

A: *I'll tell you something, Brokerage services is over 70% of our business. I need to grow that and keep that healthy. Rochelle is a strong believer in all this stuff. He says that if he has better data he can sell more. So, as far as I see it, that is the objective, SELL MORE. Everything else just gets in the way.*

Q: How do you see it achieving these objectives?

A: *When I carried a bag I knew my market. I knew the properties and I knew my clients. That was easy back then. Today I run a company that stretches across the entire U.S. Can you tell me what that market looks like? Can this thing you're putting together tell me about my clients?*

Q: Well, that is certainly what we are aiming for.

A: *Look, I'll be blunt with you. I'm spending a hell of a lot of money on this warehouse thing. Don't aim for it. Do it.*

Q: What is the most important use you could make of the data warehouse?

A: *Just as I said before, I want to know my markets and my clients.*

Q: What information do you need that you aren't getting now?

A: *Do you know what my budget is for IT?*

Q: No.

A: *Four percent of my overall budget. That's a hell of a lot of money. Do you know they can't tell me who my top five clients are? Did you know they can't tell me what are my best markets in what areas of the country? If I knew that, I would be able to go after some of these markets more aggressively. I could go after the markets and clients where I am weak. I just don't know for certain which of them are what.*

Q: Do you see this as something that you will personally use?

A: *As I said before, I have a company to run. So, no I don't see myself sitting down at my computer for a morning of working on spreadsheets. I just want to be able to turn on my computer and see a couple of key indicators and then go on with my day. That's it. If there is something that is of concern to me I can have Katie dig up the details or I can get Berry in here to brief me on it.*

Q: What parameters do you think will determine whether the data warehouse has been a success?

A: *Haven't you asked this question before? Is it going to help me sell? How is this thing going to help me bring in more revenue?*

Q: What are five questions you would expect the system to be able to answer in order to help you bring in more revenue?

1. *Who are my top ten clients?*
2. *What markets am I performing well in?*
3. *What business units are performing well?*
4. *Which regions are not performing well?*
5. *Which sales rep and managers are not performing well?*

An Interview with Peter Andrews, the CIO.   The first interview I carried out with the IT staff was with Peter Andrews, the company's CIO. Peter was brought into BBBC from the outside after a major IT shake-out. He has inherited most of his staff. The poor staff morale after a major layoff did not help Peter in winning over any friends. His acquaintance with both the CEO and Mike Rochelle has enabled him to push through most of his agenda. Part of that agenda is the data warehouse. Finding a kindred spirit in Mike Rochelle, Peter was able to find support *on the tenth floor* for his data warehouse. If successful, Peter will gain much-needed credibility throughout the entire organization. The following are the responses that I received.

Q: Are there any DSS applications currently in use within the organization?

A: *No, possibly what some people are doing with Excel spreadsheets. But there is no structured DSS in place. May have been some stuff in crude form.*

Q: What is the level of sophistication of the users?

A: *You would have to stratify that for the different users in the organization. There are some that are technically adept, and there are some that don't have any knowledge. Senior Management will not be very sophisticated. They just want to see stuff. They don't want to interact. Guys like Jim Bean won't be a power user.*

Q: Do you see him doing things like drilling down?

A: *Yes.*

Q: In other words, Jim Bean would do the easy interface stuff but nothing
     too elaborate?

A: *Jim would like see a dashboard with bar graphs or pie charts. Not neces-*
     sarily tables with rows and columns. He can then go in and do drill-
     downs from there. He wants that information in real time. While he
     may want to see details, he really wants to be able to see red-light green-
     light stuff. The next level of management would go down another level
     of detail. Even the brokers would want to have a dashboard to monitor
     their activities. The DSS would be an attribute of the sales automation
     system.

Q: What are the biggest support issues with the users?

A: *The physical things that would have to be done to touch the worksta-*
     tion. Training from the user standpoint. You will have to touch them
     several times over a period of months. Getting a group to engage at a
     point in time in training is difficult. The problem is coming up with a
     training program that is just-in-time *and just when they need it. How*
     do we direct them to the right resource? One of the ways we are trying to
     achieve this is an applications support group. There are two dimensions
     to that; one, they have a specific question, or two, a just-in-time pro-
     gram where you can connect right up with that person and give them
     the training right away. Training where you go out to the site and con-
     duct a class will not always work because of schedules and not getting
     the information to them.

Q: When interviewing Brian Berry he expressed an interest in analyzing
     customer data. Which information systems within the organization pro-
     vide data on this topic?

A: *There is the Available Properties System and the Transaction Voucher*
     System. Then there is Really Realty, the property information system. We
     also receive data from the National Listing of Properties.

Q: Really Realty? What is that?

A: *Really Realty describes commercial real estate property. We have a mar-keting information group that does nothing but gather data about com-mercial real estate. They put all their data into Really Realty. It's a terrific system; it can tell you anything you want to know about practi-cally any commercial real estate in any of our markets.*

Q: They get this information from the voucher system?
A: *The data in this system comes from all sorts of outside sources. Proper-ties within Really Realty may not even be a property we did anything with. They are in the database, however, to give an understanding of the market.*

Q: Who are the users of these systems?
A: *Each of the business units, primarily brokerage. The other business units have tailored systems that feed the voucher system.*

Q: What do you mean *"primarily"* brokerage?
A: *All business units submit vouchers to the Transaction Voucher system, they all deal with transactions, but most of the business units front-end the transaction system with a system that is specific to the business unit. They enter the transaction into their own system in terms that relate to their way of doing business. The front-end system then packs the data into a record that is acceptable to the voucher system.*

Q: How well does that work?
A: *Well enough for our purposes. It complicates the data structure of the voucher system, but the fields in which management is most interested, client and financial data, are common to all business units. Brokerage does not use a front-end system because the system was built according to Brokerage specifications.*

Q: Is there current documentation on these system? May I see it?
A: *Yes, I'll get that to you at the end of our talk.*

Q: Is there a data dictionary for these systems? May I see it?

A: *No, there isn't a data dictionary. If there was, I would be glad to show it to you.*

Q: Can you give me an overview of these systems?

A: *Why don't I set up a time with Alan the project manager for these systems to discuss them with you?*

Q: Which of these systems is your responsibility?

A: *All of them.*

Q: What do you see as the biggest challenge in integrating some of these systems with the decision support system?

A: *The platforms, they are still old COBOL mainframes. So we would expect the usual sorts of things that you would see in getting data out of legacy systems.*

Q: What about data quality?

A: *The challenge is getting the people to input good data into the system. Making sure that they put in the information that they want to get out of it. They know how to manipulate the system to put in just enough so that they can get paid. They only deal with what affects them most immediately. They are just now realizing they are getting shit out because they put shit in. The culture needs to change. These guys are not motivated to put stuff in for the corporate good. They don't want the company coming back and saying we want to get something out of the system that affects broker revenue. They are not motivated to do it unless their is money associated with the data. It doesn't mean anything what Jim says unless they get cash out of it.*

Q: What do you see as the objective of the data warehouse?

A: *The data warehouse has to unearth opportunities. It needs to point out business opportunities within a specific line of business as well as cross lines of business—in other words, vertical and horizontal.*

Q: In every system implementation there are challenges. What challenges do you see with the implementation of the data warehouse?

A: *Basically the stuff we said earlier.*

Q: How do you see the data warehouse affecting you?

A: *As a CIO it now allows me to show a real value add and a direct correlation with the bottom line and shareholder value.*

Q: This is what I am hearing concerning the mission of the data warehouse. [*Present the mission statement.*] What are your ideas? What do you think?

A: *Basically, as I said earlier, the data warehouse has to unearth opportunities.*

Q: What parameters do you think will determine whether the data warehouse has been a success?

A: *Meeting well-defined business objectives. So if we expect to have some impact on revenues and shareholder value, we need to measure it. Does it allow my sales professionals of various sorts to do their job? Does it facilitate them doing their jobs—looking, finding, and generating opportunities? A lot of it is productivity. It is professionalizing the trades. It also through this combination of things we can institutionalize some of these practices. We start raising the bar for everybody.*

Q: What are the top five questions you expect to be able to answer with the data warehouse?

1. *What is the performance of my lines of business regionally, and on a time basis? What is their performance of those operations against target?*
2. *Who are my top clients currently versus historically?*
3. *The ability to create profiles and the monitor performance based on those profiles.*
4. *Ratios, how is this line of business growing in relation to others? It is looking at the relationships between the overall business process.*

Since we are a full-service company, if we are doing business in one line of business we should be doing it in related lines. The warehouse must facilitate the entire opportunity continuum. An opportunity in brokerage should produce it in financing and appraisal.

5. *Should be able to see our financial data in real time.*

3.2.2 The Analysis Model

The preceding section discussed how the analysis process receives metadata as input. The sources of this metadata are the interviews of the user community. The architect documents what is discovered by the analysis in the analysis model. This model is verified by the interviewees to ensure that the architect has a correct understanding of the current environment. The model is also used as the basis for the detailed design. It communicates to the designers the use of the source systems.

The analysis model is a medium of communication. As such it should be clean and simple to understand. Technical and nontechnical staff should be able to easily comprehend what the model is trying to communicate. This model is accompanied by a narrative describing the process that is presented in the diagram. The goal of the model is not to be an exhaustive detailed account of the business objects and their behaviors. It is simply to communicate an understanding of the business processes. Later in the analysis process, this model will be further refined into a detailed analysis model.

The analysis model is composed of objects (circles) and behaviors (lines). You cannot get much simpler than that! Objects in the diagram perform behaviors that act on other objects. When an object acts on another object, a line is drawn pointing to the object that is being acted on. In some situations the other object responds to the actions of the first; it interacts with the first. In situations where there is an interaction the line points in both directions. Each line is labeled to define the action it represents. In this way, the analysis model is able to present a clear and concise picture of the current environment. One glance at the analysis model will give the viewer an overall feel for the interaction between the different objects in the model.

Let's use our car dealership to demonstrate the analysis model. In previous chapter, Figure 2–4 presented the objects with which we will be dealing. At the time we had two superclasses—transportation vehicles and people. All of this is rather intuitive to the architect first approaching the car dealership's data warehouse. After interviewing the different users within the organization, however, the architect quickly learns that the dealership sees things somewhat differently. While transportation vehicles are still cars, people will fall into one of three subclasses: clients, prospective clients, or salespersons. The interview process also reveals that management is concerned with the sales process. How do they identify the prospective clients who can be turned into actual clients? Basically, who is most likely to buy a car from this dealership? If we begin our analysis with the sales process, we see the analysis model presented in Figure 3–1. The accompanying text would be similar to the following:

> A prospective client enters the lot and speaks with a salesperson. In this conversation the salesperson tries to understand the needs and desires of the prospective client. Once the salesperson understands what is being sought by the perspective client, he or she will show them a car that fulfills these needs. The prospective client after viewing the car may discuss the purchase in further detail with the salesperson and negotiate a price. Once a price has been determined for the car, the prospective client makes some sort of payment. Payment may take the form of a check, a lease agreement, or financing of some sort. The salesperson receives the payment and sells the car to the client. Selling here means transferring ownership. The prospective client takes ownership of the car. This in turn transforms the client from a prospective client to an actual client.

As can be seen from the figure, the model glosses over many of the details. If only purchasing a car were as simple as this process! We left out the part where the salesperson negotiates a price and then goes to his manager. We also left out the details of the ways in which payment is made. Subsequent models will provide further detail on payment method. Remember, this is an analysis model, which is the first of several models. Its point is to present the general flow of the business process.

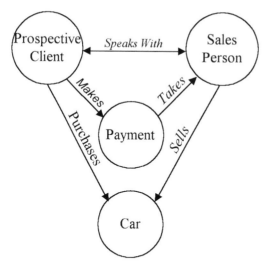

Figure 3–1   Analysis model.

The narrative should be no more than a few hundred words describing the analysis model. The users from whom the information was gathered should review both the model and its accompanying narrative, then provide any comments in writing. The architect then corrects the analysis model where appropriate. Again, it is important to note that time is of the essence. The creation of the analysis model should not become a project in and of itself. The entire interview process should take a week or two, depending on the number and availability of the users interviewed. The completion of the analysis model along with the user approvals take a matter of days, not weeks.

3.2.2.1   Big Brother & The Building Company Analysis

The interviews presented earlier have given us the information we need concerning Big Brother & The Building Company. First we have gathered the preliminary information about the environment in which the data warehouse is to exist. We have also discovered which of the operational systems will be the source of our data, specifically the Transaction Voucher System, the Available Properties System, and the real estate information system, Really Realty. There is also an external system, The National Listing of

Properties, that provides data on properties available for sale or lease. We have also learned that the users of the system, as one might expect in any organization, have a varied range of knowledge and comfort with technology. While some are quite comfortable, others still see working with information technology as an administrative task.

User training is another issue that came to light. Most users in the field offices do not have time to learn. Mostly they are driven by the task at hand and will deal only with aspects of technology that will help them at that moment. A successful user interface will, therefore, need to be intuitive and readily accessible to users. We also noted a sensitivity to cost on the part of the CEO, Jim. Several times during the interview he mentioned the cost of information technology. Most of this information does not have direct bearing on the design of a data model. This is, however, all part of the information to be gathered during the analysis process.

In turning our attention directly to the data model, we saw that the users had a pretty clear and uniform view of what analyses were to be performed. When asked about the five most important questions they would expect to be able to answer with the data warehouse, their answers were very consistent. Although several questions were common to all objects in the warehouse, the majority relate to one of three objects: markets, customers, or properties. The following list divides the questions into these three main categories.

- Markets
  - What do the specific geographic markets look like?
  - What are the trends in specific markets concerning properties?
  - What is the number of transactions by transaction type?
  - Standard variance analysis, what areas are going in the tank and where do we have to put more resources?
  - What markets am I performing well in?
  - Which business units are performing well?
  - Which regions are performing well?
  - Which regions are not performing well?
  - Which sales reps and managers are not performing well?

- What is the performance of my lines of business regionally, and on a time basis? What is the performance of those operations against target?
- Ratios, how is this line of business growing in relation to others?

- Customer
  - What are the trends in specific markets concerning clients?
  - What are the trends within certain client types?
  - Who are our top ten to one hundred clients?
  - Who are my top ten clients?
  - Who are my top clients currently versus historically?

- Property
  - What are the trends within certain property types?
  - Average rent rates by cities and locations around the globe?

- Common
  - Competitive information: Where are our competitors strong? Where are we weak?
  - The ability to create profiles and monitor performance based on those profiles.
  - Should be able to see the data in real time.

These questions define the objects needed for capture in the warehouse. When examining them, we need to read between the lines. The term *markets* could actually mean several things. There are geographic markets or sales territories. What are sales like in the Southwest? How is New York doing compared to Los Angeles? We will be able to track this information by profit center. There are also markets by property type. What is the performance of industrial property for the first fiscal quarter? How is shelter doing compared to retail? This can be tracked directly off the property object. Finally we can look at the market in terms of clients. As pointed out by Mike Rochelle, the client market can perhaps be the most complex of all to analyze. We cannot simply accept a System Industry Code (SIC) as the way to track customer type. At times a retail chain may be looking at office property. At other times RET's may be looking at shelter. Our examination of the customer markets must include not only the client's line of business; it must also consider what the client is doing with the property.

A single analysis will also cross market types. A business strategist may want to look at a geography in relation to a client and property type. We can expect these types of analysis to be common. For example, a business strategist can be proactive in looking at the types of properties that are used by different industries. Examination of the data within the warehouse, for example, can tell the strategist that a retail chain of such-and-such a size would require a certain size and type of office space. Perhaps that strategist will be able to define optimum locations for these properties. Armed with this information, the BBBC promotes itself from a reactive real estate service to a proactive consulting partner.

As noted in the second chapter, we must be careful to properly scope each iteration of the development spiral. While the intent of the warehouse is to include all the business units, tackling the entire organization at one time would be a fatal approach. We turn to our toy-box analogy. You can have only so many toys in the box. Which ones do you want to keep? Working within a finite schedule with finite resources, we must ask where these resources are best applied. Just like a parent, the data warehouse architect can recommend what to keep and what to put aside. Ultimately the decision lies with the child, or user. The warehouse is being built for them; it is their decision.

In subsequent discussions with the project sponsor and the CIO, our development team agreed that the scope of the first iteration be limited to the brokerage business unit. The voucher system, operation's primary system, is written according to brokerage's needs; all other business units have a complex translation of the data, as pointed out by the CIO. Brokerage will be the easiest business unit with which to start. Also, it accounts for the greatest percentage of revenue. Increases in brokerage performance will have greater impact than similar increases in other business units. Even a slight improvement in brokerage will produce much greater gains than larger increases in the other business units. Finally, we know that brokerage is the CEO's favorite child. In addition to its contribution to the overall organization, it is where he got his start with BBBC.

Big Brother & The Building Company Analysis Model. The   analysis
model for our case study is presented in Figure 3–2. The activity that we are
trying to capture in the first iteration of the development spiral is the sale or
lease of property by brokerage services.

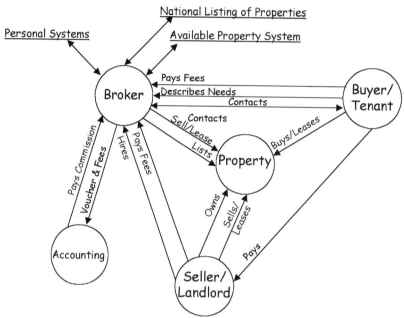

Figure 3–2   BBBC analysis model.

As we can see, four main objects are involved in this process. The following description would accompany the text for review by Mike Rochelle,
the project sponsor and head of brokerage services:

> A broker has two types of clients—one with property and one looking for prop-
> erty. The process begins when the broker makes contact with a client of either
> type. In the event that the broker is contacted by a client with property to offer,
> the broker searches his or her database for a buyer. The client has hired the bro-
> ker to represent them. Since the broker will earn commission from both the
> buyer and seller when representing both sides of the transaction, he or she
> attempts to keep news of the deal quiet. The broker will first attempt to fill any
> request from his or her own list of clients. When no ready prospect is discov-
> ered, the property is entered into the Available Property System and the National
> Listing of Properties.

If a client searching for property contacts a broker, the broker similarly will first search their personal databases for a property. Failing to find a suitable space for the client, the broker searches the National Listing of Properties and the Available Properties System for appropriate properties. If a property is found, the prospect reviews the property. The broker participates in any negotiations between the two parties to define appropriate terms. These terms could include such items as refurbishing the property to fit specific needs or several months free rent. Once the terms have been accepted, payments are made to the seller and the broker from the buying client. The property owner also pays the broker commission at the conclusion of the deal.

Upon receipt of payment the deal is recorded in the Transaction Voucher System (TVS). TVS generates the appropriate forms, which are sent to accounting along with the payments from the clients. The accounting department splits the commissions between the brokers involved in the deal and cuts the appropriate checks. Brokers are not necessarily employed by BBBC. Representatives of other organizations may also be involved in the deal.

3.3 The Design Phase

The design phase is the third phase in the development spiral. The design phase receives as input the analysis models along with the any other data collected during the analysis. From these inputs the design phase creates two outputs—the object model and the implementation model. This section will describe the construction of the object model. The implementation model is the actual schema of our database. The discussion of this model is part of our examination of the star schema and its derivatives.

3.3.1 The Object Model

The object model, the subject of this section, develops the analysis model more fully. This is, in essence, the activity of the design phase of the development spiral. One could think of the analysis model as a sketch, an outline of the reality it intends to represent. The object model is like the Sistine Chapel, rich with color and detail. Of course, Michaelangelo did not pick up his paints one day, walk into the nearest church and start to paint. Rather, he began with rough drawings that he refined to the actual work of art we see today. In creating the object model we will take the sketch in the analysis model and create a Sistine Chapel object model.

The data warehouse architect begins with the analysis model, adding more information as he or she proceeds. The model is complete when the objects within the scope of the data warehouse have been completely defined. By *complete* we mean that the object model contains all the attributes and behaviors that are relevant to our system. How do we know when we have a complete model? We don't! Complete in this context is a relative term. We can never be certain that we have completely defined all the attributes of the objects within the scope of the data warehouse, the best we can hope for is to get the majority of them. That is why the development spiral takes an object-oriented approach. We can always come back and add objects or attributes to the model in the event that some are missed.

The different symbols we will employ in creating an object model are shown in Figure 3–3. Before we look at a specific object model, let's first examine these symbols and what they represent. The first symbol that we notice in this figure is the superclass. In the previous chapter we defined a superclass as a classification of objects containing other classes. The object model represents a superclass as a rectangle with rounded corners. Within this rectangle are three main areas. The first is the name field at the top; this specifies the name of the superclass. The second is the attribute area; this specifies the attributes of the superclass. All classes subordinate to this superclass inherit these attributes. Third is the behavior area. This area specifies the behaviors that can be performed by the subordinate classes of this superclass.

The next object in the figure is that of class, represented by a rectangle with square corners. The areas within the rectangles are the same as those found in the superclass. The attributes and behaviors specified in the class object relate only to that object and do not affect those of other objects in that superclass. If a class specifies an attribute or behavior that has the same name of an attribute or behavior in the superclass, the subclass's specification is said to *override* those of the superclass. To model a class as subordinate to a superclass we employ the subclass object. A line is drawn from the superclass object to the top of the hexagon. Lines are then drawn from the hexagon to each of the subclasses.

Objects

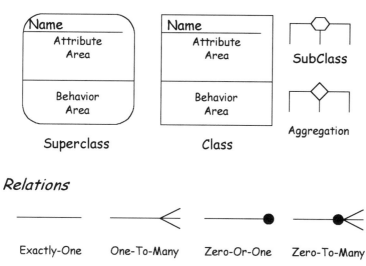

Figure 3–3   Object diagram symbols.

There are two important distinctions between class and superclass. A superclass is a higher level of abstraction. It groups together similar objects into one class defining a set of attributes and behaviors that are shared by all subordinate classes. The subordinate classes are said to inherit the behaviors and attributes of the superclass. They are passed down to the subordinate classes in much the same way that eye color or a propensity toward baldness is passed from parent to child. Another difference between class and superclass is that there are actual instances of classes. There are no actual instances of a superclass. While we may have a superclass of vehicles, there are no actual objects that are purely vehicles. There are instances of sport cars and economy cars. These are subclasses of the superclass vehicles.

The *aggregation* operator tells us when objects are aggregations. An aggregation is an object that is composed of other objects. In the preceding chapter we used the example of a car that is composed of wheels, a body, some seats, a transmission, and a steering wheel. The combination of these objects make a car, which is an aggregation. The aggregation symbol shows which objects are combined to make the aggregation.

The object model does more than present the individual objects; it also presents how the individual objects relate to one another. The relationship operators in the object model are of four types: exactly-one; one-to-many; zero-*or*-one; and zero-to-many. In relationships that are exactly-one, an instance of the first object must relate to one and only one instance of the other object. In a relationship that is one-to-many, an instance of an object may relate to many objects of the other type, but must relate to at least one. These relationships are not optional. An instance of one object *must* relate to an instance of the other object. In cases where an object's relationship to another object is optional, we have the zero-to-one and zero-to-many operators. The zero signifies that there need not be a relationship established between two instances of these objects.

All this may seem a bit confusing: superclasses, one-to-many, zero-or-one. In Figure 3–4 we return to our car-buying example to demonstrate how to create an object model. A review of Figure 3–1 shows that we are dealing with three basic objects: cars, payments, and people. In the object diagram we have four objects: cars, payments, people, and Sales Reps. In this diagram we do not recognize Sales Reps as people. (This may be something that many of you have felt for some time.) The reason for this separation is that we are interested in the car-buying habits of our target market, which is the general public. Sales Reps do not fall into this category, since their buying habits are different from those of the general public.

As shown in the diagram there are three types of abstract classes: payments, people and cars. All payments have one thing in common—an amount. Whether we purchase a car with cash, a loan, or a lease, there is always an amount. When acquiring a loan to purchase a car, however, we would like to know the bank. When leasing a car, we would like to know the terms of the lease in addition to which bank. When we pay cash for a car, all of these things are irrelevant. We, therefore, isolate each of these attributes to the related objects. We see the same type of "attribute distribution" with cars and people. The attributes that relate to a specific subclass are specified within the subclass. The diagram also demonstrates how objects inherit attributes and behaviors from a superclass. The Cars super-class has the attribute's name, engine size, doors, and price. All cars have these attributes. All cars also have the behaviors acceleration and stopping. These behaviors are passed down to each of the subclasses of cars.

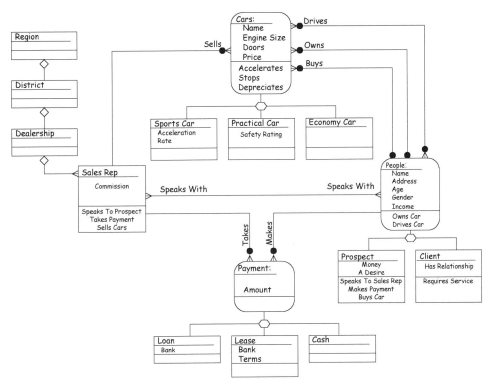

Figure 3–4 Car sales object model.

In Figure 3–4 we represent a relationship between two objects by drawing a line from one to the other. A description of the relationship labels each line with a cardinality symbol at each end. We would say, therefore, that a person makes zero to many payments, meaning that the relationship is optional. No payments are associated with prospects, while a person who has purchased many cars has made many payments. As shown in this dia-gram, if a payment does exist, it must be related to a specific person. The payment object is related also to the salesperson. A salesperson takes zero to many payments. A salesperson who has yet to make a sale would not be associated with any payments. A sales representative will receive a separate payment for every car he or she may sell, in which case the sales rep will be associated with many payments. All payments are associated with one and only one sales rep.

The relationship between the car object and the people object is also very interesting. We have two different types of people: clients and prospects. We also have three distinct types of relationship: owns, buys, or drives a car. Each of these relationships is optional from the perspective of the person object. A person may or may not own, drive, or purchase a car. Certainly a prospect may be a first-time car buyer. These relationships are also independent of one another. Although a person may buy a car, this does not necessarily mean that they will ultimately own it; they may being buying the car as a gift. By the same token, the person who receives the car as a gift will own and drive it, but did not buy it. Each of these relationships is optional from the perspective of the car as well. A car that is sitting on the lot is not owned, driven, or purchased by any person. Cars on the lot are owned by the dealership, which is also an optional relationship; this ownership relationship is broken, once the car is sold.

When constructing the model, we want to structure the objects to reflect the view of the business space that is subject to our analysis. One might look at this and say that in the *real world* things work a bit differently. We have to ask ourselves how things work in relation to what we are trying to understand. It may not be significant to our analysis that more than one person could purchase a car or that a car may be purchased with more than one payment. In these cases we do not want to cloud our understanding with unnecessary detail. In the event that we should discover that these factors are important to our analysis, the development spiral provides us with the flexibility to go back and modify the model.

3.3.1.1   Big Brother & The Building Company Object Model

The mission statement asserted that the data warehouse *is to support the analysis of the various commercial real estate markets in which the organization competes. The system is to provide management with information pertaining to clients, client behavior, BBBC's performance, and the state of each of the commercial real estate markets.* The interview process further refined this mission, describing how the users envisioned using it. Considering this information, we were able to define the objects that fell within the scope of the data warehouse.

Once the objects within the data warehouse were defined, the analysis model documented the interaction between them. In constructing the object model for BBBC we refer again to the analysis model presented in Figure 3–2. The objects presented in this model are the seller/landlord, buyer/tenant, property, broker, and accounting. From our discussions with the user community we know that accounting is just a recipient of the payments and is not really part of our analysis. We also know that at times a client will be a buyer/tenant in one deal and a seller/landlord in another. For this reason it would be most appropriate to group them into one object simply labeled client. Finally, we know from our discussions with the CIO that there are four source systems: the Available Properties System (APS), the National Listing of Properties, the Transaction Voucher System (TVS), and Really Realty, the property information system. In studying these systems in detail we are able to define both the attributes and behaviors of the objects in more detail. Figure 3–5 presents the BBBC object model that resulted from our analysis.

Traditionally the object model lists the object attributes in the diagram. For very practical reasons, however, the attributes of each of the individual objects have not been included in this diagram; there are too many of them to present within the diagram in this format. To simplify matters, the attributes have been listed separately in Table 3–1 on page 110. Most object-oriented case tools, however, provide a means to list the attributes of objects completely within a diagram.

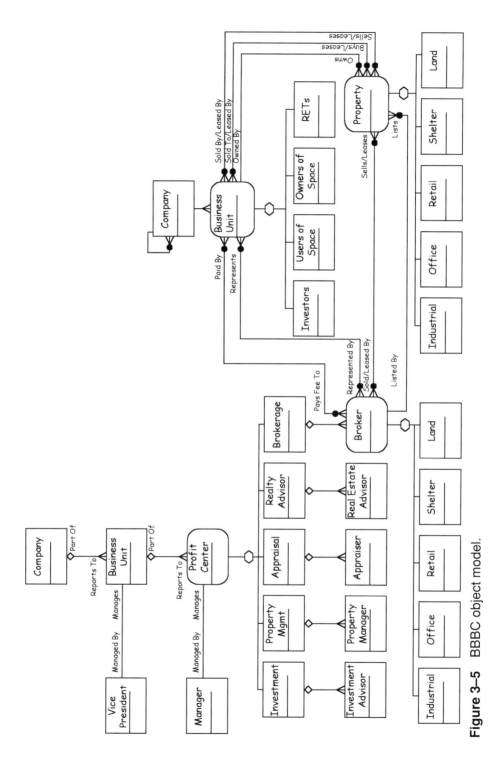

Figure 3–5 BBBC object model.

Let's examine the object model and how its structure was influenced by the business strategist's requirements. First, we see that the structure of the commercial real estate company itself has been modeled. Companies are composed of business units, and business units are composed of profit centers. The profit centers themselves are a superclass which is divided into profit-center types. Reporting to each profit center is an individual contributor, whose type is dependent on the type of profit center reported to. Brokers report to brokerage service profit centers and are the only type of contributor fully described in this model. Since the first iteration of the development spiral deals exclusively with brokerage, the model is limited to the needs of that organization. Future iterations of the spiral will be able to expand on this model.

As described in the analysis model, brokers that participate in a deal do not necessarily report to BBBC. Brokers from other organizations will also participate in deals and will receive a commission. In examining the performance of BBBC in comparison to other organizations in that market, it will be important to collect as much market information as possible. This structure will allow the warehouse to capture information pertaining to all brokers in the deal and group them according to company.

The structure above the broker also facilitates the examination of BBBC itself. By fully describing the structure of the organization, the performance of the different levels of the organization can be analyzed by the business strategist. Data pertaining to a specific business unit, profit center, or broker can be retrieved and compared to other brokers and profit centers.

Data in the property information system, Really Reality, contains property information of all buildings within a commercial real estate market. These properties may not have anything to do with a deal. This means that all the relationships to the property are optional except for ownership; a property must be owned by someone. For these same reasons, it is not necessary that a client be associated with a deal. An owner of a property that is not involved with a deal would not have any relationship with BBBC or any other commercial real estate company.

A concern brought out during the interviews was the ability to track the overall value of customers. The data warehouse would have to identify customers both at the local level and as part of a larger organization. One example provided by Mike Rochelle was that of a large retail chain. If we simply captured the individual contacts for that retail chain without associating them to the national organization, we would lose the national perspective of that client. This national perspective is critical. Recall the interview with Brian Berry. We were told that Jim Bean wanted to be able to work out strategic partnerships with large clients. The ranking of clients must, therefore, be able to look at both the national and local levels of this relationship.

The client information is *normalized* between two objects. The first object is the company. The company references itself in order to build a corporate hierarchy. This method of dealing with hierarchies will be discussed in more detail when we examine dimensions. As can be seen in Table 3–1, an attribute of the company is the company type. Types will be defined by SIC identification number. A company is related to at least one and possibly many clients. The client is a superclass that can be one of four types: investor, user of space, owner of space, or REIT. We also see in Table 3–1 that the attributes of the property include a Property Use attribute. This attribute defines how the property is used by the owner/tenant.

In our interviews, Mike Rochelle pointed out that we need the ability to track not only the business of our clients but also how they were using the property at this particular location. To meet this need the design of the database includes a type attribute for the company, business unit, and property. The business strategist is able to define behaviors at each level of the client hierarchy as well as the relationship between the different types. Large diversified corporations may have investment, retail, and manufacturing subsidiaries. Each of these in turn may have office space, and some may have retail outlets. The structure presented in the object diagram will allow each object to retain its own type. How they use a property can be defined by the use type attribute associated with the property.

The object model presented here is rather complex. In addition, it is pretty well normalized for this level of design. In fact, the preliminary designs of the development spiral can be used for either a traditional normalized transaction processing database or a denormalized subject-oriented decision support system. The difference occurs at the next step. Where the OLTP system architect would take this model and continue to normalize, the data warehouse architect goes through a process of denormalization. In this process the object model is coalesced into a star-type schema.

Before discussing this process, however, we will must first understand what is meant by multidimensional data. Armed with this understanding, we can then proceed to a discussion of the star schema structure and its variations. In the next chapter we will look at multidimensionality and how it is implemented using a star schema.

3.3.1.2 BBBC Object Attributes

In this section we will examine the attributes of the objects within the data warehouse. The tables in this section are composed of the following columns:

- **Field Name**—Specifies the name by which the data element is known to the user.
- **Format**—Specifies the layout of the data.
- **Null Option**—Specifies whether nulls are acceptable for the data element.
- **Comments**—Provides a description of the data.
- **System Of Record**—Defines which operational systems are the source of the data. Note that in some instances data may originate from more than one source. In such cases all the sources are listed in the attribute table. Part of the integration of new data into the data warehouse is to synchronize data from multiple operational systems. Valid values are:
  - APS—Available Properties System.
  - DW—Data Warehouse. Data warehouse data originates within the warehouse. Data of this type is entered by the data administrator or is interpolated during the extraction of the data from the operational environment.
  - HR—Human Resources.
  - NLP—National Listing of Properties.
  - RR—Really Realty.
  - TVS—Transaction Voucher System.

Broker Attributes. Table 3–1 describes the attributes of the Broker object.

Table 3–1 Attributes of the Broker Object

Field Name	Data Type	Null Option	Description	System Of Record
Sales Person Key	Number 9	Not Null	System Generated Primary Key	DW
Profit Center Key	Number 9	Not Null	Foreign Key to Profit Center Table	DW
Broker ID	Number 9	Not Null	Human Resources Broker Identification Number	HR
Broker Type	Character 1	Not Null	Indicates the primary type of property with which the broker deals. The following are valid codes: I = Industrial R = Retail L = Land O = Office S = Shelter	HR
Last Name	Character 20	Not Null	Employee's Last Name	HR
First Name	Character 20	Not Null	Employee's First Name	HR
Middle Initial	Character 1	Null	Employee's Middle Initial	HR
Title	Character 10	Not Null	Employee Title	HR
E-Mail Address	Character 20	Not Null	Employee E-Mail Address	HR
Street Address 1	Character 20	Not Null	First Line of Two Line Employee Home Address	HR
Street Address 2	Character 20	Null	Second Line of Two Line Employee Home Address	HR
City	Character 20	Not Null	Employee Home City	HR
State	Character 2	Not Null	Employee Home State	HR
Postal Code	Character 9	Not Null	Employee Postal Code	HR
Work Phone Number	Character 10	Not Null	Employee Work Phone Number	HR
Mobile Phone Number	Character 10	Null	Employee Mobile Phone Number	HR
Home Phone Number	Character 10	Not Null	Employee Home Phone Number	HR
Fax Number	Character 10	Not Null	Employee FAX Phone Number	HR

Business Unit. Table 3–2 describes the attributes of the Business Unit object.

Table 3–2 Attributes of the Business Unit Object

Field Name	Data Type	Null Option	Description	System Of Record
Business Unit Key	Number 9	Not Null	Foreign key to Business Unit Table, Indicates the parent business unit	DW
Profit Center Key	Number 9	Not Null	Foreign Key to Profit Center Table	DW
Vice President Key	Number 9	Not Null	Foreign Key to Vice President Table	DW
Business Unit Type	Enumerated	Not Null	Field Indicating Business Unit Type. The following are valid codes: B = Brokerage R = Realty Advisors A = Appraisal I = Investments P = Property Management	DW
Business Unit Name	Character 20	Not Null	Name of the Business Unit	DW
Street Address 1	Character 20	Not Null	First Line of Two Line Address	DW
Street Address 2	Character 20	Null	Second Line of Two Line Address	DW
City	Character 20	Not Null	Office City	DW
State	Character 2	Not Null	Office State	DW
Postal Code	Character 9	Not Null	Office Postal Code	DW
Main Office Phone Number	Character 10	Not Null	Business Unit's Main Phone Number	DW
Secondary Office Phone Number	Character 10	Null	Business Unit's Secondary Phone Number	DW
Main Fax Number	Character 10	Not Null	Business Unit's Main Fax Number	DW
Secondary Fax Number	Character 10	Null	Business Unit's Secondary Fax Number	DW

Client Business Unit Attributes.   Much of the client's business unit information can come from one of two sources: the voucher system, or Really Realty. Voucher system data pertains to those companies that are clients of BBBC. Client business unit information that originates with Really Realty pertains to those companies that own a property in the real estate information system but are not clients of BBBC. Table 3–3 describes the attributes of the Client Business Unit object.

Client Company Attributes.   Much of the client's company information can come from one of three sources: the voucher system, Really Realty, or an external source. Voucher system data pertains to those companies that are clients of BBBC. Client company information that originates with Really Realty pertains to those companies that own a property in the real estate information system but are not clients of BBBC. Companies whose information originates from an external source are those organizations that are parent companies of client companies or companies that own real estate recorded in Really Realty. The information group will be responsible for entering this information into the data warehouse from the external source. Table 3–4 describes the attributes of the Client Company object.

Commercial Real Estate Company.   Table 3–5 describes the attributes of the Commercial Real Estate Company object.

Manager.   Table 3–6 describes the attributes of the Manager object.

Profit Center.   Table 3–7 describes the attributes of the Profit Center object.

Property.   Table 3–8 describes the attributes of the Property object.

Table 3-3 Attributes of the Client Business Unit Object

Field Name	Data Type	Null Option	Comments	System Of Record
Client Business Unit Key	Number 9	Not Null	System Generated Primary Key	DW
Client Parent Company Key	Number 9	Not Null	Foreign Key to Company Table indicating parent company of the client business unit	DW
Client Name	Character 30	Not Null	Name of the Client Business Unit	VS/RR
Client Type	Character 1	Not Null	Code signifying the type of client. The following are valid client codes: I = Investor R = Real Estate Investment Trust U = User of Space O = Owner of Space	VS/RR
Street Address 1	Character 20	Not Null	First Line of Two Line Address	VS/RR
Street Address 2	Character 20	Null	Second Line of Two Line Address	VS/RR
City	Character 20	Not Null	Office City	VS/RR
State	Character 2	Not Null	Office State	VS/RR
Postal Code	Character 9	Not Null	Office Postal Code	VS/RR
Main Office Phone Number	Character 10	Null	Business Unit's Main Phone Number	VS/RR
Secondary Office Phone Number	Character 10	Null	Business Unit's Secondary Phone Number	VS/RR
Main Fax Number	Character 10	Null	Business Unit's Main Fax Number	VS/RR
Secondary Fax Number	Character 10	Null	Business Unit's Secondary Fax Number	VS/RR
Primary Contact's Last Name	Character 20	Not Null	Primary Contact's Last Name	VS/RR
Primary Contact's First Name	Character 20	Not Null	Primary Contact's First Name	VS/RR
Primary Contact's Middle Initial	Character 1	Null	Primary Contact's Middle Initial	VS/RR
Primary Contact's E-Mail Address	Character 20	Null	Primary Contact's E-Mail Address	VS/RR
Primary Contact's Work Phone Number	Character 10	Not Null	Primary Contact's Work Phone Number	VS/RR
Primary Contact's Mobile Phone Number	Character 10	Null	Primary Contact's Mobile Phone Number	VS/RR
Primary Contact's Home Phone Number	Character 10	Null	Primary Contact's Home Phone Number	VS/RR
Primary Contact's Fax Number	Character 10	Not Null	Primary Contact's FAX Phone Number	VS/RR

113

Table 3–4 Attributes of the Client Company Object

Field Name	Data Type	Null Option	Comments	System Of Record
Company Key	Number 9	Not Null	Primary	DW
Parent Company Key	Number 9	Not Null	Self-referencing key, points to company record of the Parent Company	DW
Company Name	Character 20	Not Null	Name of the Parent Company	VS/RR/EX
Street Address 1	Character 20	Not Null	First Line of Two Line Address	VS/RR/EX
Street Address 2	Character 20	Null	Second Line of Two Line Address	VS/RR/EX
City	Character 20	Not Null	Office City	VS/RR/EX
State	Character 2	Not Null	Office State	VS/RR/EX
Postal Code	Character 9	Not Null	Office Postal Code	VS/RR/EX
Main Office Phone Number	Character 10	Not Null	Parent Company's Main Phone Number	VS/RR/EX
Secondary Office Phone Number	Character 10	Null	Parent Company's Secondary Phone Number	VS/RR/EX
Main Fax Number	Character 10	Not Null	Parent Company's Main Fax Number	VS/RR/EX
Secondary Fax Number	Character 10	Null	Parent Company's Secondary Fax Number	VS/RR/EX

Table 3–5 Attributes of the Commerical Real Estate Company Object

Field Name	Data Type	Null Option	Comments	System Of Record
Company Key	Integer	Not Null	Primary	DW
Company Name	Character 20	Not Null	Name of the Parent Company	DW
Street Address 1	Character 20	Not Null	First Line of Two Line Address	DW
Street Address 2	Character 20	Null	Second Line of Two Line Address	DW
City	Character 20	Not Null	Office City	DW
State	Character 2	Not Null	Office State	DW
Postal Code	Character 9	Not Null	Office Postal Code	DW
Main Office Phone Number	Character 10	Not Null	Parent Company's Main Phone Number	DW
Secondary Office Phone Number	Character 10	Null	Parent Company's Secondary Phone Number	DW
Main Fax Number	Character 10	Not Null	Parent Company's Main Fax Number	DW
Secondary Fax Number	Character 10	Null	Parent Company's Secondary Fax Number	DW
SIC	Number 7	Not Null	Code representing companies primary line of business	VS/RR/EX

Table 3–6 Attributes of the Manager Object

Field Name	Data Type	Null Option	Description	System Of Record
Manager ID	Number 9	Not Null	Primary Key of Manager Table	DW
Manager's Last Name	Character 20	Not Null	Manager's Last Name	HR
Manager's First Name	Character 20	Not Null	Manager's First Name	HR
Manager's Middle Initial	Character 1	Null	Manager's Middle Initial	HR
Manager's E-Mail Address	Character 20	Not Null	Manager's E-Mail Address	HR
Manager's Home Street Address 1	Character 20	Not Null	First Line of Two Line Manager Home Address	HR
Manager's Home Street Address 2	Character 20	Null	Second Line of Two Line Manager Home Address	HR
Manager's Home City	Character 20	Not Null	Manager's Home City	HR
Manager's Home State	Character 2	Not Null	Manager's Home State	HR
Manager's Home Postal Code	Character 9	Not Null	Manager's Postal Code	HR
Manager's Work Phone Number	Character 10	Not Null	Manager's Work Phone Number	HR
Manager's Mobile Phone Number	Character 10	Null	Manager's Mobile Phone Number	HR
Manager's Home Phone Number	Character 10	Not Null	Manager's Home Phone Number	HR
Manager's Fax Number	Character 10	Not Null	Manager's FAX Phone Number	HR

Table 3–7   Attributes of the Profit Center Object

Field Name	Data Type	Null Option	Description	System Of Record
Profit Center Key	Number 9	Not Null	Foreign Key to Profit Center Table	DW
Manager Key	Number 9	Not Null	Foreign Key to Broker Table. Indicates the manager of the profit center	DW
Business Unit Key	Number 9	Not Null	Foreign Key to Business Unit Table. Indicates the parent business unit	DW
Profit Center Type	Character 1	Not Null	Field Indicating Profit Center Type. The following are valid codes: B = Brokerage R = Realty Advisors A = Appraisal I = Investments P = Property Management	DW
Profit Center Name	Character 20	Not Null	Name of the Profit Center	DW
Street Address 1	Character 20	Not Null	First Line of Two Line Address	DW
Street Address 2	Character 20	Null	Second Line of Two Line Address	DW
City	Character 20	Not Null	Office City	DW
State	Character 2	Not Null	Office State	DW
Postal Code	Character 9	Not Null	Office Postal Code	DW
Main Office Phone Number	Character 10	Not Null	Profit Center's Main Phone Number	DW
Secondary Office Phone Number	Character 10	Null	Profit Center's Secondary Phone Number	DW
Main Fax Number	Character 10	Not Null	Profit Center's Main Fax Number	DW
Secondary Fax Number	Character 10	Null	Profit Center's Secondary Fax Number	DW

117

Table 3–8 Attributes of the Property Object

Field Name	Data Type	Null Option	Description	System Of Record
Property ID	Number 9	Not Null	Primary Key of Property Table	DW
Acres	Number 6,2	Null	Number of acres upon which the property resides	RR
Architect	Character 20	Null	Name of Architectural Company	RR
Architect Hdqtr	Character 20	Null	Address of Architectural Headquarters	RR
Architect Hdqtr Street Address 1	Character 20	Null	First Line of Two Line Address of Architectural Company Office	RR
Architect Hdqtr Street Address 2	Character 20	Null	Second Line of Two Line Address of Architectural Company Office	RR
Architect Hdqtr City	Character 20	Null	Architectural Company Office City	RR
Architect Hdqtr State	Character 2	Null	Architectural Company Office State	RR
Architect Hdqtr Postal Code	Character 9	Null	Architectural Company Office Postal Code	RR
Architect Hdqtr Postal Code Extension	Character 9	Null	Architectural Company Office Postal Code Extension	RR
Building Ref. Num.	Number 7	Null	Really Realty Property ID	RR
City	Character 20	Not Null	City Of the Property Address	RR
Code1	Character 3	Null	User Defined Code—Value in Field varies with profit center.	RR
Code2	Character 3	Null	User Defined Code—Value in Field varies with profit center.	RR
Code3	Character 3	Null	User Defined Code—Value in Field varies with profit center.	RR
Code4	Character 3	Null	User Defined Code—Value in Field varies with profit center.	RR

Table 3–8 Attributes of the Property Object (Continued)

Field Name	Data Type	Null Option	Description	System Of Record
Code5	Character 3	Null	User Defined Code—Value in Field varies with profit center.	RR
Code6	Character 3	Null	User Defined Code—Value in Field varies with profit center.	RR
Code7	Character 3	Null	User Defined Code—Value in Field varies with profit center.	RR
Code8	Character 3	Null	User Defined Code—Value in Field varies with profit center.	RR
Code9	Character 3	Null	User Defined Code—Value in Field varies with profit center.	RR
Code10	Character 3	Null	User Defined Code—Value in Field varies with profit center.	RR
Comments	Long Varchar	Null	User Defined Comments	RR
Complex/Park Name	Character 20	Null	Name of Business Park	RR
Constructed Year	Date	Null	Year Building was Constructed	RR
Contractor	Character 20	Null	Name of Contractor Company	RR
Contractor Hdqtr	Character 20	Null	Address of Contractor Headquarters	RR
Contractor Hdqtr Street Address 1	Character 20	Null	First Line of Two Line Address of Contractor Company Office	RR
Contractor Hdqtr Street Address 2	Character 20	Null	Second Line of Two Line Address of Contractor Company Office	RR
Contractor Hdqtr City	Character 20	Null	Contractor Company Office City	RR
Contractor Hdqtr State	Character 2	Null	Contractor Company Office State	RR
Contractor Hdqtr Postal Code	Character 9	Null	Contractor Company Office Postal Code	RR

119

Table 3–8   Attributes of the Property Object (Continued)

Field Name	Data Type	Null Option	Description	System Of Record
Contractor Hdqtr Postal Code Extension	Character 9	Null	Contractor Company Office Postal Code Extension	RR
Country	Character 20	Null	Country of the Property	RR
County	Character 20	Not Null	County of the Property	RR
Cross Street 1	Character 30	Null	First Major Cross Street of Building	RR
Cross Street 2	Character 30	Null	Second Major Cross Street of Building	RR
Date Available	Date	Null	Date Property Is Available	RR
Date On Market	Date	Null	Data Property Is Placed on the Market	RR
Developer	Character 30	Null	Developer of the Property	RR
Record Date	Date	Not Null	Date Record Was Created	RR
Latitude	Number 7,4	Not Null	Latitude of the Property	RR
Longitude	Number 7,4	Not Null	Longitude of the Property	RR
Management Company	Character 30	Not Null	Name of Property Management Company	RR
Management Hdqtr	Character 20	Null	Address of Management Headquarters	RR
Management Hdqtr Street Address 1	Character 20	Null	First Line of Two Line Address of Management Company Office	RR
Management Hdqtr Street Address 2	Character 20	Null	Second Line of Two Line Address of Management Company Office	RR
Management Hdqtr City	Character 20	Null	Management Company Office City	RR
Management Hdqtr State	Character 2	Null	Management Company Office State	RR
Management Hdqtr Postal Code	Character 9	Null	Management Company Office Postal Code	RR
Management Hdqtr Postal Code Extension	Character 9	Null	Management Company Office Postal Code Extension	RR

Table 3–8   Attributes of the Property Object (Continued)

Field Name	Data Type	Null Option	Description	System Of Record
Management Contact	Character 30	Not Null	Property Management Company Contact	RR
Management Contact Phone Number	Character 10	Not Null	Phone Number of Property Management Company	RR
Number Of Tenants	Number 3	Not Null	Number of Tenants in the property	RR
Ownership	Number 8	Not Null	Foreign Key Pointing to Property Owner's Record in the Property Table.	RR
Parking Type	Character 1	Not Null	Code Indicating Type of Parking Structure. The valid codes are: N = None G = Garage C = Covered O = Open	RR
Purchase Price	Number 10	Not Null	Price for which the property was most recently purchased	RR
Purchase Year	Date	Not Null	Year in which the property was last purchased	RR
Rep ID	Number 9	Null	Foreign Key Pointing to the Employee Record of Broker	RR
Renovated Year	Date	Null	Year property was last renovated	RR
Transaction Code	Character 1	Not Null	Code indicating if the property is for sale or lease. The valid codes are: S = Sale L = Lease	RR
Sq. Ft Available	Number 7	Not Null	Total number of square feet available in the property	RR
Sq. Ft Available Contiguous	Number 7	Not Null	Total number of contiguous square feet available in the property	RR

121

Table 3–8 Attributes of the Property Object (Continued)

Field Name	Data Type	Null Option	Description	System Of Record
Sq. Ft Building	Number 7	Not Null	Total number of square feet in the building	RR
Sq. Ft Garage	Number 7	Not Null	Total square feet in parking structure	RR
Sq. Ft Improved	Number 7	Not Null	Total square feet most recently improved	RR
Sq. Ft Per Floor Max	Number 7	Not Null	Maximum square feet per floor	RR
Sq. Ft Per Floor Min	Number 7	Not Null	Minimum square feet per floor	RR
Sq. Ft Usable	Number 7	Not Null	Total usable square feet in property	RR
State	Character 2	Not Null	Property's state	RR
Status	Character 1	Not Null	Code indicating the state of the building. The following are valid codes: N = New P = Poor E = Excellent R = Repair needed G = Good	RR
Street Direction	Character 1	Not Null	Direction of property's street address	RR
Street Name	Character 30	Not Null	Name of property's street address	RR
Street Number 1	Character 5	Not Null	First number of property's street address	RR
Street Number 2	Character 5	Not Null	Second number of property's street address	RR
Use Type	Character 1	Not Null	Code Indicating the Property's Use. The following are valid codes: I = Industrial S = Shelter O = Office L = Land R = Retail	RR
Vacant Percent	Number 0,2	Not Null	Percentage of the property that is vacant	RR
Postal Code	Character 5	Not Null	Postal code of the property's address	RR
Postal Code Extension	Character 4	Not Null	Postal code extension of the property's address	RR

Vice President. Table 3–9 describes the attributes of the Vice President object.

Table 3–9 Attributes of the Vice President Object

Field Name	Data Type	Null Option	Description	System Of Record
VP ID	Number 9	Not Null	Primary Key of VP Table	DW
VP's Last Name	Character 20	Not Null	VP's Last Name	HR
VP's First Name	Character 20	Not Null	VP's First Name	HR
VP's Middle Initial	Character 1	Null	VP's Middle Initial	HR
VP's E-Mail Address	Character 20	Not Null	VP's E-Mail Address	HR
VP's Home Street Address 1	Character 20	Not Null	First Line of Two Line VP Home Address	HR
VP's Home Street Address 2	Character 20	Null	Second Line of Two Line VP Home Address	HR
VP's Home City	Character 20	Not Null	VP's Home City	HR
VP's Home State	Character 2	Not Null	VP's Home State	HR
VP's Home Postal Code	Character 9	Not Null	VP's Postal Code	HR
VP's Work Phone Number	Character 10	Not Null	VP's Work Phone Number	HR
VP's Mobile Phone Number	Character 10	Null	VP's Mobile Phone Number	HR
VP's Home Phone Number	Character 10	Not Null	VP's Home Phone Number	HR
VP's Fax Number	Character 10	Not Null	VP's FAX Phone Number	HR

3.4 Summary

This chapter has presented the first three phases of the development spiral: definition, analysis, and design. These three phases form the foundation upon which the current and future iterations of the spiral will be based. In this chapter we have learned how to develop an understanding of user needs. We have also seen how to develop a design based on that understanding. We have bridged the chasm between the needs of the user and the high-level design of a working system.

The chapter has discussed how in the first phase of the spiral the data warehouse architect collaborates with the project sponsor to define the mission of the data warehouse. This mission is defined, appropriately enough, in the mission statement. This statement determines the scope and direction of the data warehouse.

The second phase of the spiral is the analysis. In the analysis phase the data warehouse architect gains an understanding of the user's needs. This is done by interviewing key people within the organization who will interact with the data warehouse. It is also during this phase that the architect gathers an understanding of the environment in which the warehouse is to reside. The term *environment* here means everything from the operational systems that will provide the warehouse with data to the desktop of the business strategist who will be accessing that data.

The third and final stage discussed in this chapter is the design phase. In this phase we refine our understanding of the data warehouse environment. Objects are examined more closely than in the analysis phase. Within this phase the behaviors and attributes of the objects are defined in enough detail to allow the architect to go on and develop the detailed implementation model. In the next chapter we will examine the implementation model, in which the star schema takes shape.

3.5 Glossary

Analysis Model   Preliminary model in the design process. Identifies the objects within the analysis and their interaction with one another.

Mission Statement Defines the objective, or mission, of the data warehouse in a simple single statement.

Model An abstraction of reality. A model of an object is something with which an analyst works when the actual object cannot easily be manipulated or modified.

The Implementation Model

In this chapter we take the step from the theoretical to the actual. In the preceding chapter we built the analysis and design models. These models provided a conceptual view of the objects within the scope of the data warehouse. In their creation we developed an understanding of how things work. We now take these conceptual models and build the implementation model.

The structure we are about to design supports the way in which strategists view their environment. In Chapter 1 we discussed how the strategist is looking for behaviors in the marketplace, searching for ways to understand the current environment and predict its future. As we shall see in this chapter, the architect must create a data structure that is natural to the business strategist. It must allow strategists to think in terms of the objects they are studying. To achieve this end the warehouse architect structures the data dimensionally. Dimensions draw borders around the area of study, and they also provide a way to define specific relationships between objects within the business environment. The construction of the implementation model builds this multidimensional structure, known as a star schema, within a relational database.

To fully appreciate the way in which we use dimensional analysis and construct the implementation model, let's begin at the very beginning. When we count, we begin with one, two, three. When we build, we begin with dimensionality, dimensionality. The first section of this chapter discusses dimensionality in its most basic form. In this section we explore coordinate systems and how they are used to define space. In the second section we relate dimensionality to information systems. We first explore traditional applications and how they fall short in providing a multidimensional environment for the strategist. Then we discuss multidimensional databases (MDDB) as an alternative. Although multidimensional systems provide the desired environment for the business strategist, certain limitations make them unsuitable for many environments. Another solution to multidimensional analysis is the star schema. The last two sections of this chapter present the star schema as a means to implement multidimensionality in a relational environment.

The structure of this chapter is important. It is simple enough to present the basic star schema. It would not take an entire chapter to explain the tables and how they are related. What is most important, however, is an understanding of what the star schema creates. The beauty of the star schema is its ability to provide a very complex multidimensional view of data in a very simple structure. The goal of this chapter is to develop an appreciation for the multidimensional nature of the star schema. This chapter develops the concept that the star is in fact a multidimensional model implemented within a relational environment. It shows how the dimensions create a space within which the strategist can perform analyses.

4.1 Dimensionality

In this section we will discuss multidimensional data and what we mean by multidimensional analysis. A *dimension* is an axis of a coordinate system that binds a space. The prefix *multi-* means multiple or more than one. *Multidimensionality*, then, refers to more than one dimension or to binding a space in multiple ways. This is natural to our way of thinking. The universe in which we live exists in multiple dimensions—height, depth, width, and time. In our daily lives we deal with these four dimensions, although we may not be consciously aware of them as we go about our business. What about data, though? How does this all relate to data and our understanding of the objects with an organization's environment?

Let's step back in time for a moment to review what we all learned in junior high. We studied the cartesian coordinate system, in which we started out working with two dimensions. We called those dimensions the X and Y axes and divided each into equal units, as shown in Figure 4–1. The space *dimensioned by* these axes is a plane. That is, the plane is bound, or contained within, these axes.

Envision a space whose edges are the dimensions. Every point within that space has some relationship to the binding dimensions. This relationship is defined by the point's coordinates. To locate a point using its coordinates we move along each axis the specified number of units and draw a line perpendicular to the axis at that coordinate. The intersection of these lines is our point. In Figure 4–1 we have the point (3, 4). We have moved 3 units along the X axis and 4 units along the Y. As you may recall, in the cartesian coordinate system the first number represents the X-axis and the second the Y.

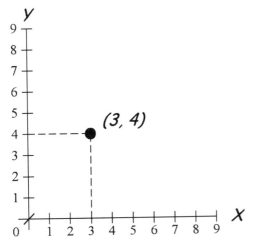

Figure 4–1   Cartesian coordinate system.

The point at which the two axes meet, point (0, 0), is referred to as the point of origin. The set of axes emanating from a single point of origin is a coordinate system. When we plot a point or a graph on some coordinate system, we are expressing that the point's X-coordinate is some function of its *Y*-coordinate. This is true of all dimensions within the coordinate system; all dimensions are related to one another.

Perhaps we are representing a sine wave or the fluctuations of the stock market over a period of time. The points along the *X*-axis are related to the points along the *Y*-axis by some function. Look at any stock market report and you will see this relation. Typically what you will see is the *X*-axis representing time and the *Y*-axis representing the value of the stock market. The relation between the two axes is the set of all possible values of the market for all points within a given time period.

In looking at these dimensions, note how they represent objects of analysis. The objects in the stock market report are time and the value of the market. When we organize related objects into dimensions, creating a coordinate system, the space formed by this coordinate system is the *analysis space*. In our stock market report the points in the analysis space are the values of the market at a particular time.

In a two-dimensional world we are limited to existence on a plane. This world exists in only two dimensions: height and width. There is no depth. This world of two dimensions differs drastically not only from our physical existence but also from the way in which we view our business environment. Organizations work in a universe of complex issues composed of not just two or even three objects, but many objects. We must work with all of them in our analysis to understand their impact on the organization.

To add another object we must add another axis—that is, another dimension. We have done this in Figure 4–2. We can go beyond three dimensions and extend our analysis to as many dimensions as we like. The general rule of thumb, however, is that you should not have more than six or seven dimensions in any one analysis. As you will see later in this chapter, working in many dimensions at one time can become quite confusing and result in clouding an issue that you actually hope to clarify.

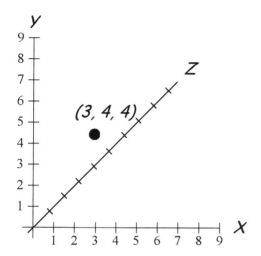

Figure 4–2 Three-dimensional coordinate system.

4.2 Dimensionality and Information Systems

When we look at a relational table we can almost see a two-dimensional space. We have columns that serve as the *X*-axis and rows that serve as the *Y*. In actuality a relational table has a single dimension. In Figure 4–3 we see a typical relational database table of employee records. In a normalized database each row in the table represents a different employee. The columns represent different characteristics of that employee—name, address, and phone number, for example. The primary key of this table is the employee ID. Every employee characteristic is referenced by this primary key. We locate the record by its single coordinate, employee ID. There is no second dimension. Compare the relational table with a two-dimensional space. The second axis in a two dimensional space, the *X*-axis, contains all the possible values for the second object. The columns of the relational table, however, contain different characteristics of the same *Y*-axis object, employee.

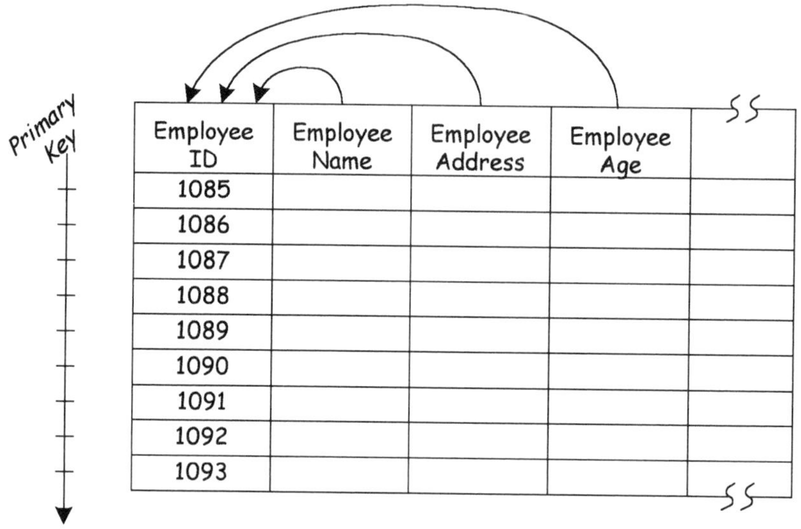

Figure 4–3   Relational database table.

A possible common multidimensional tool is the spreadsheet. Note
that it is only a possible multidimensional tool. A spreadsheet that simply
lays out data and performs a calculation has no dimensionality. If, for example, a CFO uses a single spreadsheet to lay out an income statement, there
is no real axis to determine upon which row or in which column a data
item will appear. We could also lay out a table of a relational database on a
spreadsheet, in which case we would be working in a single dimension.
Spreadsheets can also be used in a multidimensional fashion. Figure 4–4
demonstrates one such use. In this diagram we see that the Y-axis represents the different products for a chain of car dealerships. Each column, the
X-axis, in the spreadsheet represents time. The cells define the sales for a
particular product for a particular month. The individual worksheets each
represent a particular dealership. These worksheets could be viewed as the
Z-axis.

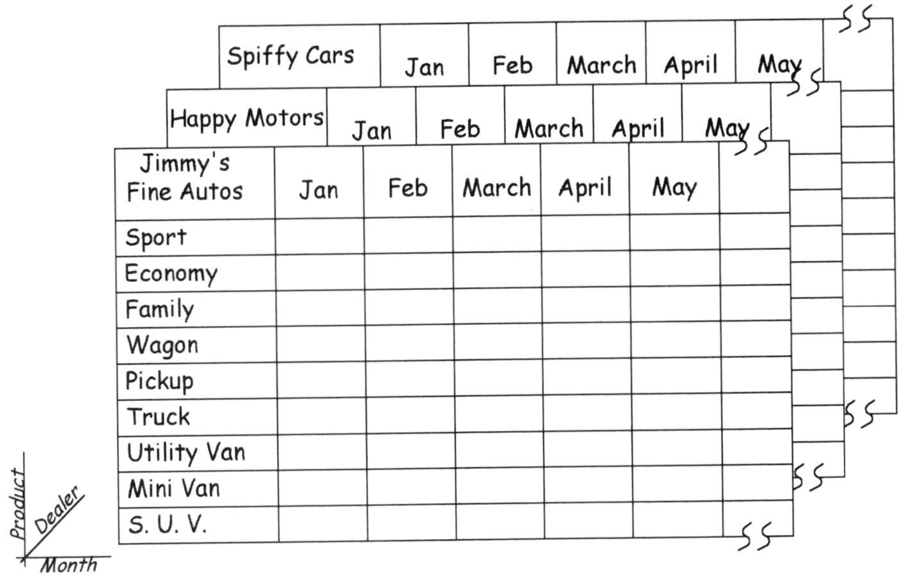

Figure 4–4 Multidimensional spreadsheet for auto sales.

Although spreadsheets do lend themselves to working in multiple dimensions, they are limited to only three in one file. Working with multiple dimensions in a spreadsheet is cumbersome even for the most technically astute business strategist. Consider what it would take in our example to show a user the sales by product—say, the sales for sports cars—for all dealerships in the month of March.

In the first chapter we discussed how the decision support system must be a tool that facilitates the business strategist's interactive dialog with the data. Imagine your CEO or CFO attempting to gather answers using the spreadsheet presented in Figure 4–4.

4.2.1 Multidimensional Databases

As we have stressed throughout this book, the strategist is interested in the behavior of objects. In discussing object-oriented analysis in Chapter 2 we showed how the strategist will look at a set of objects and group them into categories. The example shown in Figure 4–4 organizes objects into three dimensions. The products are ordered along the *Y*-dimension, time along the *X* and dealerships along the *Z*. Each dimension represents a different object. The relationship between the objects is described within the cells of the worksheet. A dealership sold a car. Information about the sale is stored in the cell. Perhaps the cell contains the price for which the car sold or the dealer's profit from that sale. In either case we see the world from the eyes of the business strategist, objects interacting with objects.

The question is how to create an environment in which the strategist can work with these multiple dimensions. As we have seen, traditional databases and spreadsheets fall short of this goal. Typical normalized relational databases work in one dimension. A spreadsheet can work in only three dimensions, and even then it is cumbersome. Just our simple auto-sales example requires more than three dimensions. Let's refer back to the object model in Figure 3–4. We have four objects: people, cars, dealership, and payment. We also need to add the all-important dimension of time. This gives our analysis a total of five dimensions. A strategist might ask *what types of cars* are being sold by *which dealerships* in *which months* to *what customer type*.

Figure 4–5(c) presents the resultant analysis space. Since things get complicated once we move beyond three dimensions, we will take a moment to build this space. We begin with Figure 4–5(a). In it we present a simple data cube. The data cube is dimensioned by the product, time, and dealership dimensions. Adding a fourth dimension is similar to creating a data cube of data cubes; this is referred to as a hypercube. We see this in Figure 4–5(b). One could imagine the lower front left corner of one cube touching the upper back right corner of another. The new fourth dimension moves up and at an angle to the other three dimensions. To build the fifth dimension we create a hypercube of hypercubes. This is presented in Figure 4–5(c).

It is rather difficult in two dimensions to present four- and five-dimensional objects. Although I have presented hypercubes as best I could here, future representations will be limited to three dimensions, data cubes.

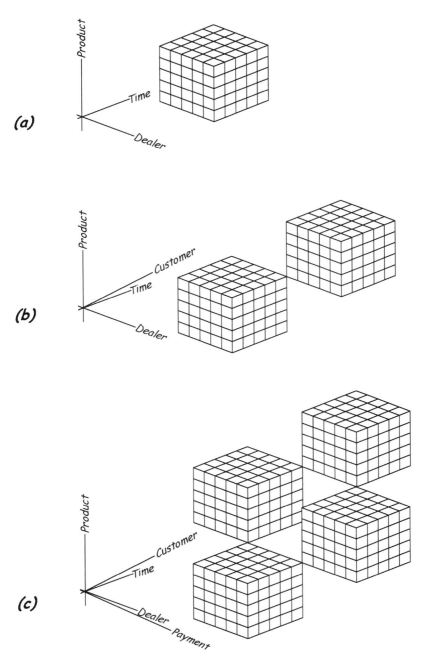

Figure 4–5   Auto sales hypercube construction.

Technically, the term data *cube* is a misnomer. A cube is a three-dimensional object whose sides are of equal length. It is a three-dimensional extension of a square, which is a quadrilateral having four right angles and four sides of equal length. Squares are actually a subset of rectangles, which are quadrilaterals having four right angles. A rectangle does not have the additional constraint of having equal sides. The three-dimensional extension of a rectangle is a parallelepiped. The length of a data *cube*'s side is determined by the number of values for that dimension within that analysis space. The sides of a data *cube*, therefore, would most probably not be equal. The more technically correct terms would be data parallelepipeds and hyperparallelepipeds. As it is, data warehouse architects speak in a strange enough language; I believe that for simplicity's sake we can all live with the terms data cubes and hypercubes.

The points within the analysis space are the individual sales. The business strategist thinks of these sales in terms of a specific car sold by a specific dealership in a specific month. The units along an axis are referred to as *values*. Just as in a coordinate system, the multidimensional database defines a cell in the data cube by the values of its dimensions. To access a specific sale the strategist defines the coordinates of that sale. The coordinates are the values for each of the respective dimensions: car, dealership, and time. For example, we specify the values (Testosterone 400, Don's Spiffy Cars, July '99) to access the cell containing the sales of the Testosterone 500 for Spiffy Cars in July 1999. Figure 4–6 demonstrates how we reference the sale.

The business strategist now has a tool to analyze the relationships between the objects in the business space. The cube becomes an object that can be manipulated. Rather than being lost in the details of storing and retrieving data, the strategist is able to focus on the thing that is most important, the analysis of the data. In looking at Figure 4–6 one can almost imagine the business strategist holding this cube. Simply by turning it, the strategist can view the business space from different perspectives. Perhaps the strategist could even break off sections of the cube and perform analysis on subsets of the data. Well, that is exactly the point of multidimensional data. The strategist can now easily gain different perspectives on the data as well as focus his or her analysis on subsets of the data.

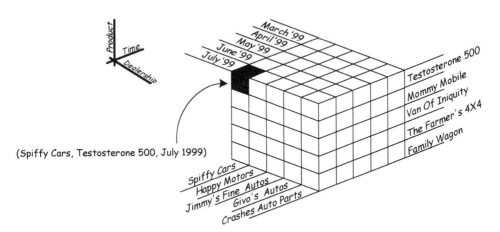

Figure 4–6   Data cube for auto sales model.

4.2.2 Working in Multiple Dimensions

Think of some of the possible questions a business strategist might attempt to answer with a data cube. Perhaps the district manager is interested in how well Spiffy Cars performed over the past few months. In such a case the spreadsheets presented in Figure 4–4 would perform well. What if the district manager would like to see the performance of all dealerships in the district for the month of May for all products? The spreadsheet distributes the sales for the month across the different worksheets; creating a view that presented all sales for an individual month would be difficult. A multidimensional tool, however, makes such a change in perspective easy.

By simply rotating, or pivoting, the cube you could change the perspective of the data. As we can see in Figure 4–7, rotation about one axis switches the other axes. In Figure 4–7(a), for example, rotation about the Z-axis, dealership, moves product to the X-axis and month to the Y. Similarly, we could rotate the cube about the Y- and X-axes. We could easily combine these rotations to provide any perspective that might be convenient to our analysis. The cube could first be rotated about the Z-axis and then about the Y-axis.

The number of possible different views of an analysis space is a function of the number of dimensions used to construct the space. For example, we could create two views out of a two-dimensional analysis space. We could view product along the X-axis and month along the Y-axis, or we could view month along the X and product along the Y. Data cubes—three dimensions—have six possible different views. Hypercubes of four dimensions have twenty-four possible views.

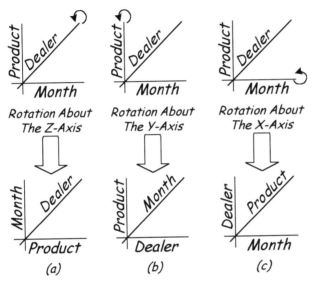

Figure 4–7   Rotation about an axis.

Let's return to the business strategist to see how we can use this to our advantage. To change the display to show the sale of all products in all dealerships for a particular month, we would perform the rotation in Figure 4–7(b). This would display all the products along the Y-axis and the dealerships along the X-axis. Units of time, or months, are displayed along the Z-axis. To move from one month to another we would simply change the value of the time axis, the Z-coordinate.

Another benefit of multidimensional databases is the ability to segment the data. As shown in Figure 4–8, the business strategist can easily extract a subset of the data from the entire cube. This is referred to as *slicing*. In essence we are contracting the analysis space. The analysis space initially contains all possible values for each of the dimensions. We create a slice of this space by defining a subset of values for one or more dimensions. In our example diagram we see where the number of rows has been limited to just two products, while all the values from the time and dealership dimensions have been maintained. We could do this for the other dimensions of the analysis space as well. In Figure 4–8 we have restricted the number of dealerships to three values while accepting all values for the time and product dimension. Although our examples slice along one dimension at a time, there is nothing to prohibit a strategist from slicing along multiple dimensions. Slicing along multiple dimensions at one time is sometimes referred to as dicing.

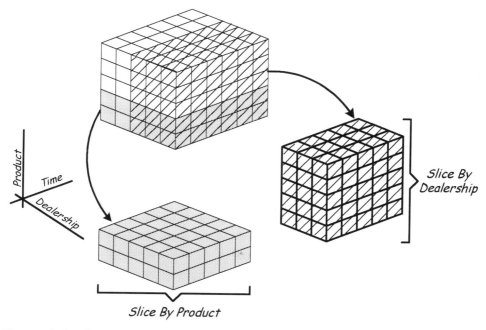

Figure 4–8 Slicing data.

The business strategist would not think in terms of cutting dimensions along rows and columns. The strategist would think in terms of objects. He or she might be interested in an analysis space of one fiscal quarter for all sport utility vehicles in the Northwest Region. While architects realize that these objects are in fact values of a dimension, strategists are simply working with the objects in their day-to-day world.

There are actually some subtle benefits to slicing data. First, it provides better performance. When working with a slice, we are defining a subset of the data. We can rotate this smaller set of data faster than the entire cube. Slicing also provides better control of the data. It extracts a subset of the data from the multidimensional database and passes it to the user. Users only have access to the information they are given. They can't see what they haven't received.

In these examples the strategist is examining very detailed data—specific dealerships, products, and months. Business strategists, however, are interested in differing levels of detail. We saw this earlier in our case study. The CEO and the CFO were interested in a *dashboard* of their organization's leading indicators. The regional managers were interested in a regional level of details. Lower-level managers and individual contributors were interested in very detailed information, often down to the level of individual transactions. Typically the level of detail is commensurate with the business strategist's position within the organization. High-level strategists, such as CEOs, CFOs, and CIOs are interested in high-level summaries of the organization's performance. Individual contributors and line managers are interested in the most detailed data.

Data can be summed along the different axes of the data cube to provide this higher-level view. This is presented in Figure 4–9. We could determine the total sales for each dealer for each month for all products by simply summing the cells in the columns. To determine the total sales for each car for each dealer for all time, we perform our summation on the cells along the Z-axis. There are times, however, when we like to group the sums according to some characteristic of the objects, such as the total sales of sport cars of dealerships in the Western Region. This is where aggregation comes into play.

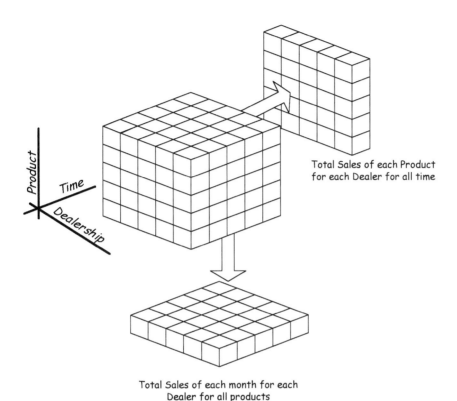

Total Sales of each Product
for each Dealer for all time

Total Sales of each month for each
Dealer for all products

Figure 4–9   Data summation.

In Chapter 2 our discussion of objects presented the concept of aggregation. We defined aggregation as a unique relationship between objects that form a new object. For example, a disk drive, memory, terminal, motherboard, CPU, and keyboard are combined to make a computer. The computer is an aggregation. In the object model presented in Figure 3–4 we see two sets of objects that are aggregations. These are the objects that were created by joining other objects together. Refer back to this diagram to see if you could identify the two aggregations.

The organization itself is the first aggregation. It is composed of regions, which are composed of districts, which are composed of dealerships. These levels of aggregation parallel management's level of interest. The CEO is interested in the performance of the company and at times may look down into the region. The regional manager is interested in the region and at times may look down into the district. This flows down the corporate hierarchy to the individual sales rep, who is interested in the most detailed level of information. Another term for aggregation is *roll-up*. A roll-up is a summation of cells to provide a higher-level view of the data. We roll-up the dealership sales numbers into district numbers. The district numbers are rolled-up into regional numbers.

Figure 4–10 demonstrates how an aggregation is performed in a multidimensional database. The lowest level of detail is the dealership data. This cube contains the sales data for the individual dealerships. This data is then divided by district and summed. The sales data for all the dealers for each district is added together into another cube. This process is then repeated for each level of aggregation up the hierarchy. Note that the other dimensions of the cube have not changed. If the detailed data cube's other dimensions were months for time and individual makes of cars for products, the aggregate cubes would have the same time and product dimensions. The aggregations of these other dimensions are built separately.

Aggregations can be created for each of the hierarchies within the data warehouse. Time, customer, and product dimensions each have a hierarchy for which aggregations can be created. They can also be created across different levels of hierarchies. A sum can be created for each district or region by product or product category. These sums can be compiled for any desired time period, weekly, monthly, or even annually.

The reverse of a roll-up is a *drill-down*, which is the examination of the data at a deeper level of detail. Perhaps a CEO notices on the corporate dashboard that there is a problem in a particular region. The drill-down will allow the CEO to select that indicator and examine the detailed data underneath. In a multidimensional environment the drill-down moves from one cube to next, slicing the detailed data to only those records that formed the aggregation.

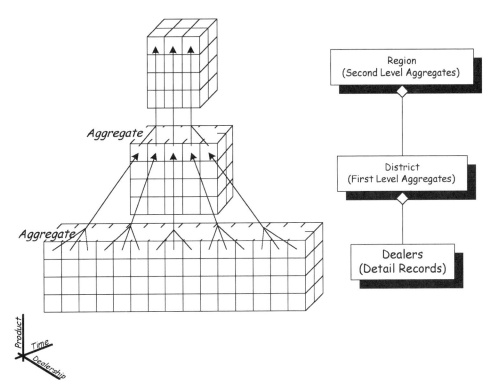

Figure 4–10 Data aggregation.

4.2.3 Multidimensional Database Issues

As we can see, multidimensional databases offer the business strategist significant advantages over traditional information systems. Considering all these benefits, one might ask why all data warehouses aren't implemented with multidimensional databases. As with most things in life, there are trade-offs. The most significant drawback to multidimensional databases is the size requirements. Adding dimensions to an analysis space and values to existing dimensions increases the size of a multidimensional database much more dramatically than adding attributes to a relational table.

The number of cells in a hypercube is the product of the number of values in each of the dimensions defining the analysis space. The cells increase geometrically with each additional value. Figure 4–11 demonstrates this relationship. Let us assume that we have 100 different cars sold by 200 different dealerships. We collect data from each of these dealerships on a daily basis. The number of cells in the data cube would therefore equal the number of dealerships times the number of cars times the number of days. If we retained just one year's worth of information the data cube would contain 7,300,000 cells (100 × 200 × 365). If the data warehouse architect were to add payment type as a fourth dimension we would see a dramatic increase in the number of cells. Just three different values for the payment-type dimension increases the number of cells to 21,900,000 (100 × 200 × 365 × 3). Obviously the number of cells could increase quite rapidly for even our modest data cube. These calculations do not include any aggregations associated with the cube, either. As we add these supporting data structures, the size requirements continue to increase.

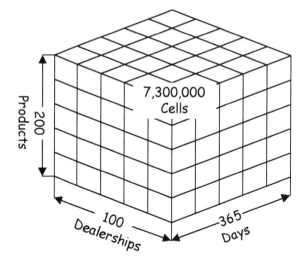

Figure 4–11   Data cube size.

Unlike records in a relational database, a cell is created whether it contains a value or not. As a result, many of the cells in a multidimensional database are empty. Consider our simple auto-sales example. Few dealerships will actually sell at least one car of each type in a particular day. The probability that more than one dealership will do the same is almost nonexistent. Consider the example of a national tire-store chain. Stores in New York and Minnesota will probably be selling a good number of snow tires for at least half the year. On the other hand, stores in Southern California or Nevada probably will not be selling a lot of snow tires, especially in June and July. The cells for these stores for these products will be empty. We would say that the data in the data cube is sparse; there is a lot of space between the data points in the cube. We can see that having many multidimensional databases can give rise to creating very large storage areas that have significant percentages of empty space.

Multidimensional databases are beginning to deal with the problem of sparse data, otherwise known as *sparcity*. Many of the approaches used, however, require the data warehouse architect to anticipate which dimensions will have sparse data.

4.2.4 Big Brother and the Building Company's Analysis Space

In this section we will build the BBBC analysis space. We construct this space by identifying the objects in the object model that are to be part of our analysis. These objects will dimension, or define, the analysis space. We can then go on to develop the implementation model that provides the structure to our database.

In reviewing the BBBC object model we see that there are three main objects: broker, property, and client. Although it is not specifically called out in the analysis model, we know simply by the fact that we are implementing a data warehouse that we will want to examine the data in terms of the time dimension. With rare exceptions, all analysis spaces will contain the dimension of time. We will also see that the structure of the time dimension can be fairly standardized from one implementation to the next. The resulting analysis space is presented in Figure 4–12.

It may seem at first glimpse that we have not included all the objects in our object model. So let's look at how we selected these dimensions. First, we discussed in the preceding chapter that we are trying to achieve the greatest possible impact with our first iteration of the data warehouse. In

Section 3.2.2.1, "Big Brother & The Building Company Analysis" on page 94, we agreed with the user community that to achieve this end we will limit the initial scope to the brokerage business. We chose brokerage because it provides a significantly larger percentage of revenue to BBBC than any of the other business units. A slight increase in the profitability of brokerage will have greater effect on the overall organization than increases in the other business units.

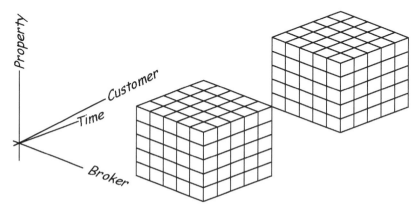

Figure 4–12   BBBC analysis space.

We also see that we have several objects that are a superclass. These are the broker, client, and property objects. Attributes that are common to all subclasses of a superclass are contained within the superclass. Each subclass, however, has its own private set of attributes. In constructing a dimension we reverse what we have done in creating the superclass. We collapse all the subclasses into one object that contains all the attributes of all the subclasses. Although it may seem as if we are simply creating something to subsequently destroy it, we are actually making progress. In the process of expanding the different subclasses out in the object model we gain a better understanding of the variety of attributes pertaining to the object. When we collapse the subclasses into one object, we can contain the attributes of all subclasses in one dimension. This simplifies the overall design of the structure. An example of a superclass and a subclass within the BBBC analysis space is property. All properties have an address and an owner. These would be attributes of the superclass property. An industrial property, however, may have the attribute of a crane. The crane would be an attribute of the industrial subclass property.

Management will want to view information based on the different levels within the organization. The organization, therefore, will be implemented as an aggregate. In examining the object model we see that this aggregation extends from the broker up to the company. The company is composed of business units that are composed of profit centers. The profit centers are a superclass. The subclass brokerage profit center is also an aggregate, which is composed of brokers. Time is also part of an aggregation. It is only logical that the business strategist will want the ability to see information on each of the different time aggregates: weekly, monthly, quarterly and annually. We should plan on it. We will see in the next chapter how to structure these aggregates.

Our final aggregation is that of client. A client may be a completely independent company or a subsidiary of a large corporation. BBBC Management stressed that it was important to look at activities with an individual client as well as any parent company or companies. Management would like to capture this information and roll-up the performance for the entire corporation as well as its subsidiaries. The customer dimension, therefore, will require an aggregation as well.

In the next section we will review how to create an implementation model. In that model we will design the database structures that will store the information for the BBBC analysis space.

4.3 Star Schema

As we shall see, the star schema overcomes the shortcomings of a multidimensional database by providing a multidimensional analysis space within a relational database. The structure of the star schema is actually quite simple. Figure 4–13 presents a star for our auto-sales example. In this diagram we see two basic types of tables, dimension and fact. The primary keys of the dimension tables are foreign keys in the fact table. Each of these tables correlates nicely to the basic elements of the hypercubes discussed earlier in this chapter. The dimension tables are the dimensions of our cube, our axes. The fact-table records are the cells.

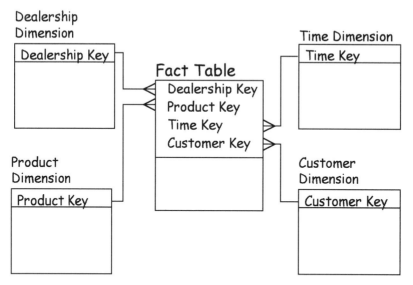

Figure 4–13   Star schema.

At this point we should briefly discuss the keys that link the tables in the star. The temptation is to use the primary keys from the operational environment as the data warehouse primary keys. The consistency between the two environments makes the option attractive. Don't do it! While it is useful to maintain the operational primary keys as attributes of the objects in the data warehouse, they should not be used as data warehouse keys. Data warehouse keys should be anonymous, system-generated keys. These are often referred to as surrogate or synthetic keys. We will discuss the use of keys in more detail in Chapters 5 and 6.

The star schema creates a multidimensional space out of relational tables. This is presented in Figure 4–14. As we noted in the beginning of this chapter, to form a coordinate system the dimensions of the coordinate system must be related to one another. We also noted how relational tables are one-dimensional structures. The relationship between the dimensions in the star schema is described within the fact table. Just as a coordinate system joins related dimensions, the star schema joins the single-dimensional dimension tables to one another. This forms a multidimensional analysis space within the relational database. Examining Figure 4–14, one could almost imagine these tables as planes *glued* together to form a cube. The glue is the fact table. It does this with keys. The primary key of the fact table is a composite of the dimension-table keys. How a record or set of records in one dimension is related to a record or set of records in another is defined by the keys contained in the primary key of the fact-table record.

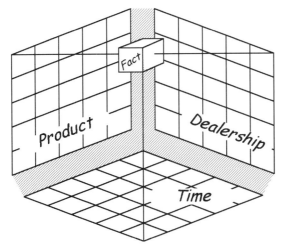

Figure 4–14 Star schema dimensionality.

The fact table does more than just bind the dimensions together to form a multidimensional space. The fact table contains the facts—numbers that describe the characteristics of the relationship between the dimensions. It contains the points in the analysis space. In our auto-sales example, the product, dealership and time dimension are related at a specific point. If we are tracking sales, the point at which Spiffy Cars is related to the Testosterone 500 and July 1999 is defined by the fact in the fact-table record. In this record we might see number of cars sold or perhaps the total sales revenue for those cars by that dealership. These are the characteristics of the relationship between those three objects. Fact-table records will tend to be much shorter than dimension-table records, as we shall see in the discussion to follow. The length of the fact table, however, will be much longer than the length of its surrounding dimensions.

As we can see, the interesting part of the star schema to the business strategist is the fact table. This is where the data is located. To get there, though, we need the dimensions. The dimensions in both the hypercube and star schema are entry points. When working with hypercubes we access the cells by specifying the values (coordinates) of the dimensions. In a similar fashion we define the records of interest within the fact table via the dimension specifications. Although the fact table is where the action is, everything begins with the dimension. One could imagine the dimension tables as doorways through which the business strategist enters a room containing the facts, the fact table.

As we have said earlier, the values of the dimension are the different objects of that dimension. In the star schema each record or row of the dimension table is the equivalent of the dimension values, the objects of that dimension. The rows in the product table of our auto-sales example are the different makes cars sold by the dealerships. To gather facts on any of these products we select the product(s) of interest from the dimension table. The primary keys of the product records are the foreign keys in the fact table.

At times the business strategist may select specific products or groups of products. At other times, however, the strategist may select products based on a set of common characteristics or attributes. The strategist may be interested in the sales data for cars with four-cylinder engines or cars with certain performance characteristics. These attributes are included as columns of the dimension table. The attributes included in the dimension tables are only those that may be the basis of some future analysis. In the customer dimension we may want to include demographic information, but we would probably not include descriptive information such as a client name or social security number. We will discuss attribute selection in more detail in the next chapter. What we need to understand at this point is that the selection of records from the dimension table is based on the attributes of the objects contained in that table's record. These records in turn will provide the keys for entry into the fact table.

A typical analysis may ask how well certain cars with a specific engine size, seating capacity, and fuel efficiency sold to a specific market segment.

These are all object attributes. All the attributes of an objects should be located within that object's dimension-table record. Normalizing these attributes across several tables will greatly complicate the data-retrieval process. Architects coming from the OLTP environment may balk at this level of denormalization. After all, won't this create long tables of wide records that will ultimately lead to poor performance? Well, yes and no. Yes, this will lead to tables of wide records, but it will not lead to poor performance. Denormalizing the dimension tables will actually improve performance. The queries of the database will be kept much simpler by keeping all the attributes in one place, thus reducing the number of joins. That's the short answer.

In looking at this question in more detail, keep in mind that normalization is a tool of the OLTP world. Distributing the data across a normalized structure improves the performance of searching for a specific record. It takes much longer to search through a long table of very wide records than a table of the same length with significantly shorter records. It also eliminates the data redundancy that occurs in environments where data is frequently updated. The difference within the star schema is that the number of records in the dimension table is *relatively* static and small. In our simple auto-sales example the product, dealership and time dimensions will not grow nearly as fast as the fact table. The relationship between the dimension and fact tables is one-to-many. We expect to have for every product, dealership, and time record many fact records. This translates to many sales for every product for every dealership within a particular period of time. True, new records will be added to each of the dimension tables, but these tables will grow slowly in comparison to the fact table.

The denormalization of the dimension tables also greatly simplifies queries against the database. In the star schema there is a join between each of the dimension tables and the fact table. A query searching for the sales of large sport utility vehicles for dealerships in the southwest would simply join three tables. Now imagine if the tables were normalized. We could easily double the number of dimension tables to create a query against five tables or more. In a fully normalized database, it would not be surprising to experience an exponential growth in the number of tables as the number of dimensions increases. Denormalization, however, simplifies the queries and ultimately enhances overall performance.

The star schema takes significantly less space than a multidimensional database with the same dimensions. Remember, the multidimensional database will create a cell regardless of use. The star schema will create a fact record only when there are facts to record. If a dealership does not sell a particular car in a particular month, no fact record is created. Even those multidimensional databases that provide for sparcity require some knowledge on the part of the architect to predict where sparcity will occur. None of this is required with the star schema.

4.3.1 Working with the Star Schema

Although the data warehouse architect is well aware that the structure of the database is a star schema, this should be invisible to the business strategist. In a well-designed system, the strategist will have a multidimensional view of data contained within a relational database. All of the advantages of working in a multidimensional environment are available to the strategist using the star schema.

Let's begin by looking at rotation. In the multidimensional world the Y-axis becomes the rows of our reports and the X-axis becomes the columns. The Z-axis is what we refer to as a *page item*, in which each page of the report, or display, is a separate value of the Z-axis. The strategist specifies the orientation of the data, and the presentation layer displays the data accordingly. How the data is retrieved from the database is independent of the orientation of the display. Each point in the analysis space is the equivalent of a cell in a data cube, which is the equivalent of a record in the fact table. Each record contains the coordinates of its respective position within the analysis space. It is a simple matter for the presentation layer to change the orientation of the data to suit the specifications of the strategist.

The second feature of multidimensional data we discussed was the ability to slice data. In this discussion we noted how slicing data is merely the constriction of the analysis space by the specification of a subset of dimensional values. In our auto-sales example we might specify one product or one dealership. In the star schema we would do almost the same thing. We would simply select the fact-table records based on the keys of a subset of the dimensions. We would select the record from the fact table whose product key matched the key to the product table, regardless of the values of the other keys. We can apply the same technique to the other dimensions or multiple dimensions at one time, just as we did with in the multidimensional environment.

In the next chapter we will examine dimension tables in more detail. As part of this discussion we will look at slicing data within the star schema. The next chapter will also discuss how hierarchies are implemented within the star schema.

4.3.2 Big Brother and the Building Company's Implementation Model

Now that we understand the star schema, we are ready to construct the implementation model for BBBC. This model is presented in Figure 4–15. When we last visited our case study we defined the analysis space as being dimensioned by the broker, property, customer, and time dimensions. The implementation model creates a separate dimension table for each of these objects.

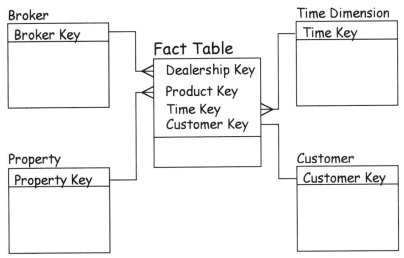

Figure 4–15 BBBC star schema.

The fact table will initially contain revenue information for the broker-age business unit only. The facts in the fact table represent either the sale or lease of property. We could have chosen to create two fact tables, one for the sale of property and another for the lease. In a sense they represent two distinct ways in which the organization has interacted with the client. This would give us problems in future iterations of the data warehouse. As we added other business units such as Appraisal and Realty Advisors, we would have to create additional fact tables to reflect the different ways in which these units interacted with the user. By combining them into one table we haven't lost anything. It still provides the business strategist with the ability to view lease and sale information individually. Creating multiple fact table would only slow down our queries through multiple joins when examining the overall organization.

In the case study we have not yet discussed the detailed attributes of the dimension tables or the facts in the fact table. We will discuss each of the topics in more detail in subsequent chapters. In Chapter 5 we will present the dimension table as well as discuss the inclusion of object attributes. In Chapter 6 we will present the issues that relate to facts within the fact table.

4.4 Summary

When developing a strategy, the business strategist seeks to understand the behaviors of objects that relate to his or her organization. We have defined behaviors as predictable responses to a set of stimuli. Multidimensional analysis allows the strategist to study the relationship between several objects at one time. He or she is able to stand back and look at the entire picture to see the ebb and flow of activity relating to the organization.

Multidimensional analysis begins with dimensions. These are the objects that relate to our organization. We create a dimension for every object that is to be part of our study. We can group related objects, dimen-sions, into a single coordinate system. While there is no limit on the number of dimensions that can be in one coordinate system, working beyond six or seven begins to get rather cumbersome. The coordinate system defines a space; we describe this as binding the space. We call the space defined by the objects relating to our organization our analysis space. All points in a space exist within the dimensions that comprise the coordinate-system binding space. We identify points relative to each of these dimensions.

While multidimensional analysis is important to the business strategist, many traditional information systems are not well adapted to such uses. Relational databases work in only one dimension, and spreadsheets are inflexible in the manipulation of data. Multidimensional databases allow the strategist to create structures that fit his or her view of the analysis space. Objects are translated into dimensions forming a data cube or hypercube. The cells of these *cubes* contain the characteristics of the behavior between the objects that form the dimensions. Multidimensional databases, however, have a size limitation that makes them inappropriate for very large data warehouses.

A star schema allows the data warehouse architect to create a multidimensional space within a relational database. Dimensions are implemented as tables with wide records containing complete descriptions of the objects that make the dimensions. In the middle of these dimension tables is the fact table. Records of the fact table contain the facts of the relationship. This is the data one would expect to find in the cells of the data cube. The fact table's primary key is a composite of the keys of the surrounding dimension tables. In this way the fact table *glues* the single-dimensioned dimension tables together into an analysis space.

4.5 Glossary

Analysis Space   Space defined by the dimensions of an analysis.

Coordinate System   The set of related dimensions emanating from a point of origin.

Data Cube   Three-dimensional object composed of columns and rows of cells. The edges of the cube are the dimensions of the analysis space.

Dimension   The axes of a coordinate system that bind the space defined by that coordinate system. In an analysis space the dimensions are the objects of the analysis.

Dicing   A constriction of the analysis space across multiple dimensions. Dicing selects a subset of the data to form another cube.

Drill-Down   Presentation of the data at a deeper level of detail.

Hypercube   An object of four dimensions or more composed of columns and rows of cells. The edges of the cube are the dimensions of the analysis space.

Multidimensional   A space or database that exists in more than one dimension.

Point of Origin   The point at which all axes of a coordinate system meet. The value of all dimensions in the coordinate system at this point is 0.

Roll-Up   The presentation of data at a higher level of detail.

Slicing   A constriction of the analysis space to include only a subset of the data. Slicing can occur along any of the dimensions.

Surrogate Keys   Keys generated by the data warehouse, used in place of keys from the operational environment. Also known as synthetic keys.

Synthetic Keys   Keys generated by the data warehouse. Also known as surrogate keys.

CHAPTER 5

Dimension Tables—the Nouns of the Data Warehouse

The development spiral views the organization's environment, including its business processes, as objects and behaviors. This view is developed as an evolving series of models. The definition phase establishes the project's scope as described in the mission statement. The first model, the analysis model, identifies the objects, that fall within this scope as well as their associated behaviors. The second model, the object model, refines the description of the objects, providing the details of the object's attributes and behaviors. The object model also describes how the objects relate to one another. The next step, as described in the preceding chapter, is the implementation model.

The implementation model first presents the star schema. We saw that the construction of this model requires that the objects in the analysis be translated to dimensions in the implementation model. The dimensions are the persons, places, and things that are related to the business. In short, they are the nouns of the data warehouse. As we look at a schema, we see the star from which it gets its name. The points of the star are the dimensions. They are the entryway to the facts contained within the nucleus of the star. It seems logical, therefore, to proceed with our examination of the star schema by first examining the dimensions. While some of this may be a bit repetitious, this chapter will provide a complete discussion of dimensions. It shows how the different variations of dimension are used to implement structures described in the object model.

157

5.1 Dimension-Table Characteristics

In the preceding chapter we described the relationship between space and dimensions. A space is defined by a coordinate system composed of axes or dimensions that define the space. The points within the analysis space are identified by its coordinates, which are values for each of the axes. In translating this to the decision support environment, we have an analysis space. We noted how the business strategist works in terms of objects within an analysis space. The classes of the different objects in our object model define the dimensions in our analysis space. In our example the product class has a corresponding product dimension. Each of the different instances of the object class defines a unique value for the dimension. The Testosterone 500 is a car, a particular instance of a car object. The instance of the car object has a corresponding value in the auto product dimension.

The analysis space is entered via the dimensions. A user cannot identify a point or work within the analysis space without specifying a set of coordinates. The star schema creates an analysis space within a relational environment by binding single dimension tables together. The dimension tables are single-dimensional data structures that are used to form the walls of our analysis space. This is shown in Figure 5–1.

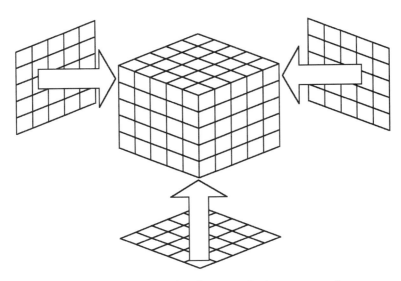

Figure 5–1   Dimension tables form analysis-space walls.

The business strategist specifies the specific instances that are to comprise the analysis. The strategist may specify a specific product in a specific region at a specific time. The definition of analysis-space coordinates, however, is not limited to specific items within a dimension. The strategist may select a set of items based on some attribute. Perhaps the strategist is interested not in the sales performance of a particular sports car but in the performance of all sports cars, or some subset of sports cars. Rather than sports cars the analyst may be interested in cars with eight-cylinder engines or with four doors. These characteristics are the attributes of the objects. Attributes that can be used to define a set of objects for analysis are known as *analytical data elements*. The dimension table should primarily contain only those attributes that are analytical data elements.

Analytical data elements are used to group objects. Remember that the business strategist is looking for behaviors in the analysis space. To recognize and define these behaviors the strategist is collecting information from many records at one time. The attributes of the objects are one way for the strategist to define which objects are of interest. A car's engine size is an analytical data element. Business strategists can group the different types of cars together by their engine size. The car's serial number is not an analytical item; each car has its own. It would be foolish for the strategist to perform an analysis on cars based on their serial number. Only one car would show up in the analysis. These types of queries are better delegated to the operational transaction-processing system.

Analytical data elements also have a finite domain of possible values. This is actually a natural conclusion drawn from the fact that an analytical data element is used to select groups of records from the database. What could possibly be the analytical value of a free-formatted comment space in a dimension table? While the strategist may be able to select records based on the presence or absence of some key words, it would be extraordinarily difficult to develop a method to detect behaviors based on those comments. The types of elements one would expect to see within the dimension table are either numeric fields or text fields with a limited number of possible values.

Although the dimension table is composed *primarily* of analytical data, it is not exclusively so. There are times when it is impractical to exclude certain nonanalytical data elements. There is always a need to make the data within the table meaningful. It is inconvenient to see the product number "678-489A-892" in a report. The business strategist would, of course, prefer to see the product name—"Mommy Mobile," for example—in any reports or analyses. At other times nonanalytical data's space requirements are trivial and its inclusion would greatly simplify working with the structure. Although the number of nonanalytical data elements should be kept to a minimum, the selection of which ones to include within the dimension record is a matter of the architect's judgment.

5.2 Slowly Changing Dimensions

We have noted how the data warehouse is nonvolatile; the data once written is referenced many times. The warehouse creates a history of activities, which are composed of nouns and verbs. Once the event occurs, the information surrounding it remains unchanged. If a person purchases a particular car for a specific price, no amount of time will change the characteristics of that particular event. The price at the time of purchase will remain the same; so will the actual car that was purchased. This is the information that is contained within the fact table. Once something is a fact, it's a fact, and that is basically all there is to it.

The objects represented in the dimension are another matter, however. Objects change over time. The demographics of a particular customer will change. A customer can easily go from single, to married, to divorced, to married and back to divorced. (With that kind of record I am not sure if they would be able to afford a car, but that is beside the point.) All of the objects represented in the dimensions of the star schema can easily change with time. We describe the dimensions representing these objects as *slowly changing dimensions*. This poses an interesting challenge to the data warehouse architect. The data structure of the warehouse must be able to adapt to these changes and still maintain its data integrity. In other words, how does the warehouse accurately reflect the changing environment without corrupting history? There are actually five basic solutions to this problem. Some are better than others. Their inclusion here does not imply a recommendation. The main intent here is to describe what may be encountered by the data warehouse architect. He or she must decide which is the most appropriate.

The first solution is the most straightforward; simply change the dimension record. This is most appropriate when correcting errors in the data. This is also used when the view of the past as well as the future changes permanently. An example of such a change is an organizational change. Perhaps corporate management decides to take the organization from three regions to four, and the business strategist has assured the data warehouse architect that all analysis will be in terms of the new structure. In such a case we could simply destroy the old data, replacing it with the new.

Unfortunately not all changes are this clear cut. Let's say that we have a middle-aged married woman who purchases a car from a dealership. In entering the sale into the data warehouse, however, we discover that this same client purchased a car from the same dealership 15 years ago. At that time the client was a single man. (Modern medicine seems to complicate everything these days.) We could simply go into the dimension record for that customer and change the marital status and gender attributes from single to married. The problem with this solution is that it corrupts the integrity of the data warehouse. Both current and past sales to that client will now be referenced as the purchases of a married woman. If this occurs within one or two dimension records the difference may be negligible, but if it is in fact part of a larger trend within the general population it could lead to the loss of confidence in the data warehouse. Perhaps a strategist performs an analysis showing sales of particular cars by fiscal quarter for the last several years. Then there is a mass migration of young married male clients to single women. After this migration occurs, the strategist runs the same sales report noticing the change in demographics. How will the data warehouse architect explain the change in results? How could the architect even know what caused the results to change?

A more nefarious and ultimately more damaging effect of the first solution is undetected errors. Changing history could lead the business strategist to inaccurate conclusions. Looking at sales history, the strategist could incorrectly conclude that a certain type of car is popular within a certain demographic. Marketing decisions made under these false assumptions could have serious and far-reaching effects for the overall organization. The source of these incorrect assumptions could go undetected. While this may temporarily save the data warehouse architect's hide, these incorrect assumptions could lead the organization into strategies that would lead to its ultimate demise.

A second alternative is to simply create a new dimension record. This maintains the past history while accurately reflecting the current state of the market. Certainly the user community will not notice anything wrong with the data, and for the most part they will be correct—the data is not wrong. The problem with the solution is that it hides valuable market information. The change in the dimension in and of itself could be of significant value to the business strategist. It would be of tremendous value to track how the behaviors of a subject change in relation to changes in the customer's demographics. What are the buying habits of a person as he or she moves from single to married and then to married with children?

A third alternative is to alter the structure of the dimension record to contain both the new and old values of the dimension record. If we return to our previous example, one would expect the marital status of a client to change over time. We could, in fact, create a current and past field. Initially we may have single for the marital status. When the client marries, we move the current status to past status and then change the current to married. We also have to record the date the change took place, so that we can accurately reflect the state of the client when purchasing the car.

There are two problems inherent in this solution. First, which of the object's attributes do we expect to change? Do we create a current and past field for every dimension attribute? If not, the architect must select which fields are allowed to change and which fields are not. In all seriousness, one would expect the marital status to change over time for most of the population while the gender would stay pretty constant, at least for most people. An attribute's potential for change may not be as clear as in these examples. Second, how many times will the architect allow a field to change? How many changes does the architect plan to capture for a particular field. Sadly, marital status for a very large portion of society changes more than twice. I have relatives whose marital status has changed as many as eight times!

A fourth alternative is a slight modification to the second. In this alternative we create a new record every time there is a change in the dimension record. To track these changes, however, we create a revision number, which is appended to the end of the primary key. The system-generated key field will define which records of the dimension represent that same instance of an object. The revision numbers will identify the order in which the attribute changes occurred. In addition to the revision number we add a simple binary field to signify the most recent. In this way we are able to easily identify which records represent the most recent attributes of the object. This alternative allows the warehouse architect not only to capture the current state of an object, but to track the changes as they occur and what effects they may have on the object's behaviors. The problem with this method is that it complicates the link between the dimension tables and the fact table. Rather than joining the two tables with a single field, we now have a concatenated key. This also lengthens the records in the fact table by one field.

The fifth and final solution combines the second and fourth methods of dealing with slowly changing dimensions. When a dimension changes, a new record is created with a new primary key, just as in the second method. The client ID is carried over from the operational system and is used to link the different versions of the dimension to one another. A flag is included to indicate which version of the dimension record is the most recent. In this way we retain the history of the objects described by the dimension while simplifying the link between the fact table and the dimension. Although this solution may seem optimum, it is not always available. The data stored within the data warehouse is integrated from many disparate systems. When bringing in dimension data, the primary keys from these systems may overlap or be inconsistent in format. In such cases one cannot count on using the operational system's ID to identify records.

Let's take a look at each of these alternatives and examine how it might be used in our auto-sales example. In Figure 5–2 we have an example of the application of each of these methods to the client dimension. A phone number is not usually an attribute that is a subject of analysis. There is, therefore, no real danger in overwriting the information. The data warehouse architect could simply overwrite the old phone number. We can safely conclude that when dealing with changes to nonanalytical attributes the overwrite method would be appropriate.

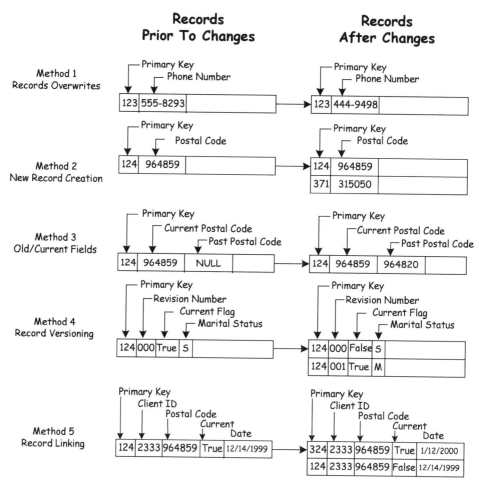

Figure 5–2 Slowly changing dimensions.

In the example we chose to create a new record to deal with changes in the postal code. Postal codes will be useful in understanding market behavior. For example, the business strategist might use the postal code as a method of mapping the customer base. How far are customers willing to travel to purchase a car from a particular dealership? This would be of great interest to a strategist. This information could also be linked to promotion campaigns. The strategist may wish to determine the effectiveness of specific campaigns in specific areas. On the other hand, the strategist would probably not be interested in tracking the movement of clients from one area to another. Creating new records would be sufficient. Perhaps we submit this design to the project sponsor, only to discover that he or she would like to have a record of when a client moves between zip codes. Since this is a relatively infrequent occurrence, the architect might choose to keep current and past fields in the record. This would allow the strategist to look back at least one move into the client's history.

In the final example we track the marital status of the client. Note that the number of revisions acceptable to the warehouse is determined by the number of digits in the revision number. In this case, the client can change his or her marital status as many as 100 times. The architect is probably safe with this one. The only problem with this solution is that we have created a compound key that joins the dimension table to the fact table. We will, therefore, opt for the fifth alternative, in which we create a new record for the new data. We were able to preserve the client ID from the operational system, so we will use this to link the dimension records together to track the client's history.

One should also note that these methods could be used in different combinations. Perhaps the data warehouse architect decides to overwrite nonanalytical data and keep record versions for all other attribute revisions. As the previous example demonstrates, each of the four alternatives presented in the section has a use within the data warehouse. The architect must keep each of these methods of dealing with slowly changing dimensions in mind and determine where they can best be applied. Each attribute and dimension will be different. These are all just tools in the architect's toolbox.

5.3   Constellations and Conforming Dimensions

Whenever I think of constellations, I think back to one night in the eighties. As I watched *Gandhi* steal the Academy Award away from *ET* for best picture, my niece and I arranged little stick-'em stars onto a large black poster board. We would then draw lines between the stars showing the different constellations in the evening sky. It was her fifth grade science fair and she actually got a pretty good grade for it. Well, that's what the data warehouse architect does to construct a warehouse containing multiple facts. He or she simply connects the different stars in the schema. The final product is a constellation.

We have established that dimensions are the objects of our analysis. So far we have worked with an analysis space whose dimensions are dealership, product, and time. We are able to put these objects together into an analysis space because they are related to one another. Dealerships sell cars within certain months. What about other objects—objects that are not part of this relationship? Many possible analysis spaces could be created for a car dealership. Perhaps the strategist would like to study the purchase of parts that make the car. In this new analysis the strategist may want to track the average monthly costs of parts for each product. The dimensions in this analysis space are parts, products, and time. Although two of the dimensions are part of the auto-sales analysis space, the third dimension, parts, is not. Parts are not related to dealerships. Their data points can not be defined in relation to any values in the dealership dimensions. This places the parts outside the auto-sales analysis space.

To create an analysis space that includes the parts dimension, we must create a new analysis space. We have demonstrated this in Figure 5–3. The new data cube, the parts-cost data cube, sits beside the auto-sales data cube. This new space shares two dimensions with the existing auto-sales analysis space. These are the product and time dimensions. They exist in both the auto-sales analysis space and the parts-cost analysis space. The dealership and parts dimensions, however, exist in two separate analysis spaces, the auto-sales analysis space and the parts-cost analysis space, respectively.

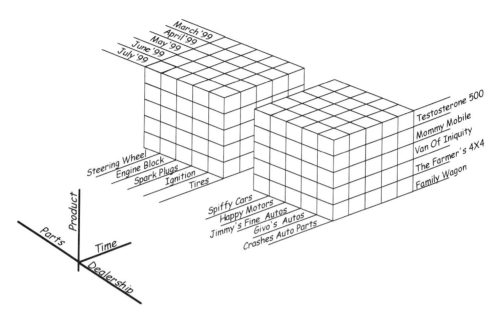

Figure 5–3 Auto-sales analysis space.

We can now build an implementation model for these cubes. One alternative is for the warehouse architect to actually create a completely separate schema where the dimensions are duplicated and a new parts-cost fact table is created. This will limit the effectiveness of our data warehouse. First, keeping the common dimension tables synchronized will complicate the administration of the warehouse. Second, it limits the functionality of the warehouse. Creating two separate schemas isolates the information within the stars. There is no way for the strategist to move from one analysis space to another.

Another alternative implementation model creates a second fact table linked to the first via the common dimensions. This is shown in Figure 5–4. In the example we have two stars, the auto-sales star and the parts-cost star. The sales fact table is linked to the salesperson, customer, product, and time dimensions. The cost fact table is associated with the product, time, supplier and parts dimensions. The two stars are linked together to form a constellation by the common dimensions product and time.

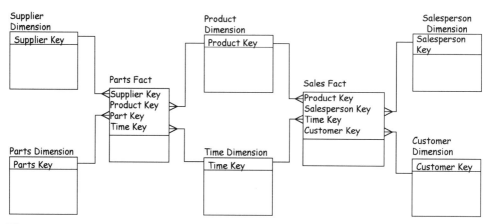

Figure 5–4   Constellation with conforming dimensions.

By linking the two stars into a single constellation we eliminate the duplication of dimensions and the synchronization requirements. This method also provides the business strategist with a way to *drill-across* into different fact tables. Drilling-across relates different fact tables by the common dimension. In Figure 5–4, an analysis could examine how costs of parts relate to sales. The constellation provides the structure to allow the strategist to traverse the schema to perform this type of analysis. As we expand this constellation, we can perform more advanced financial analyses. The challenges in constructing a constellation, however, are the links between the fact tables, the dimensions.

In order for a dimension to act as a link between two fact tables it must be a *conforming dimension*. Despite what may have been said in the sixties, sometimes conformity is a good thing. It certainly is when we are discussing a constellation schema. A conforming dimension simply is one whose values are consistent between the two stars. The values of the time and product dimension must be sufficient to meet the needs of both the parts-cost star and the auto-sales star. A problem in conformity usually occurs when the source of the information originates in different operational systems. Consider our simple auto-sales example. The sales information may come from the accounts receivable system and the parts information may come from an accounts payable system. The product data may not be the same between the two systems.

We have defined a conforming dimension as being consistent between two stars. So far we have used conforming dimensions to link stars into a constellation, but we can take them even further. The stars with which the dimensions are consistent do not necessarily have to be in the same system. A conforming dimension could be used between stars in a data warehouse and a dependent data mart. This is demonstrated in Figure 5–5.

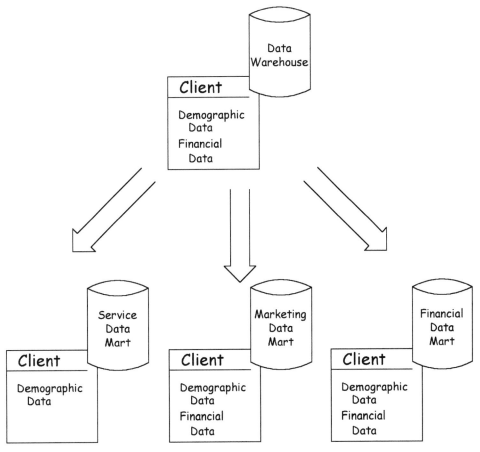

Figure 5–5   Dependent data marts with conforming dimensions.

The base dimension for clients is in the data warehouse. It contains the client data that is used across all systems that use the client dimension. The data from this dimension is extracted and transported to dependent data marts. This dimension is then used in the schema of the dependent mart. Note how the service data mart extracts only a subset of the data. The dimensions are still conforming, even though the service data mart uses only a subset of the base dimension. This subset is still consistent with the data warehouse's base dimension; that is, the client dimension is still conforming to the standard established by the data warehouse.

5.4 Snowflakes

A variation on the star schema theme is the *snowflake*. There are situations where the temptation to normalize a dimension is too great to resist. In these situations the architect must decide whether the benefits outweigh the cost. A snowflake schema is employed. Figure 5–6 shows a snowflake schema for the auto-sales example.[1] We see that the same basic structure employed in the star schema is maintained—a fact table surrounded by dimension tables. The dimension tables in this structure, however, are normalized. This normalization gives the schema a snowflakelike structure; arms extend from a central point, where each arm branches off into other structures.

Snowflaking the warehouse schema has some rather serious implications. First, the queries themselves are complicated. This will reduce the system's retrieval performance. Multiple tables will be joined together, forming more complex queries. This may also hide the star schema from the database's query engine. Many relational database systems can recognize when a query is being made against a star schema and will optimize the query accordingly. In some instances the complex snowflake schema will inhibit this optimization, further reducing the system's performance. The

---

1. The diagram includes several fact tables. These have been shadowed to differentiate them from the dimension tables. Also, not all the joins have been included in the schema. Rather than include all the fine details and create an incomprehensible morass of lines, I felt it best to simply provide the appropriate keys, letting the reader fill in the obvious omissions.

snowflake schema also reduces the system's usability. The star schema is a simple concept that most business strategists can easily grasp; sales data is in the fact table and the pointers to the sales data are in the dimension table. As we complicate the schema, we decrease the intuitiveness of the warehouse structure. The net result is that the business strategist will be more dependent on the architect for data retrieval than with a star schema.

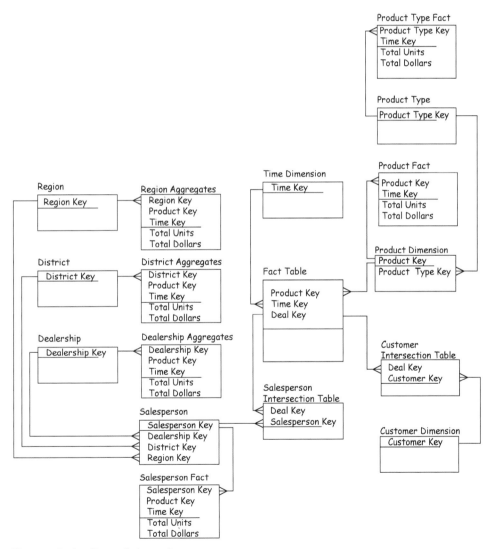

Figure 5–6 Snowflake schema.

There are instances when a snowflake schema may be appropriate in spite of the drawbacks described above. Snowflakes allow us to deal with such structures as many-to-many relationships, nonanalytical data, and hierarchical structures. The following subsections will discuss these topics in detail.

5.4.1 Many-to-Many Relationships

In our auto-sales example we assumed that a car may be sold by only one salesperson and purchased by only one customer. This may not be a correct assumption. Perhaps the auto manufacturer would like to track the demographics of couples who purchase vehicles. How do the combined demographics of a couple affect auto purchases? What about a wife's age versus a husband's—are there any patterns there? What if a parent and child purchase a car jointly? What about couples with the same gender?!—a very real question in today's marketplace. Would not an auto manufacturer have an interest in these demographics as well? If the demographics of individuals in a marriage are clumped together into one customer, this information is lost.

The method of capturing a many-to-many relationship used in the star schema is common to the transaction-processing world. Between the fact table and the dimension table is an *intersection table*. The records in this table are composed of the client key and a deal key. There is a one-to-many relationship between the customer table and the intersection table and a one-to-many relationship between the fact table and the intersection table.

Referring to Figure 5–5, we see this method of resolving many-to-many relationship employed for the salespersons and customer dimensions. Sitting between the salesperson dimension and the fact-table dimension is an intersection table. The intersection table's record contains two keys. The first is a deal key which points to a particular record in the fact table representing a specific deal. The second key points to a salesperson involved in the deal. Each record in the intersection table will have a unique pairing of salesperson key and deal key. Although a deal may have multiple records in the intersection table, each salesperson key for those records will be unique. The same is also true for salespeople. A salesperson may have multiple records in the intersection table, but each will be for a different deal.

An alternative method of dealing with many-to-many relationships is to create multiple fact records within fact table relating to the same event. We can use this method in the auto-sales example to allow multiple salespersons to be included in an individual deal. A new record is entered in the fact table for every salesperson involved in the sale. Calculating aggregates is somewhat complicated, since there is a danger of double-counting the data. To prevent this we assign each event a unique ID number. Each fact record relating to a deal will contain the same deal number. To collect all the data for a particular deal we retrieve all the fact records with the same deal number. When calculating aggregates, we include the UNIQUE clause in the SQL statement to make sure that deal information is included only once.

5.4.2 Hierarchies and Aggregations

There are several methods of dealing with hierarchies within the star schema. The simplest is to embed the hierarchy within the dimension. The granularity of the dimension is at the lowest level of detail for our analysis. Each dimension record contains a field for every level in the hierarchy above it identifying exactly where the object belongs in the hierarchy. We have applied this method to our auto-sales example in Figure 5–7. Each salesperson record contains a dealership, district, and region key. We can now look at an individual salesperson record and know exactly where the record fits within the company hierarchy. If corporate were to add another level in the hierarchy, we would have to change the design of our dimension to provide for the additional pointer.

The hierarchy keys in the salesperson record are used to join the record directly to each of its ancestors in the hierarchy. The architect can then join aggregate tables to each level in the hierarchy. To see the aggregate sales in the Western District, the query can be redirected to the actual Western District aggregate tables. From this structure, the strategist can also drill-down into the detailed records by traversing dealership records into the fact table.

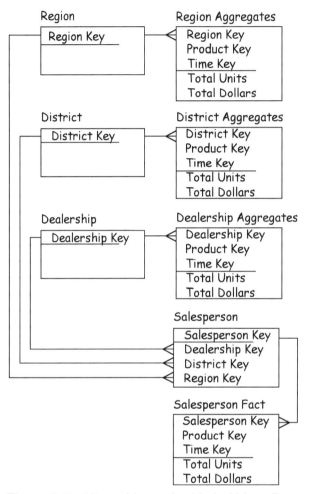

Figure 5–7   Hierarchies embedded within a dimension.

In spite of what we may have previously discussed, this is a partial normalization of the dealership dimension. The alternative would be to duplicate the district and region data in each of the dealership dimension records. This would greatly increase the size of the dealership dimension records, resulting in poorer performance. The only possible justification for this performance degradation would be to fulfill a theoretical design constraint. While it is important to work according to design principles, the data warehouse architect must realize that, unlike life, it is not always a character flaw to trade principles in the face of practical realities.

A second alternative is demonstrated in Figure 5–8. In this diagram we have included the hierarchy data directly in the fact table. The advantage is that the strategist no longer needs to traverse the dealership record to drill-down to the detailed data. The problem, especially for organizations with organizational hierarchies that have many levels, is an increase in the size of the records in the fact table. While this method may be appropriate in some environments, it should be avoided when possible.

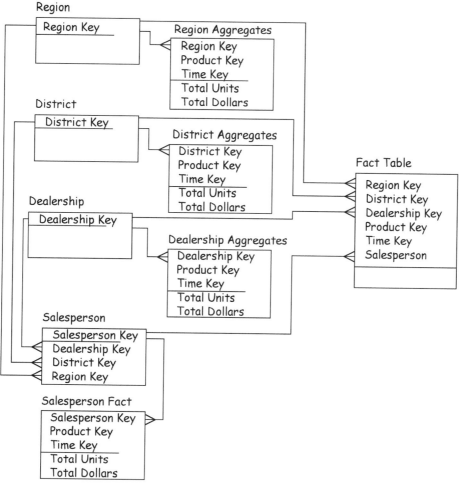

Figure 5–8   Hierarchies within fact tables.

One problem is common to both methods described above. In order to build such a structure, the data warehouse architect must know in advance the number of levels in the hierarchy. Any change in the hierarchy will also cause a change in the structure of the database. As we shall see in our case study, this isn't always the case. There are times when we do not know how many levels a corporate structure may have. We may also be tracking multiple companies in a dimension, and the number of levels in the corporate structure may change from one company to the next.

When the number of levels in a hierarchy is unknown, the data warehouse architect may choose to use a recursive table structure. This is demonstrated in Figure 5–9. The record points to its parent which is defined within a record in the same table. The record also indicates at which level in the hierarchy it resides with a level indicator. This is a very common method for dealing with hierarchies. Most databases can traverse such structures by employing a CONNECT BY clause in the SQL statement.

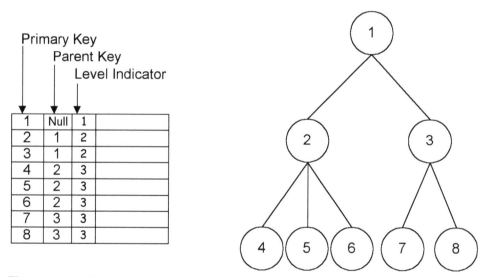

Figure 5–9   Recursive data structure.

5.4.3 Nonanalytical Data

In describing a star schema we emphasized the importance of denormalizing the dimension tables. In this way we are able to improve performance by simplifying the database queries. This does not mean that we throw every little possible detail concerning an object into the dimension table. To do so would frustrate our goal of improving performance. Although a denormalized structure improves performance, the architect must be judicious in selecting the attributes to be included in the dimension. There will be data that is not useful for analysis yet necessary to maintain within the data warehouse. By including these fields in the dimension tables we will create large, unwieldy tables that will slow down our queries and ultimately the effectiveness of our data warehouse.

The standard in a star schema limits the data within the star to only the data that can be included in the analysis. Data that is not likely to be included in an analysis should be pushed out of the star *when it is practical to do so*. When we talk about data that is to be part of an analysis we are talking about attributes that are not specific to any one object but can be used for grouping occurrences of the object. Customer demographics can be used to group the customers. Such information as their gender, age, and postal code can be used to categorize customers in a way that would be meaningful to the business strategist. Other attributes such as street address or name may be of little use to the strategist's analysis. We would, therefore, resist the urge to include these attributes within the dimension table.

The business strategist, however, may wish to drill-down to a level of detail that might require nonanalytical data in a report. The manager of a dealership may drill-down to the most detailed level of information and wish to see the individual sales records. In such a case the manager would probably want to see the names and address of the customers. While there may be no real query value to this information, the strategist may gather value from identifying specific customers. In our case study, the business strategist wanted to know who were the top customers. In such a case we would most certainly want to display the names. So, how do we limit the number of attributes in the dimension to analytical type attributes while providing for the needs of our users?

An alternative to including nonanalytical data in a dimension is to create a *shadow dimension*. This is shown in Figure 5–10. A shadow dimension creates a separate table that contains all the nonanalytical data for the dimension. It is not a true dimension in the sense that it binds the analysis space. The shadow dimension merely provides additional information concerning the values—that is, objects—within the actual dimension. The shadow dimension is joined to the dimension table it shadows in a one-to-one relationship. It is also joined to that fact table in a one-to-many relationship.

In Figure 5–10 we see the benefits of shadow dimensions. On the one hand we retain the basic structure of the star schema. A single fact table remains at the center of our structure, surrounded by denormalized dimension tables. The original set of dimension tables contain only analytical data. The business strategist retrieves data from within the analysis space based on these original dimensions. This optimizes performance by minimizing the size of the tables that have to be searched. Nonanalytical data is retrieved from the shadow dimensions. When the business strategist drills to the deepest level of detail and requires the names of individual products and customers on a report, for example, this data is retrieved from the product and customer shadow dimensions.

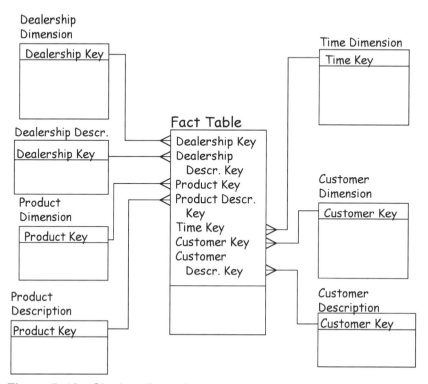

Figure 5–10   Shadow dimensions.

5.5 Dimension of Time

In the physical world, time is as real a dimension as width and depth. Its effects are felt in everything from borderlines to hairlines. In the data warehouse, time is equally important. The very description of a data warehouse is that of a *time-variant* collection of data. In the data warehouse time becomes a variable; we are able to manipulate it as we would any other parameter in our analysis. Time becomes one of those objects that is translated into a dimension of our analysis space. We specify a point in the analysis space by defining a value for the time dimension. The basics of time are understood relatively (forgive the inadvertent pun). Identifying a point in analysis space by its time value is a simple enough matter. The warehouse architect simply provides the data of the sale—November 7, 1992, or June 15, 1994.

Time becomes more complex when the architect starts to establish a hierarchy. A simple raw date would hardly suffice for the needs of most analyses. Consider some basic queries. Perhaps the strategist would like to examine the data on a quarterly basis, reviewing the past year in terms of the past four quarters. Once this data is examined, the strategist would like to compare it to the same quarters in the previous year. This all requires the construction of a time hierarchy. Years are composed of quarters. Quarters are composed of months. Months are composed of weeks and days. The time hierarchy is also complicated by the type of calendar employed by the warehouse. While some data warehouse environments may be satisfied with a standard calendar, others will be based on a fiscal calendar. Rarely will these fiscal periods coincide with the standard calendar. This is demonstrated in Figure 5–11.

Let's return again to our auto-sales example, using Figure 5–11 as our fiscal calendar. As we can see, the fiscal year begins in June. It is reasonable to expect a strategist to consider auto sales on a quarterly or weekly basis. It is also reasonable to expect the strategist to track such things as promotions, test drives, and sales based on the characteristics of different dates such as a holiday, weekday, or weekend. Consider trying to calculate where a date may fall in this calendar. If we close the books for the first fiscal year on May 27, the remaining days in that month will fall in a different fiscal quarter in a different fiscal year.

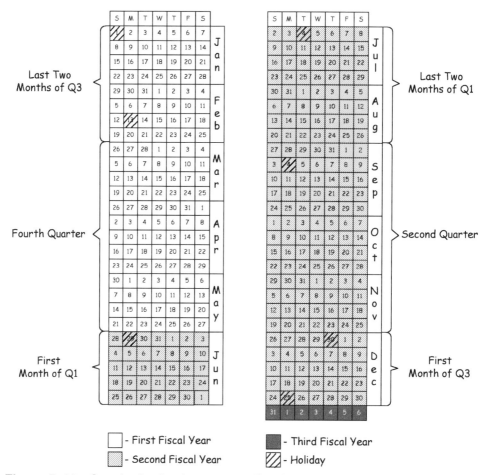

Figure 5–11   Standard calendar versus a fiscal calendar.

As one can see, developing an algorithm to accurately translate a standard date into a fiscal date would be no simple task. Figure 5–12 shows how to resolve the time issue within the star schema. The time key points to a specific record within the time dimension that specifies the fiscal year, quarter, month, week, and day of that particular date. The fiscal day is the number of days into the fiscal calendar the date occurs. January 1 would be the first fiscal day, February 12 the forty-third fiscal day, and so on. Dates that fell on the weekends and holidays would have their appropriate flags set. A season flag would define the time of year in which the date fell—summer, autumn, winter, or spring. The strategist could easily retrieve sales records from the sales table based on any of these categories.

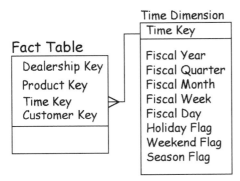

Figure 5–12   Time dimension.

5.6 THE DIMENSIONS OF BBBC

The next step in the development of our case study is to take the object model and transform it to a star schema. Referring back to Figure 3–5, we see that there three main objects: broker, property, and client. In converting from the object model to the implementation model, the superclasses become the dimensions of our implementation model—our star schema. The BBBC implementation model is presented in Figure 5–13. As we noted in the preceding chapter on multidimensionality, what binds these objects together to form an analysis space is the interactions between the objects. These interactions or behaviors are maintained in the fact tables, which are the subject of the next chapter.

Examining Figure 5–13, we see two places where the implementation model varies slightly from the object model. First, we have added the dimension of time. As we have noted throughout this text, the business strategist is interested in the detection and prediction of behaviors. This, of course, requires that the analysis varies time. As we discussed when examining the dimension of time, the data warehouse architect can pretty much be assured that every implementation model will include a time dimension.

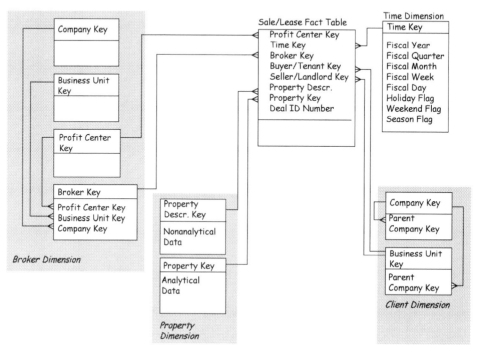

Figure 5–13 BBBC implementation model.

5.6.1 Broker Dimension

The broker dimension is distributed across two tables—the broker table itself and the broker/deal intersection table. The attributes of the broker table are described in Table 5–1. The broker table has combined all of the attributes described in the object model, both analytical and nonanalytical, into one table. We could have created a shadow dimension and separated the two data types. The table is relatively small, however, so there would be little if any performance gain. In addition, any possible gain would be offset by the additional overhead in joining the two tables.

Table 5–1   Broker Table

Field Name	Data Type	Null Option	Description	System of Record
Broker Key	Number 9	Not Null	System-Generated Primary Key	DW
Record Version Number	Number 3	Not Null	Indicates the version of the record. New versions will be applied only when the broker changes profit centers.	DW
Current Flag	Boolean	Not Null	Flag to indicate the record is the most current. When True the record is the most recent version of the broker record. All previous records will be set to False.	DW
Company	Number 9	Not Null	Foreign Key to Company Table	DW
Business Unit	Number 9	Not Null	Foreign Key to Business Unit Table	DW
Business Unit Record Version Number	Number 3	Not Null	Indicates the version of the Business Unit Record	DW
Profit Center Key	Number 9	Not Null	Foreign Key to Profit Center Table	DW
Profit Center Record Version Number	Number 3	Not Null	Indicates the version of the Profit Center Record	DW
Broker ID	Number 9	Not Null	Human Resources Broker Identification Number	HR

Table 5–1 Broker Table (Continued)

Field Name	Data Type	Null Option	Description	System of Record
Broker Type	Character 1	Not Null	Indicates the primary type of property with which the broker deals. The following are valid codes: I = Industrial R = Retail L = Land O = Office S = Shelter	HR
Last Name	Character 20	Not Null	Employee's Last Name	
First Name	Character 20	Not Null	Employee's First Name	HR
Middle Initial	Character 1	Null	Employee's Middle Initial	HR
Title	Character 10	Not Null	Employee Title	HR
E-Mail Address	Character 20	Not Null	Employee E-Mail Address	HR
Street Address 1	Character 20	Not Null	First Line of Two Line Employee Home Address	HR
Street Address 2	Character 20	Null	Second Line of Two Line Employee Home Address	HR
City	Character 20	Not Null	Employee Home City	HR
State	Character 2	Not Null	Employee Home State	HR
Postal Code	Character 9	Not Null	Employee Postal Code	HR
Work Phone Number	Character 10	Not Null	Employee Work Phone Number	HR
Mobile Phone Number	Character 10	Null	Employee Mobile Phone Number	HR
Home Phone Number	Character 10	Not Null	Employee Home Phone Number	HR
Fax Number	Character 10	Not Null	Employee FAX Phone Number	HR

The broker dimension is also an example of a slowly changing dimension. Much to the regret of BBBC management, brokers do not make a career with one commercial real estate company. It is very common for a broker to move from one company to another. To make sure that we capture these career changes, employ record versioning. The record will change versions only as related to changes in employment. Changes in the nonanalytical data within the brokerage record, such as home address or marital status, will not cause a new version of the record to be generated.

As noted in the analysis in Chapter 3, more than one broker can be involved with a deal. This creates a many-to-many relationship between the broker and the fact table. In addition, these brokers are not necessarily employed by BBBC. To provide a means to associate more than one broker with a specific deal we have created an intersection table. The attributes of the intersection table are described in Table 5–2.

Table 5–2 Broker/Deal Intersection Table

Field Name	Data Type	Null Option	Description	System of Record
Broker Key	Number 9	Not Null	System-Generated Primary Key	DW
Broker Record Version Number	Number 3	Not Null	Version of the broker record that was the most recent at the time of the deal.	DW
Deal Key	Number 9	Not Null	Foreign Key to Fact Table	DW

5.6.2 Client Dimension

There is an intentional ambiguity in terminology within the client dimension. The term *business unit* is meant to cover a plethora of organizational structures. These units are the base node of the client hierarchy. In some cases a business unit may be an office of a division of large multinational corporation. In other instances it may be the only office owned or leased by a small *mom & pop shop*. This would indicate that a snowflake approach to the hierarchy would not work. The number of levels in this hierarchy, the hierarchy height, is not consistent from one client to the next. To allow for such an unpredictable hierarchy height, we have chosen to implement the client hierarchy with a self-referencing table at the company level.

The client business unit contains the foreign key of the company table. This key points to the parent company of the business unit. This record is the topmost node of the client hierarchy where the company is not part of some larger organization. If the company is some subdivision of a much larger organization, the parent company key will point to company record of the parent company. It is one thing to have the structure to contain the data, but it is a completely separate issue to have the data. This data will be retrieved from an external source. A variety of information providers are able to supply data pertaining to company structure.

As can be seen in the attribute table, a number of attributes have the potential of changing. The majority of these attributes are not significant to any analysis performed by a business strategist. There are instances when a business unit will change ownership. This could mean that a division or subsidiary is sold to another organization. Of course BBBC will be interested in tracking this new information while retaining a history of the past relationship. Consider the purpose of tracking the client information and how the CEO might be able to use this historical information when attempting to establish a national relationship.

Perhaps a division of a large corporation is sold to another large corporation. BBBC when negotiating a relationship with the original owner of the division would need an accurate history of the relationship. Certainly BBBC would want to include the business done with the old division as part of the total business done with the corporation. At the same time BBBC would not want to include any business after the change. Consider the ramifications of presenting erroneous data that makes BBBC's relationship appear more favorable than what reality might suggest. Such an error at best would reflect poorly on BBBC's competence, at worst it would reflect poorly on its ethics. For marketing purposes, BBBC would want to detect any change in business that might result from the change in ownership.

Table 5-3 Client Table

Field Name	Data Type	Null Option	Comments	System of Record
Client Business Unit Key	Number 9	Not Null	System-Generated Primary Key	DW
Record Version Number	Number 3	Not Null	Indicates the version of the record. New versions will be applied only when a business unit is sold to another corporation.	DW
Current Flag	Boolean	Not Null	Flag to indicate the record is the most current. When True the record is the most recent version of the business unit record. All previous records will be set to False.	DW
Client Parent Company Key	Number 9	Null	Foreign Key to Company table indicating parent company of the client business unit.	DW
Client Parent Company Record Version Number	Number 3	Null	Most recent version of the parent company record when the relationship was established.	DW
Client Name	Character 30	Not Null	Name of the Client Business Unit	VS/RR
Client Type	Character 1	Not Null	Code signifying the type of client. The following are valid client codes: I = Investor U = User of Space O = Owner of Space R = Real Estate Trust	VS/RR
Street Address 1	Character 20	Not Null	First Line of Two Line Address	VS/RR
Street Address 2	Character 20	Null	Second Line of Two Line Address	VS/RR
City	Character 20	Not Null	Office City	VS/RR
State	Character 2	Not Null	Office State	VS/RR

Table 5–3 Client Table (Continued)

Field Name	Data Type	Null Option	Comments	System of Record
Postal Code	Character 9	Not Null	Office Postal Code	VS/RR
Main Office Phone Number	Character 10	Null	Business Unit's Main Phone Number	VS/RR
Secondary Office Phone Number	Character 10	Null	Business Unit's Secondary Phone Number	VS/RR
Main Fax Number	Character 10	Null	Business Unit's Main Fax Number	VS/RR
Secondary Fax Number	Character 10	Null	Business Unit's Secondary Fax Number	VS/RR
Primary Contact's Last Name	Character 20	Not Null	Primary Contact's Last Name	VS/RR
Primary Contact's First Name	Character 20	Not Null	Primary Contact's First Name	VS/RR
Primary Contact's Middle Initial	Character 1	Null	Primary Contact's Middle Initial	VS/RR
Primary Contact's E-Mail Address	Character 20	Null	Primary Contact's E-Mail Address	VS/RR
Primary Contact's Work Phone Number	Character 10	Not Null	Primary Contact's Work Phone Number	VS/RR
Primary Contact's Mobile Phone Number	Character 10	Null	Primary Contact's Mobile Phone Number	VS/RR
Primary Contact's Home Phone Number	Character 10	Null	Primary Contact's Home Phone Number	VS/RR
Primary Contact's Fax Number	Character 10	Not Null	Primary Contact's FAX Phone Number	VS/RR

Table 5–4 Client Company Table

Field Name	Data Type	Null Option	Comments	System of Record
Company Key	Number 9	Not Null	Primary	DW
Record Version Number	Number 3	Not Null	Indicates the version of the record. New versions will be applied only when a division or subsidiary is sold to another corporation.	DW
Current Flag	Boolean	Not Null	Flag to indicate the record is the most current. When True the record is the most recent version of the company record. All previous records will be set to False.	DW
Parent Company Key	Number 9	Not Null	Recursive key, points to company record of the parent company	DW
Parent Company Record Version Number	Number 3	Not Null	Indicates the version of the parent company record	DW
Level Indicator	Number 3	Not Null	Indicates at what level in the hierarchy the current record resides.	DW
Company Name	Character 20	Not Null	Name of the Parent Company	VS/RR/EX
Street Address 1	Character 20	Not Null	First Line of Two Line Address	VS/RR/EX
Street Address 2	Character 20	Null	Second Line of Two Line Address	VS/RR/EX
City	Character 20	Not Null	Office City	VS/RR/EX
State	Character 2	Not Null	Office State	VS/RR/EX
Postal Code	Character 9	Not Null	Office Postal Code	VS/RR/EX
Main Office Phone Number	Character 10	Not Null	Parent Company's Main Phone Number	VS/RR/EX
Secondary Office Phone Number	Character 10	Null	Parent Company's Secondary Phone Number	VS/RR/EX
Main Fax Number	Character 10	Not Null	Parent Company's Main Fax Number	VS/RR/EX
Secondary Fax Number	Character 10	Null	Parent Company's Secondary Fax Number	VS/RR/EX

To allow the business strategist to track the ownership of companies we have again implemented record versioning. Changes in the ownership of a business unit or parent company will result in a new version of the record being generated. Any other data changes in the record will be simply overwritten. The user community may request a change in design, requiring that new versions of the record be generated when other attributes of the record are modified. The data structure would accommodate such design changes. Caution: Any such design change request should be well documented and agreed to by the project sponsor.

5.6.3 Commercial Real Estate Company Dimension

The commercial real estate company is an aggregation. We have implemented this hierarchy by normalizing the structure along the lines of the organization's structure. The aggregation is the object model's way of presenting a hierarchy. In contrast to the client company object, the commercial real estate company has a well-defined structure. We have implemented a three-level hierarchy consisting of profit center, business unit, and company. Since we can be sure of a consistent height, we will implement the hierarchy by normalizing the dimension. The attributes of the Profit Center, Business Unit, and Company are described in Tables 5–5, 5–6, and 5–7, respectively.

In both the profit center and the business unit tables we have used record versioning to track changes. Specifically we are interested in tracking changes to the management of either object. In this way the CEO will be able to compare performance of the business entity over time as well as changes in the management. For example, the CEO can compare the performance of a particular profit center over several fiscal periods that span a change in the management of the profit center. As noted in previous discussions on record versioning, users may request a design change that would extend the generation of new versions of the record for changes to data other than management information. While the data structure is sufficient to provide for these changes, they should be well documented and agreed to by the project sponsor.

Table 5–5 Commercial Real Estate Company Profit Center

Field Name	Data Type	Null Option	Description	System of Record
Profit Center Key	Number 9	Not Null	Foreign Key to Profit Center Table	DW
Record Version Number	Number 3	Not Null	Indicates the version of the record. New versions will be applied only when a profit center experiences a change in management.	DW
Current Flag	Boolean	Not Null	Flag to indicate the record is the most current. When True the record is the most recent version of the company record. All previous records will be set to False.	DW
Profit Center Type	Character 1	Not Null	Field indicating profit center type. The following are valid codes: B = Brokerage P = Property Management A = Appraisal R = Realty Advisors I = Investments	DW
Profit Center Name	Character 20	Not Null	Name of the profit center	DW
Street Address 1	Character 20	Not Null	First Line of Two Line Address	DW
Street Address 2	Character 20	Null	Second Line of Two Line Address	DW
City	Character 20	Not Null	Office City	DW
State	Character 2	Not Null	Office State	DW
Postal Code	Character 9	Not Null	Office Postal Code	DW
Main Office Phone Number	Character 10	Not Null	Profit Center's Main Phone Number	DW
Secondary Office Phone Number	Character 10	Null	Profit Center's Secondary Phone Number	DW
Main Fax Number	Character 10	Not Null	Profit Center's Main Fax Number	DW

Table 5–5 Commercial Real Estate Company Profit Center (Continued)

Field Name	Data Type	Null Option	Description	System of Record
Secondary Fax Number	Character 10	Null	Profit Center's Secondary Fax Number	DW
Manager ID	Number 9	Not Null	Primary Key of Manager Table	DW
Manager Employee ID	Number 9	Not Null	Manager's Employee ID	HR
Manager's Last Name	Character 20	Not Null	Manager's Last Name	HR
Manager's First Name	Character 20	Not Null	Manager's First Name	HR
Manager's Middle Initial	Character 1	Null	Manager's Middle Initial	HR
Manager's E-Mail Address	Character 20	Not Null	Manager's E-Mail Address	HR
Manager's Home Street Address 1	Character 20	Not Null	First Line of Two Line Manager Home Address	HR
Manager's Home Street Address 2	Character 20	Null	Second Line of Two Line Manager Home Address	HR
Manager's Home City	Character 20	Not Null	Manager's Home City	HR
Manager's Home State	Character 2	Not Null	Manager's Home State	HR
Manager's Home Postal Code	Character 9	Not Null	Manager's Postal Code	HR
Manager's Work Phone Number	Character 10	Not Null	Manager's Work Phone Number	HR
Manager's Mobile Phone Number	Character 10	Null	Manager's Mobile Phone Number	HR
Manager's Home Phone Number	Character 10	Not Null	Manager's Home Phone Number	HR
Manager's Fax Number	Character 10	Not Null	Manager's FAX Phone Number	HR

Table 5–6 Commercial Real Estate Company Business Unit

Field Name	Data Type	Null Option	Description	System of Record
Business Unit Key	Number 9	Not Null	Foreign key to business unit table, indicates the parent business unit.	DW
Record Version Number	Number 3	Not Null	Indicates the version of the record. New versions will be applied only when a business unit experiences a change in management.	DW
Current Flag	Boolean	Not Null	Flag to indicate the record is the most current. When True the record is the most recent version of the company record. All previous records will be set to False.	
Business Unit Type	Enumerated	Not Null	Field indicating business unit type. The following are valid codes: B = Brokerage A = Appraisal P = Property Management R = Realty Advisors I = Investments	DW
Business Unit Name	Character 20	Not Null	Name of the business unit	DW
Street Address 1	Character 20	Not Null	First Line of Two Line Address	DW
Street Address 2	Character 20	Null	Second Line of Two Line Address	DW
City	Character 20	Not Null	Office City	DW
State	Character 2	Not Null	Office State	DW
Postal Code	Character 9	Not Null	Office Postal Code	DW
Main Office Phone Number	Character 10	Not Null	Business Unit's Main Phone Number	DW

193

Table 5–6 Commercial Real Estate Company Business Unit (Continued)

Field Name	Data Type	Null Option	Description	System of Record
Secondary Office Phone Number	Character 10	Null	Business Unit's Secondary Phone Number	DW
Main Fax Number	Character 10	Not Null	Business Unit's Main Fax Number	DW
Secondary Fax Number	Character 10	Null	Business Unit's Secondary Fax Number	DW
VP ID	Number 9	Not Null	Primary Key of VP Table	DW
VP Employee ID	Number 9	Not Null	VP Employee ID	HR
VP's Last Name	Character 20	Not Null	VP's Last Name	HR
VP's First Name	Character 20	Not Null	VP's First Name	HR
VP's Middle Initial	Character 1	Null	VP's Middle Initial	HR
VP's E-Mail Address	Character 20	Not Null	VP's E-Mail Address	HR
VP's Home Street Address 1	Character 20	Not Null	First Line of Two Line VP Home Address	HR
VP's Home Street Address 2	Character 20	Null	Second Line of Two Line VP Home Address	HR
VP's Home City	Character 20	Not Null	VP's Home City	HR
VP's Home State	Character 2	Not Null	VP's Home State	HR
VP's Home Postal Code	Character 9	Not Null	VP's Postal Code	HR
VP's Work Phone Number	Character 10	Not Null	VP's Work Phone Number	HR
VP's Mobile Phone Number	Character 10	Null	VP's Mobile Phone Number	HR
VP's Home Phone Number	Character 10	Not Null	VP's Home Phone Number	HR
VP's Fax Number	Character 10	Not Null	VP's FAX Phone Number	HR

Table 5-7 Commercial Real Estate Company

Field Name	Data Type	Null Option	Comments	System of Record
Company Key	Number 9	Not Null	Primary	DW
Company Name	Character 20	Not Null	Name of the Parent Company	DW
Street Address 1	Character 20	Not Null	First Line of Two Line Address	DW
Street Address 2	Character 20	Null	Second Line of Two Line Address	DW
City	Character 20	Not Null	Office City	DW
State	Character 2	Not Null	Office State	DW
Postal Code	Character 9	Not Null	Office Postal Code	DW
Main Office Phone Number	Character 10	Not Null	Parent Company's Main Phone Number	DW
Secondary Office Phone Number	Character 10	Null	Parent Company's Secondary Phone Number	DW
Main Fax Number	Character 10	Not Null	Parent Company's Main Fax Number	DW
Secondary Fax Number	Character 10	Null	Parent Company's Secondary Fax Number	DW

Also note that both the profit center and the business unit contain geographic data. This data defines the sales territories of each. Since the business unit is an aggregation of profit centers, the sum of all territories for all business units within a profit center should equal the territory of a business unit.

5.6.4 Property Dimension

The property table is relatively large, containing both analytical data and nonanalytical data. To provide for better performance while maintaining the ability of the data warehouse to provide complete information to the business strategist, the implementation model breaks the property dimension into two tables. The first contains purely analytical data and is presented in Table 5–8. The second contains the nonanalytical data and is presented in Table 5–9.

5.6.5 Time

A standard dimension within data warehouses is time. The very definition of the data warehouse contains the term *time-variant*. To allow the business strategist to vary time, to use it as a variable, the data warehouse includes a time dimension. The structure presented earlier in this chapter would be sufficient for the BBBC data warehouse. The attributes of this dimension are presented in Table 5–10.

The primary key of the time table is the Julian date of the fact. The Julian date is a nominal noninteger that represents a continuous date from a common reference point, January 1, 4712 B.C. The fractional portion of the number presents the time of day. For simplicity's sake, however, the Julian date used as the time dimension's primary key will be integer value. The Julian date for April 8, 1993, would be 2449086.

Table 5–8   Analytical Property Data Table

Field Name	Data Type	Null Option	Description	System of Record
Property Key	Number 9	Not Null	Primary key to the property table.	DW
Record Version Number	Number 3	Not Null	Indicates the version of the record.	DW
Current Flag	Boolean	Not Null	Flag to indicate the record is the most current. When True the record is the most recent version of the company record. All previous records will be set to False.	DW
Nonanalytical Property Data Key	Number 9	Not Null	Foreign Key to the nonanalytical property table	DW
Nonanalytical Property Data Record Version Number	Number 3	Not Null	Indicates the version of the nonanalytical property record.	DW
Acres	Number 6,2	Null	Number of acres upon which the property resides	RR/VS
Constructed Year	Date	Null	Year building was constructed	RR/VS
Date Available	Date	Null	Date property is available	RR/VS
Date on Market	Date	Null	Data property is placed on the market	RR/VS
Number of Tenants	Number 3	Not Null	Number of tenants in the property	RR/VS
Parking Type	Character 1	Not Null	Code indicating type of parking structure. Valid codes are: N = None G = Garage C = Covered O = Open	RR/VS
Renovated Year	Date	Null	Year property was last renovated	RR/VS

197

Table 5–8 Analytical Property Data Table (Continued)

Field Name	Data Type	Null Option	Description	System of Record
Sqr Ft Available	Number 7	Not Null	Total number of square feet available in the property	RR/VS
Sqr Ft Available Contiguous	Number 7	Not Null	Total number of contiguous square feet available in the property	RR/VS
Sqr Ft Building	Number 7	Not Null	Total number of square feet in the building	RR/VS
Sqr Ft Garage	Number 7	Not Null	Total square feet in parking structure	RR/VS
Sqr Ft Improved	Number 7	Not Null	Total square feet most recently improved	RR/VS
Sqr Ft Per Floor Max	Number 7	Not Null	Maximum square feet per floor	RR/VS
Sqr Ft Per Floor Min	Number 7	Not Null	Minimum square feet per floor	RR/VS
Sqr Ft Usable	Number 7	Not Null	Total usable square feet in property	RR/VS
Status	Character 1	Not Null	Code indicating the state of the property. Valid codes are: N = New G = Good E = Excellent P = Poor R = Repair Needed	RR/VS
Use Type	Character 1	Not Null	Code indicating the use of the property. Valid codes are: I = Industrial R = Retail O = Office S = Shelter L = Land	RR/VS
Vacant Percent	Number 2,2	Not Null	Percentage of the property that is vacant	RR/VS

Table 5–9 Nonanalytical Property Data Table

Field Name	Data Type	Null Option	Description	System of Record
Nonanalytical Property Data Key	Number 9	Not Null	Primary key to the nonanalytical property table	DW
Nonanalytical Property Data Record Version Number	Number 3	Not Null	Indicates the version of the nonanalytical property record.	DW
Current Flag	Boolean	Not Null	Flag to indicate the record is the most current. When True the record is the most recent version of the company record. All previous records will be set to False.	DW
Analytical Property Data Key	Number 9	Not Null	Foreign key to the analytical property table	DW
Analytical Property Data Record Version Number	Number 3	Not Null	Indicates the version of the analytical property record.	DW
Architect	Character 20	Null	Name of Architectural Company	RR/VS
Architect Hdqtr	Character 20	Null	Address of Architectural Headquarters	RR/VS
Architect Hdqtr Street Address 1	Character 20	Null	First Line of Two Line Address of Architectural Company Office	RR/VS
Architect Hdqtr Street Address 2	Character 20	Null	Second Line of Two Line Address of Architectural Company Office	RR/VS
Architect Hdqtr City	Character 20	Null	Architectural Company Office City	RR/VS
Architect Hdqtr State	Character 2	Null	Architectural Company Office State	RR/VS
Architect Hdqtr Postal Code	Character 9	Null	Architectural Company Office Postal Code	RR/VS
Architect Hdqtr Postal Code Extension	Character 9	Null	Architectural Company Office Postal Code Extension	RR/VS

199

Table 5–9 Nonanalytical Property Data Table (Continued)

Field Name	Data Type	Null Option	Description	System of Record
Complex Park Name	Character 20	Null	Name of Business Park	RR/VS
Contractor	Character 20	Null	Name of Contractor Company	RR/VS
Contractor Hdqtr	Character 20	Null	Address of Contractor Headquarters	RR/VS
Contractor Hdqtr Street Address 1	Character 20	Null	First Line of Two Line Address of Contractor Company Office	RR/VS
Contractor Hdqtr Street Address 2	Character 20	Null	Second Line of Two Line Address of Contractor Company Office	RR/VS
Contractor Hdqtr City	Character 20	Null	Contractor Company Office City	RR/VS
Contractor Hdqtr State	Character 2	Null	Contractor Company Office State	RR/VS
Contractor Hdqtr Postal Code	Character 9	Null	Contractor Company Office Postal Code	RR/VS
Contractor Hdqtr Postal Code Extension	Character 9	Null	Contractor Company Office Postal Code Extension	RR/VS
Country	Character 20	Null	Country of the Property	RR/VS
County	Character 20	Not Null	County of the Property	RR/VS
Cross Street 1	Character 30	Null	First Major Cross Street of Building	RR/VS
Cross Street 2	Character 30	Null	Second Major Cross Street of Building	RR/VS
Developer	Character 30	Null	Developer of the Property	RR/VS
Record Date	Date	Not Null	Date Record Was Created	RR/VS
Management Company	Character 30	Not Null	Name of Property Management Company	RR/VS
Management Hdqtr	Character 20	Null	Address of Management Headquarters	RR/VS

Table 5–9   Nonanalytical Property Data Table (Continued)

Field Name	Data Type	Null Option	Description	System of Record
Management Hdqtr Street Address 1	Character 20	Null	First Line of Two Line Address of Management Company Office	RR/VS
Management Hdqtr Street Address 2	Character 20	Null	Second Line of Two Line Address of Management Company Office	RR/VS
Management Hdqtr City	Character 20	Null	Management Company Office City	RR/VS
Management Hdqtr State	Character 2	Null	Management Company Office State	RR/VS
Management Hdqtr Postal Code	Character 9	Null	Management Company Office Postal Code	RR/VS
Management Hdqtr Postal Code Extension	Character 9	Null	Management Company Office Postal Code Extension	RR/VS
Management Contact	Character 30	Not Null	Property Management Company Contact	RR/VS
Management Contact Phone Number	Character 10	Not Null	Phone Number of Property Management Company	RR/VS
State	Character 2	Not Null	Property's State	RR/VS
Street Direction	Character 1	Not Null	Direction of Property's Street Address	RR/VS
Street Name	Character 30	Not Null	Name of Property's Street Address	RR/VS
Street Number 1	Character 5	Not Null	First Number of Property's Street Address	RR/VS
Street Number 2	Character 5	Not Null	Second Number of Property's Street Address	RR/VS
Postal Code	Character 5	Not Null	Postal Code of the Property's Address	RR/VS
Postal Code Extension	Character 4	Not Null	Postal Code Extension of the Property's Address	RR/VS

Table 5–10 The Time Dimension

Field Name	Data Type	Null Option	Comments	System of Record
Time Key	Integer 7	Not Null	The Julian date of the fact.	DW
Fiscal Year	Number 4	Not Null	The fiscal year in which the Julian date occurs.	DW
Fiscal Quarter	Number 1	Not Null	The fiscal quarter in which the Julian date occurs.	DW
Fiscal Month	Number 2	Not Null	The fiscal month in which the Julian date occurs.	DW
Fiscal Week	Number 2	Not Null	The fiscal week in which the Julian date occurs.	DW
Fiscal Day	Number 3	Not Null	The fiscal day in which the Julian date occurs.	DW
Holiday Flag	Character 1	Not Null	A Boolean field where the value T (True) indicates the Julian date is a holiday. All other dates are set to False.	DW
Weekend Flag	Character 1	Not Null	A Boolean field where the value T (True) indicates the Julian date is a weekend day. All other dates are set to False.	DW
Season Flag	Character 1	Not Null	Indicates the season in which the Julian date occurs. The following are valid season codes: W = Winter S = Spring H = Summer (H for hot) A = Autumn	DW

5.7 Summary

This chapter reviewed the dimensions of the star schema. As shown, the transformation of objects in the object model to dimensions in the implementation model entails more than simply denormalizing the dimension tables. Dimension tables must be structured to provide for such issues as slowly changing dimensions, hierarchies within the data, and many-to-many relationships, to name a few. In this chapter we reviewed dimensional structures that deal with each of these contingencies.

Another dimensional issue discussed in this chapter is that of time. Standard calendars do not map easily to the types of analyses performed by business strategist. There is no algorithm that can easily transform standard days, weeks, and months. The time dimension presented in this chapter and applied to the case study maps a standard date to its fiscal equivalent.

The broker dimension within the case study provided an example of how to deal with slowly changing dimensions as well as with a many-to-many relationship. The client dimension provided an example of one alternative to dealing with hierarchical data by using a recursive table. The company dimension, on the other hand, used a more normalized structure in more of a snowflake approach. Finally, we demonstrated the separation of analytical from nonanalytical property data with shadow dimensions.

5.8 Glossary

Analytical Data   Object attributes used to select objects or groups of objects for analysis. The domain of values for an analytical data element is finite.

Conforming Dimensions   A dimension that is common to two or more analysis spaces. The values of the dimension are sufficient to bind both spaces. In a star schema a conforming dimension is joined to multiple fact tables, allowing the business strategist to traverse the structure from one fact table to another.

Constellation   A schema containing multiple fact tables joined together by conforming dimensions.

Drill-Across Traversal of constellation from one fact table to another via a fact table.

Intersection Table An intermediate table used to link two tables in a many-to-many relationship. Each record in the intersection table has a unique combination of the foreign keys of the tables it is linking, creating a many-to-one relationship between the intersection table and each of the linked tables.

Nonanalytical Data Data elements included in the dimension for reporting purposes but having little analytical value. Their domain of values is not necessarily finite and they cannot be used to create groups of objects.

Shadow Dimension A separate table of nonanalytical data linked to a dimension table in a one-to-one relationship.

Slowly Changing Dimension A dimension whose object attributes change infrequently over time.

Snowflake A star schema whose dimension tables have been normalized.

Fact Tables—the Verbs of the Data Warehouse

The objective of a decision support system is to give the business strategist a tool to examine the behavior of objects connected to the organization. In the preceding chapter we noted how the dimensions are the nouns of our analysis—the persons, places, and things related to our organization. It is the behavior of these nouns, these objects, in which the strategist is interested. Where the dimensions record the attributes of objects, the facts record the attributes of behavior. These are the verbs of the data warehouse. These facts are stored in the fact table, the nucleus of the star schema.

The fact table does more than record facts. In Chapter 4 we noted that the dimensions in a coordinate system are related to one another. We also noted that the fact table binds the single-dimensioned dimension tables into a multidimensional space within a relational environment. The fact table in essence becomes the glue that binds the dimensions together. We will explore this in the first section below.

In this chapter we are going to look at the facts, or at least the fact tables. We will look at some of the issues in recording the facts. The chapter will conclude by presenting the fact table for our case study and the final version of the star schema for BBBC.

6.1 Fact Tables

The fact table is at the heart of the star schema and serves two purposes. First, it pulls together the dimension tables into a multidimensional analysis space. Second, it contains the points in the analysis space. If we were to relate the star schema to the data cube, the fact-table records would be the cells of the cube. The structure of the fact-table records parallels the functions it performs in the warehouse. The first group of fields form the links between the fact table and the different dimensions. The second group contains the actual data points.

A point's coordinate uniquely identifies that point in space. In a two-dimensional space there is only one point with the coordinates (4,3). There is no other. In the same way, the primary key of a relational table is the coordinate of the record; it uniquely identifies the record. The primary key of the fact table is a composite of the dimension-table keys. The combination of the dimension keys uniquely identifies the data point. There is no ambiguity when the strategist asks for the data point (Spiffy Cars, Testosterone 500, July 1999). The strategist is asking for the number of Testosterone 500's sold by Spiffy Cars in July 1999.

In Figure 6–1 we present the star schema of the auto-sales example with a fully described fact table. The upper half of the fact-table record contains the keys to the record, the coordinates. The importance of using system-generated surrogate keys should be noted once again. The data warehouse architect should resist the urge to use the keys in the operational environment as the data warehouse primary keys. While at first glimpse this may appear to be a good idea, it will actually complicate the administration of the data warehouse. First, any changes in the keys in the operational environment will force a similar change in the data warehouse. Also, as the scope of the data warehouse expands and additional operational systems contribute data, the architect must then contend with how the data from these other systems will be merged into the data warehouse without corrupting the keys.

It is, however, beneficial to maintain the operational environment's keys as attributes of the dimension. First, the architect will use these keys in the extraction and transformation process. In bringing data from the operational world the operational keys will identify which data is new dimension data and which is update data. We have also seen, when working with slowly changing dimensions, the use of operational-system primary keys.

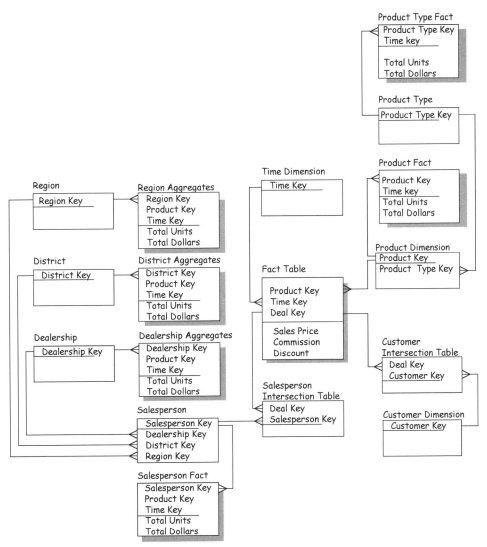

Figure 6–1 Auto-sales star schema.

The fact table links each of the different dimensions together. It serves as the central hub for the star schema. Each dimension is joined to the central fact table. An instance of an object in one dimension is related to an instance of an object in another dimension via the fact table. Let's look at the salesperson dimension. Taking the key of a particular salesperson, we can identify his or her records in the fact table. These records will tell us which products were sold by this salesperson and which customer bought them. We have established a relationship between these objects. Without the fact table there would be no association between the salesperson and a product.

Figure 6–1 also demonstrates the ease with which an analyst can slice and dice information with the star schema. In selecting a particular salesperson we have sliced the data cube. Since the keys are the actual coordinates of the hypercube created within the relational database, specification of a range of values for a coordinate or set of coordinates will specify a slice of the data. We have demonstrated this in Figure 6–2. In this diagram we see a reference that specifies the month June 1999. This specification will return all facts of all actions that were carried out in June 1999. This means all sales by all dealerships for the month of June 1999. The slice is a set of records whose time coordinate meets the month of June. The other dimensions are not taken into consideration for this selection.

Fact Table

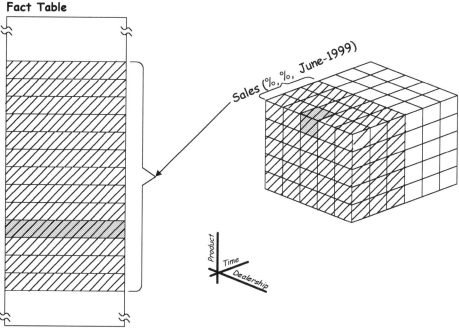

Figure 6–2   Star schema slicing.

We could also dice the data where we cut away a smaller cube of data. We do this by specifying a range of values for the other dimensions. Perhaps we could specify the sales of all sports cars for the month of June 1999. This would create a data cube with the sales of all sports cars in the month of June 1999 for all dealerships. We could also limit the data cube to all dealerships in a particular region of the country. As we shall see in the next chapter, bitmapped indexing will assist us in slicing and dicing a star schema's hypercube.

The second half of the fact-table record contains the attributes of the behavior. These attributes are measures of the actions that occur between the different objects. In our auto-sales example these measures might include the sale price of the car or the commission paid to the salesperson. They might even include the discount given to the customer to purchase the car. All of these are measures of the action of selling the car.

It is important not to confuse a fact with a dimension's attribute. A fact is something that can be measured only when a sale occurs. In our auto-sales example the sale price, commission, and discount can only be determined once the sale of the car occurs. Prior to the sale all these measures are unknown. There are other numeric measures that are more appropriately defined as attributes of the dimension, such as the car's fuel efficiency or the age of the person purchasing the car. These are all measures, true, but they are measures of the dimensions, not facts pertaining to the interaction between the dimensions.

Since facts are measures, we expect them to be numeric. When looking at the fact table we expect to see two types of data: foreign keys and numeric data. Unfortunately, in the star schema there is no such thing as a simple fact. Many things need to be considered by the data warehouse architect when designing a fact table. Such issues as precision and granularity, among others, must be resolved. The following subsections will discuss each of these issues in detail.

6.1.1 Measure By Measure

In the preceding section we noted that the facts in the fact table are measures of the verbs or interactions between objects in our analysis space.

There are, however, measures and then again there are measures. We measure according to a scale. A scale is a way to organize items according to a predefined arrangement. There are four generally recognized scales: nominal, ordinal, interval, and ratio. In addition, the data warehouse employs counts and ranks. The data warehouse architect should understand the differences between each of these scales when selecting one to measure a particular fact. These differences will determine the ways in which that fact can be analyzed by the business strategist.

Nominal scales are simple labels. District names can be thought of as nominal scales. They simply label each of the districts. When we divide a company into the Los Angeles, New York, and Chicago districts, we are applying a nominal scale. There is no relationship between the different elements in the scale. There is no way to evaluate the Los Angeles district in relation to the New York district simply in terms of this nominal scale. Measurement with a nominal scale has no real value other than the identification of the elements being measured.

An ordinal scale is a ranking of objects. We place the objects in an order according to some criterion. Perhaps in the auto-sales data warehouse we wanted to evaluate the sales experience as perceived by the customer. We could have a fact named "Sales Experience," whose domain of values is "Excellent," "Good," "Fair," or "Poor." An ordinal scale is useful for grouping, but it is not possible to calculate any distance between two measures on the scale. What if one customer ranked the sales experience as "Excellent" and another ranked it as "Fair"? What is the distance between "Excellent" and "Fair"? Where does "Good" fit into the range?

If we hope to be able to measure a distance between two objects on a scale, we would need to use an interval scale. An interval scale, besides ordering objects, measures the distance between them in units of equal intervals. The origin of the scale, however, is arbitrary. It may or may not start at zero. The most common interval scale is time. The time origin does not start at zero. In our case study we use a Julian date where the origin is January 1, 4712 B.C. The distance between the objects, however, is equal. The distance between today and this same day last year is equal to the distance between this same day last year and today, as well as today and this same day a year from now.

Scales that start with an origin of zero are ratio scales. Ratio scales measure according to some multiple of a common unit. Typically one sees ratio scales pertaining to physical attributes such as height or weight. A common unit is a pound, and objects are weighed in multiples of that common unit. In our auto-sales example the financial facts are based on a ratio scale. The common unit is a dollar, and we start at an origin of zero.

In data warehousing we have two additional scales that are not generally discussed as such. The first is count. We simply select an object and count the number of occurrences. We also have rankings. A ranking can be seen in an organizational structure. There are staff members, managers, directors, vice presidents, and presidents. While there is a hierarchy to the data, there is no distance between the objects as in the ratio or interval scales.

6.1.2 Precision

Not too long ago I took my children on a tour of the museum of natural history. As we were going through the tour, our guide pointed to a Neanderthal skull and said it was 125,010 years old. At the end of the tour I asked him about the dating of these objects. He replied, "Well, when I started training to be a tour guide they told me those skulls were 125,000 years old, and I have been here for ten years." Obviously the guide had a slight problem with precision.

Precision deals with the decimal position of the last significant digit. This means that the method of measuring something will determine its precision. Just as with fossils, the precision of a number is only as good as the measurement tool. Carbon dating of an object could only give us an approximate measurement. To suggest that it could precisely date an object to within a year or two would be like trying to time a sprinter with a sundial. So when we are told that a certain object is several thousand years old, the precision of that number is in the thousands.

Note that there is a significant difference between the precision of a measurement and its correctness. In our auto-sales example the number of cars sold in a particular month is exact; we simply count the number of cars sold. There are measurements used within the warehouse, however, that are not so precise. Consider our case study in which we measure the square footage of a building. Certainly the appraiser of the property does not go to each and every room and measure the square feet in it. Typically the length and the width of the floors are multiplied and the square footage is estimated. This is why we will discuss several thousand square feet or several hundred square feet. This is the most precise measure with which we have to deal.

When working with numbers of different precision we must be careful to report the results of the computation accurately. If we go back to our museum story, the problem is that the guide combined two numbers that did not have the same precision. The result was to present a number having a level of precision that was not consistent with the actual data. If the guide had been working there for ten thousand years instead of ten, he could have accurately said that the skull was now 135,000 years old. In combining numbers of different precision, we must report the results to the least precise value used in the calculation.

This has a severe effect on the data warehouse—one that can give the data warehouse architect considerable problems if the user community's expectation is not properly set. Remember that the data warehouse collects data from a variety of sources. As we have discussed in the first chapter, these sources do not always agree on the definition of data. One part of an organization may need data that is much more precise than that required by other parts of the organization. Perhaps a carpeting company tracks what is on hand to a precision of 10 square yards, while sales deals with square yards. When the data from these two systems are combined into one, there will be differences in the precision of the numbers. The warehouse will have to transform the more precise number to the less precise number. The data warehouse architect must set the expectation of the user community, especially the community that is contributing a data that is more precise.

6.1.3 Granularity

The grain of the data warehouse determines the most basic element of data. If the business strategist were to drill-down into the data until there was no deeper level of detail, that would be the grain. In some situations an acceptable level of granularity is the individual transaction. In the example we have worked with in this book the granularity has been to the transaction level. There are many applications where a transaction granularity level would be inappropriate. Consider a telephone company that was tracking the calling pattern of its clients. The sheer number of calls over any significant period would make the size of the data warehouse so unwieldy that no meaningful analysis of the data could be made in a timely manner.

When considering the level of granularity, the data warehouse architect must look at what is desired by the user and what is deliverable by the system. On the one hand, the user may wish to see the detail of individual transactions. On the other hand, the performance of the underlying hardware and software platform would be unable to deliver this level of detail. Again referring to the telephone industry, imagine tracking every call made by every customer of a large telephone company for an entire year. We can quickly start talking about a data warehouse in the petabyte range. Rather than provide data down to the transaction level, it may be acceptable to sum the data at a higher level. Perhaps individual calls could be summed on an hourly or daily basis. The business strategist can then examine behaviors over larger periods of time.

The warehouse architect should also keep in mind that establishing a higher level of granularity will affect the dimensions within the data warehouse. Consider our auto-sales example. If the warehouse is being implemented by the auto manufacturer, there may not be an interest to track sales down to the individual deal. Perhaps the manufacturer will be satisfied with daily totals from each of the dealerships. In this case the bottom level of the dealership hierarchy, salespeople, would be eliminated. Compare the star schema in Figure 6–1 with a revised schema in Figure 6–3. As shown in the two diagrams, the schema is simplified by the removal of the salesperson table and the salesperson summation table. Removal of these dimensions, of course, renders the business strategist unable to perform an analysis to that level of detail.

Deciding the granularity of the data warehouse is one of the most far-reaching design decisions that the data warehouse architect can make. It will affect not only the fact table, but the structure of the star schema itself. Ultimately it will define how detailed an analysis can be performed by the business strategist.

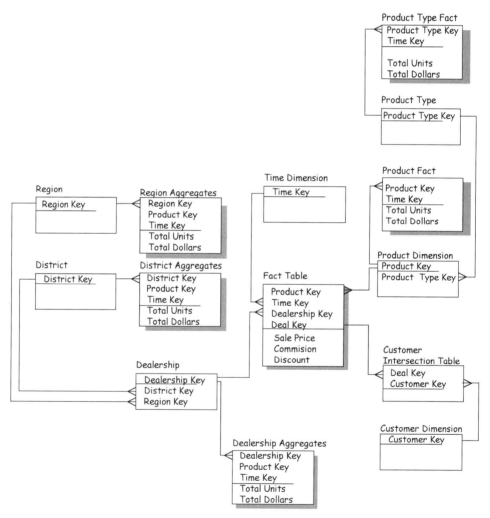

Figure 6–3 Revised auto-sales star schema.

6.1.4 Additive, Semiadditive, and Nonadditive

There are three types of facts: additive, semiadditive, and nonadditive. The additive you can add. The semiadditive you can kind of add, and the non-additive you cannot add at all. Nothing more needs to be said, right? Well actually, there is a bit more to it.

Additive data is pretty straightforward. It is typically the kind of raw data that one expects to find in the fact table. It is composed of a basic number, sale price, commission, or cost. If we want to get the total revenue for the day or the total commissions paid in a week, we simply go to the fact table and add the data. When working with a count measure we are working with an additive value, most of the time.

There are times when data is not so straightforward. For example, there are times when we could inadvertently double-count an item. These are semiadditive values—we can add them but must be careful not to add them together incorrectly, thereby giving a false picture of the state of the business. Typically these are derived facts—facts that were created by the system based on some basic additive facts. Imagine a situation where the auto dealership would like to know the margin as a percentage of cost of goods sold. If we stored this value in the fact record for each sale, we would know it for the individual item, but we could not add these numbers together to come up with a grand total. Since the fact is derived from the facts within the warehouse, we have a solution. Take a step back and look at the data from which the fact is derived. Sum those numbers and derive the new grand total from that. So in our example we could calculate a total cost of goods sold for the requested time period. We could then do the same for margin. With these numbers we could then perform the calculation for the grand total.

Some facts are nonadditive. These are facts that cannot simply be combined to get a grand total. Take headcount, for example. In the first three months of the year we might have three different sets of numbers. In January we might have 24 employees; in February, 35; and in March, 29. What is the total headcount for the quarter? It would certainly be incorrect to add these numbers together. The business strategist could determine the beginning and ending headcount, but this would hide the fact that February had a spike in headcount. We could also give the average headcount for the quarter. The total headcount for the quarter, however, is a question that really cannot be answered because it is asking the data warehouse to add a set of numbers that cannot be added.

6.2 Factless Fact Tables

As we mentioned earlier, the fact-table records are similar to the cells of the data cube. They contain the attributes of the action between the objects that are the dimensions in the analysis space. We have also noted that these attributes or facts are the measures of those verbs or actions. There are instances, however, in which no measures are associated with an action—instances in which the mere existence of an action is enough information for the business strategist. A class roster is an example of such a relationship. There is really nothing to measure. The simple acknowledgment that the student attended a particular class session says all there needs to be said.

A factless fact records the occurrence of events without measuring any of the attributes of those events. It is sufficient for the analysis to simply record that something happened. Let's return to our auto-sales example to demonstrate this point. In the example we had the one sales fact table. This was loaded with several facts concerning the auto sale.

What if the business strategist wanted to understand the relationship between customer test drives and resulting purchases? Test drives is an interaction between objects but does not necessarily mean a sale. Therefore, we would not include test drives in the sales fact table. The objects related to the test drive are the customer, salesperson, product, and time dimensions. This additional test-drive fact table becomes the second fact table in our constellation. Figure 6–4 presents the auto-sales schema with a Test Drive factless fact table.

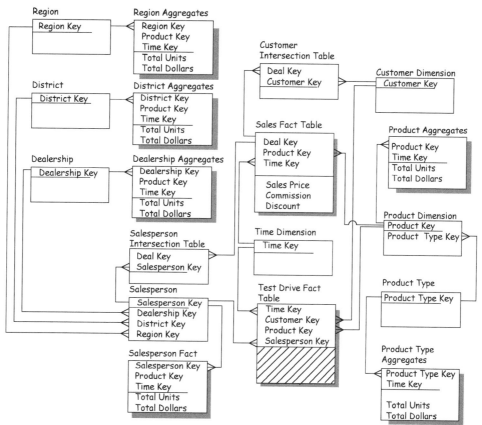

Figure 6–4 Factless fact table.

In the Figure 6–4, we see that the test-drive fact table contains the foreign keys of the different dimensions. The second half of the fact table, the measures portion, is empty. There is nothing to measure. All questions that one might ask of a test drive are answered by the intersections of the dimensions. From the intersections we can determine the salesperson, the prospect, and the time when the test drive occurred. Note that an intersection table has been added to the schema. Many people when shopping for a car will test drive several cars before making a final decision. The intersection table allows the business strategist to track a prospect that test drives more than one particular car. From this schema the business strategist is able to determine any relationships that might exist between test drives and actual purchases of cars.

6.3 Degenerate Dimensions

When purchasing a car, the customer and dealer complete a written contract that documents the terms of the purchase. The contract specifies the seller, the buyer, the product to be purchased, and the purchase price. Basically, everything that is described in our star schema is described in the contract with one exception, the contract itself. The question is where to store this information. On the one hand, the contract is a document, an object. This would suggest that we create another dimension. The contract dimension could contain all the attributes of the sale, which would be redundant, since the rest of the tables in schema contain this data. The alternative would be to limit the data to only what is unique to the contract, which is the contract number.

Rather than create an additional table we could simply store the contract number in the fact table. Although it is technically a dimension, we have stored it as an attribute of the sale—a fact, in other words. We refer to this as a *degenerate dimension*. This is useful when attempting to associate the facts in the data warehouse with original source documents. One could imagine situations in which the degenerate dimension is used as a foreign key to a document-imaging system. While this would provide little in the way of analytical data, especially since most of the analytical data is already recorded elsewhere in the data warehouse, it could be viewed as a shadow dimension. The document image is nothing more than an elaboration of nonanalytical data.

6.4 Degenerate Facts

Just as we have degenerate dimensions, we can also have degenerate facts. A *degenerate fact* is a measure recorded in the intersection table of a many-to-many relationship. It allows the data warehouse architect to record a measure for each instance of the many-to-many relationship. Again returning to our auto-sales example, we can create an intersection table between the sales fact table and the salesperson table. The records in this intersection table contain both the foreign key into the sales fact table and the salesperson table. This is the same as with other intersection tables. The intersection table containing a degenerate fact, however, includes the fact of the salesperson's commission.

As we look at the degenerate fact, we see that we can now associate a separate fact for each salesperson. The fact included in the fact record is the commission that salesperson received for that particular deal. The sum of the commissions in the degenerate fact table for a particular deal will equal the commissions for the deal in the central sales fact table.

6.5 Heterogeneous Fact Tables

Earlier we discussed how the subclasses of a superclass are merged into one general class. The measures of the behavior between this one general class and other objects defining the analysis space can all be captured within one fact table. There are instances, however, when the superclass is composed of a subclass of objects so unique that there are many distinct measures of each of the behaviors. In such cases the data warehouse architect can employ heterogeneous fact tables.

Figure 6–5 applies heterogeneous fact tables to our auto-sales example. The only dealership sales we have discussed at this point is the sales of automobiles. Dealerships, like many other businesses, sell products that are quite diverse. In addition to cars, dealerships sell parts and services. The measures of each of these products may be just as distinct as the products themselves. To be able to provide a set of measures that are tailored to the specific interaction between objects, the data warehouse architect employs a heterogeneous fact table.

At first Figure 6–5 may not be recognizable as a star schema. We have moved the dimensions to the center and the central fact table to the side. The central fact table contains the base measures of the schema. These are the measures that are common to all sales. Perhaps we would include here total sales price and cost of goods. We may also include a flag to indicate which type of product was sold. In this example the flag will indicate a service, part, or vehicle. Joined to the central fact table is central product dimension. This dimension contains all the attributes that are common to all products sold. These are the same as the attributes of the superclass that are inherited by the subclasses.

Each subclass and the behaviors related to it are recorded in separate fact and dimension tables. Referring to our diagram, we see the three tables we have created for each of the subclasses. In the service fact table we may have an hourly rate and the number of hours required to deliver the service. Neither of these measures would have any meaning when discussing parts or vehicles. We would, therefore, limit them to the service subclass fact table. While this diverges from the models presented in the design phase, I have taken this detour simply to demonstrate a point.

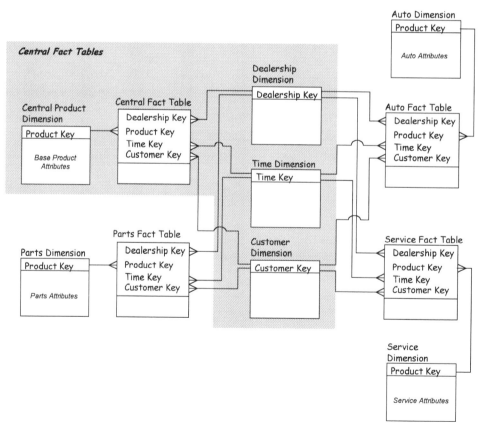

Figure 6–5   Heterogeneous fact table.

6.6 BBBC Fact Tables

The final piece in the case-study puzzle is the fact table. Figure 6–6 presents the schema for BBBC. This diagram lists the measures to be recorded for each deal done by BBBC.

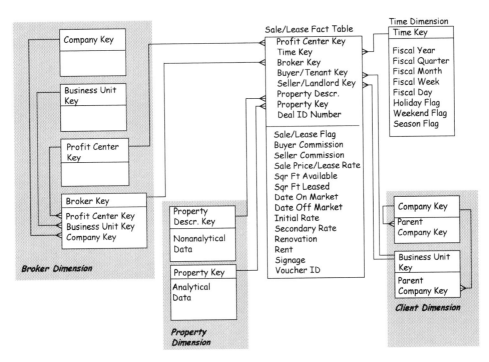

Figure 6–6 BBBC star schema.

The first field we added to the fact table is the Deal ID Number. Note that this number is NOT the primary key. The primary key for the fact table is a composite of the dimension keys and the Deal ID Number. This field is used for handling the many-to-many relationships in the star schema. Our design allows multiple brokers to participate in an individual deal. In this design every broker that participates in a deal will have a separate record in the fact table. To prevent a record from being double-counted in aggregates the Deal ID Number will define which fact records are associated with the same deal.

The table also includes a *degenerate dimension*. The Voucher ID field points to records in a separate document-imaging system. The vouchers are legal documents that record the agreement between the parties in a deal. Technically, it may not be the typical field one would expect to find in a data warehouse. After all, it provides no analytical value. DSS developers, however, can include the option to retrieve an image of the voucher from the document-imaging system when the business strategist drills-down to the deal level.

Another important field in the fact table is the sale/lease flag. In our initial design we opted to include both the sale and lease of a property in one star schema. This distinguishes between the two types of records. We could have created a constellation with two fact tables and the same set of dimensions. One fact table would have included leases and another, sales. We chose not to do this, however, because both are engagements with the client. If we were to begin to split the deals by type, we would have to continue to do so as we brought the other business units into the scope of the data warehouse. This would have greatly complicated the ability of top management to look at the entire organization at one time. We shall see in the next chapter how we might achieve the same ends while maintaining this structure. The remaining fields in the fact table are described in Table 6–1.

In examining the star schema for BBBC it seems that we have wrapped up the design of the project and it is time to start putting this thing together. All the relationships with the clients have been defined and we have included them all in our analysis space. Once we build this structure and load it with data from the operational environment we are all set to go. Right? Actually, no, we really messed up big time in our design. (This is the part of the book that is supposed to be a surprise ending.) Figure 6–7 presents the object model for BBBC. This is the same model that we saw in Figure 3–5. To determine if our schema meets all our needs, let's check to make sure we can find all the relationships between the objects.

Table 6-1 Sale/Lease Fact Table

Field Name	Data Type	Null Option	Description	System of Record
Time Key	Integer 7	Not Null	The Julian date of the fact.	DW
Property Key	Number 9	Not Null	Primary key to the property table	DW
Property Record Version Number	Number 3	Not Null	Indicates the version of the record.	DW
Property Description Key	Number 9	Not Null	Primary key to the table of nonanalytical property data.	DW
Property Description Record Version Number	Number 3	Not Null	Indicates the version number of the non-analytical property data record.	DW
Buyer/Tenant Key	Number 9	Not Null	System-Generated Primary Key.	DW
Buyer/Tenant Record Version Number	Number 3	Not Null	Indicates the version of the record. New versions will be applied only when a business unit is sold to another corporation.	DW
Seller/Landlord Key	Number 9	Not Null	System-Generated Primary Key.	DW
Seller/Landlord Record Version Number	Number 3	Not Null	Indicates the version of the record. New versions will be applied only when a business unit is sold to another corporation.	DW
Broker Key	Number 9	Not Null	System-Generated Primary Key.	DW
Broker Record Version Number	Number 3	Not Null	Version of the broker record that was the most recent at the time of the deal.	DW
Deal ID Number	Number 9	Not Null	Identifies the deal to which this record belongs.	DW
Sale/Lease Flag	Character 1	Not Null	Flag to indicate if the transaction was a Sale or a Lease. The following are valid codes: S = Sale L = Lease	VS

Table 6–1 Sale/Lease Fact Table (Continued)

Field Name	Data Type	Null Option	Description	System of Record
Commission	Number 7.2	Not Null	Commission paid to broker for the sale or lease of the property. Commission is that which was paid to the individual broker represented in this record. It is NOT a total commission	VS
Sale Price/Lease Rate	Number 10.2	Not Null	Price at which the property was sold or leased. This will contain the initial lease rate for lease agreements with two rates.	VS
Sqr Ft Available	Integer 10	Null	Number of Sqr Ft available. This field is ignored for leases.	VS
Sqr Ft Leased	Integer 10	Null	Number of Sqr Ft leased as part of the deal.	VS
Date On Market	Date	Not Null	Date the property was put on the market.	VS
Date Off Market	Date	Not Null	Date the property was taken off the market.	VS
Secondary Rate	Number 10.2	Null	Secondary lease rates apply to lease agreements where the lease agreements increase after a specified period of time. The secondary rate will be the new lease rate after the increase.	VS
Renovation	Number 10.2	Null	Renovation allowance. As part of the agreement the owner may grant a renovation allowance.	VS
Rent	Number 3	Null	Landlord may agree to a number of months of free rent as part of the lease agreement.	VS
Signage	Number 10.2	Null	As part of the lease agreement the landlord may agree to provide signs for the tenant. This field will contain the cost of the sign.	VS

We can determine the relationship between the company, business unit, profit center, and broker in our schema by traversing the company hierarchy. The schema presents not only the structures of the organization, but also the managers in charge of each structure as well. Although we have not built a structure for business units other than brokerage into our schema, this is acceptable because we limited the initial scope of the warehouse to the brokerage business unit. We will add those other structures in future iterations of the data warehouse.

The client company is also defined in the schema in much the same way as we see it in the object model. The only difference in the star schema is that we have collapsed the business-unit superclass into one object. The same is also true of the property object.

All the objects are represented in our star schema, but what about the relationships between these objects? In looking at the relationship between client and property we are covered. Using our star schema, we can identify the buyer/tenant and the seller/landlord. We can also associate the brokers to the different deals. What about the properties that are not sold or leased? Nothing in our star schema deals with property listings. Also, we noted in our analysis that a broker is paid both by the client leasing the property and the landlord. The same is also true of a sale. There are times when the broker is paid by both parties in the transactions. This is not accommodated in our schema, either.

To correct these mistakes we have to make two changes to our schema. The first is rather simple. We have to change the fact table to include commissions from both parties in the deal. This can be done by adding a field. Second, we need to include the listing of a property. But how? On the one hand, we could make this part of the current star; certainly all the measures for a listing are present. This would be in keeping with our logic to include the sale and lease in one fact table. All the interactions with the client will be included in one table. Although we could build such a structure, this would be incorrect. We may want to consider a constellation—that is, create another star and link it to the current star by way of conforming dimensions.

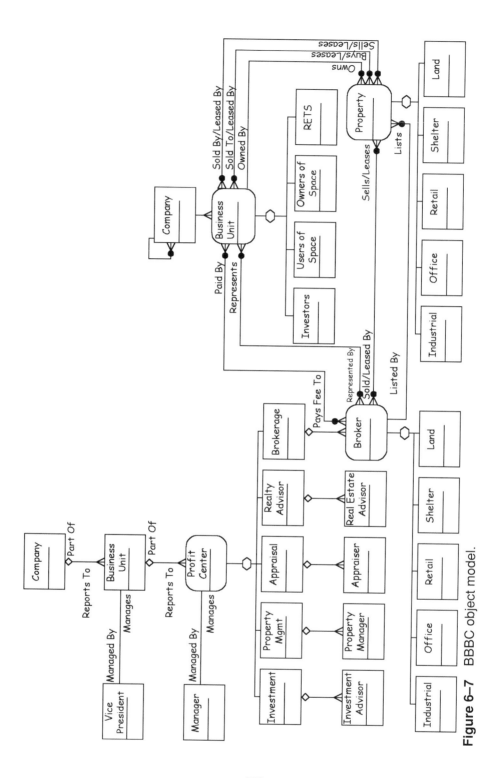

Figure 6–7 BBBC object model.

The reasoning for creating the second star is twofold. First, the listing does not generate revenue. A broker can have as many listings as he or she can get, but until something sells, or is leased, no revenue is generated. Second, the listing does not have a buyer and a seller. The listing transaction is a relationship between BBBC and one client. This would violate the cardinality between the fact table and the client table. The schema currently requires both relationships. We could always say just change the cardinality—but think of the implications of such a change.

Remember, the dimension tables establish a multidimensional space in a relational environment. If we glibly remove a relationship, we produce dramatic effects on our analysis space. We present the BBBC analysis space in Figure 6–8. Note this is a five-dimensional analysis space. How can we omit one of the two dimensions that relate to client? Whether we select Seller/Landlord or Buyer/Tenant, making one of these optional would create points in space that cannot relate to one of the dimensions that define the space! Although we could do it within the relational database, the structure would create an incorrect analysis space.

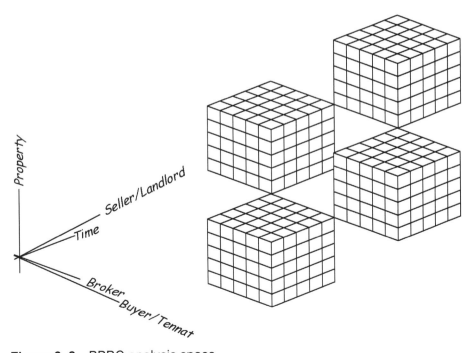

Figure 6–8 BBBC analysis space.

When we introduced the concept of a constellation, we noted how the two spaces created by the stars in the constellation sit next to one another. This is also the case with the BBBC constellation. Since we are working in more than three dimensions, I will not attempt to draw the spaces. The listing analysis space sits next to the sale/lease analysis space. The two spaces share the broker, property, and time dimensions. The listing has a completely separate dimension, which is the owner dimension. The owner is not a seller/landlord, because they may not want to sell or rent the property. Neither is the owner a buyer/tenant; the owner owns the property. The dimensions of the listing analysis space are defined by the broker, property, time, and owner dimensions. Figure 6–9 presents the revised schema, which includes the constellation that creates the two analysis spaces.

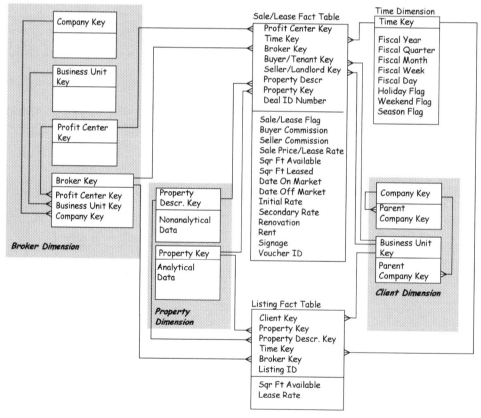

Figure 6–9   BBBC constellation.

Note that we have added the buyer/tenant and seller/landlord commissions to the sale/lease fact table. The listing fact table uses the client table that already exists as its own client dimension. Although this dimension is used for buyer/tenant and seller/landlord in the other star, it only makes sense to share this dimension table across the constellation. We would expect the same client that lists property with BBBC to sell and buy property. Keeping all the clients in the same table would eliminate duplicate client data as well as the problems associated with synchronizing duplicate data. Table 6–2 describes the listing fact table in detail.

Examining the resulting constellation, we see that the business strategist is able to perform some interesting analyses. In addition to being able to examine the listing, we can also see the relationships between the listing analysis space and the sale/lease analysis space. The analyst is able to traverse the constellation to relate listings to sales which result in BBBC revenue. Also remember that the broker does not have to be a BBBC broker. The schema we have created allows the entry of brokers from other commercial real estate companies. We could, therefore, rank which companies provide listings resulting in BBBC sales.

6.7 Summary

This chapter delivered us to our ultimate destination, the fact table—the heart of the star schema. We call it the heart of the star schema because it pulls together the different dimensions into a single coordinate system. Each single-dimensioned dimension table is glued to the other dimension tables by way of the fact table. One could almost view the joins between the fact table and the dimension tables as cords that bind the analysis space.

The fact table is composed of two major sections. The first contains the keys from each of the dimensions for the analysis space. The primary key of the fact table is a composite of these foreign keys. The second section of the fact table contains measures. These are the attributes of the actions that occur between the object that form the dimensions. A variety of issues relate to the measures stored within the fact table.

Table 6-2 Listing Fact Table

Field Name	Data Type	Null Option	Description	System of Record
Time Key	Integer 7	Not Null	The Julian date of the fact.	DW
Property Key	Number 9	Not Null	Primary key to the property table.	DW
Property Record Version Number	Number 3	Not Null	Indicates the version of the property record.	DW
Property Description Key	Number 9	Not Null	Primary key to the table of nonanalytical property data.	DW
Property Description Record Version Number	Number 3	Not Null	Indicates the version number of the nonanalytical property data record.	DW
Client Key	Number 9	Not Null	System-Generated Primary Key.	DW
Client Record Version Number	Number 3	Not Null	Indicates the version of the record. New versions will be applied only when a business unit is sold to another corporation.	DW
Broker Key	Number 9	Not Null	System-Generated Primary Key.	DW
Broker Record Version Number	Number 3	Not Null	Version of the broker record that was the most recent at the time of the deal.	DW
Listing ID Number	Number 9	Not Null	Identifies the deal to which this record belongs.	DW
Sale/Lease Flag	Character 1	Not Null	Flag to indicate if the transaction was a Sale or a Lease. The following are valid codes: S = Sale L = Lease	VS
Sale Price/Lease Rate	Number 10.2	Not Null	Price at which the property was sold or leased. This will contain the initial lease rate for lease agreements with two rates.	VS
Sqr Ft Available	Integer 10	Null	Number of Sqr Ft available. This field is ignored for leases.	VS
Date On Market	Date	Not Null	Date the property was put on the market.	VS

230

When combining measures from multiple sources, the data warehouse architect must contend with the precision of the different measures. Precision deals with the level of accuracy of the measurement. When values of different accuracy are combined, the least precise measure determines the precision of the result. The data warehouse architect must also deal with the granularity of data. What is the lowest level of detail to be tracked by the data warehouse? The architect must determine whether the warehouse will track down to the individual transaction or roll-up the data to a higher granularity.

The types of operations that can be performed on a measure is also an issue. Some measures can be easily added together to form a total. These are referred to as additive facts. Other facts—those that are already the result of a previous calculation, for example—are semiadditive facts. These facts must be broken down to their component additive facts and then aggregated. Finally, there are facts that just cannot be added. These are nonadditive facts.

The fact table itself can come in a variety of flavors. There is the factless fact table that contains no measures. Typically the fact that there is a relationship between the objects in the analysis space is information enough. In contrast to this, there are fact tables that contain dimension information in the measure section. These are known as degenerate dimensions. Just as we have degenerate dimensions, we also have degenerate facts, these are facts that are contained within the intersection tables of dimensions that have a many-to-many relationship to the fact table.

6.8 Glossary

Additive Facts   Facts that can be combined to form aggregates.

Counts   A type of measure employed in the data warehouse. Counts provide a count of a particular object.

Degenerate Dimensions   Dimensions whose single attribute is stored within the fact table.

Degenerate Facts   Measures stored within the intersection table of dimensions that have a many-to-many relationship with the fact table.

Drill-Across   Traversal from one star in a constellation to another via the common dimensions.

Factless Fact Table   Fact tables containing no measure. The existence of a relationship between the dimensions is significant in and of itself.

Granularity   The level of detailed captured by the data warehouse. Granularity can be at the transaction level or rolled-up to a higher level.

Interval Scale   A scale with equal distance between ordered units. The origin of an interval scale is not zero.

Measure   The facts of the fact table. Measures describe some attribute of the relationship or action between the dimensions of the analysis space.

Nominal Scale   Labels of objects within a set. A nominal scale does not provide an ordering between the labels.

Nonadditive Facts   Facts that cannot be added together into aggregates.

Ordinal Scale   The ordering of objects based on some criterion.

Precision   The number of significant digits within a measure.

Rank   The placing of objects in a hierarchical structure such as an organization chart.

Ratio   A scale with equal distance between ordered units and having an origin of zero.

Semiadditive Facts   Facts that must be broken down to their additive components to form aggregates.

CHAPTER 7

Implementation Considerations

The next step in the development spiral is the implementation of the system. While this text does not deal with the four remaining phases of the development spiral, we will conclude our examination of the methodology with a discussion on some implementation considerations. These are issues that the architect should consider prior to selecting the hardware and software with which he or she may plan to implement the system.

Before we begin looking at some of these issues, let me offer a word of caution to any prospective data warehouse architect. There are two pits into which we can easily fall. The first deals with hardware. The architect may look at the proposed system and think that the requirements are not so severe as to require anything more than a minimal system. After all, it is only a data mart. Four processors are enough; why worry about things like parallel processing and running massive queries? The answer to this question is the very point of this methodology.

The focus of the methodology, from the object-oriented approach to the spiral-like development process, is upon the fact that a successful data warehouse grows. The initial iteration or even the first two or three iterations of the data warehouse may be sufficiently served by a minimal system. Subsequent iterations of a successful data warehouse will, however, quickly outgrow these systems. If the architect is lucky, the second or third iteration will outgrow a system architecture that is too small. In such a case the volume of software to be ported to a more appropriate platform will not be as large as it would be if the system outgrew the platform in latter iterations of the spiral. The few pennies that may be saved by going to an underpowered system will be quickly eaten by the porting cost.

The best advice I can give the architect is to look at his or her environment. What type of system would it take to support a truly enterprise data warehouse? Imagine every possible business strategist examining every possible piece of information. What system would it take to support that data warehouse? True, your data warehouse may never get that large, but how large could it get? Remember, the data warehouse is not like a traditional OLTP system, where the scope stays relatively static. If it is successful and you achieve the goal of assisting management in making decisions, IT WILL GROW!

The second issue is that of software cost. When you put together your budget what do you think is going to be your greatest expense? Hardware? Software? Pizzas for the folks who are working late? Actually the largest single cost is going to be the cost of your software engineers. If they are good (and who really wants an engineer that isn't good), they are going to cost you. Compare this to the cost of software. Any DBMS that is to be used for a data warehouse must have at a minimum the capabilities described in this chapter. You may think you are going to save a few dollars per seat, but at what cost? Everything that the DBMS doesn't have, you are going to have to build. Every line of code that you write is going to cost you development and support dollars.

An example will demonstrate this point. In previous chapters we discussed aggregations. Some database engines have summary redirection built into the basic DBMS. We will discuss this in more detail latter in this chapter. Let's say you save $100 per seat by buying the database without summary redirection. How many seats do you need in order to offset the cost of having an engineer build this into your data warehouse? Don't forget—after you build the tables you will have to maintain them and analyze the warehouse queries to see what new data elements need to be preaggregated. How many DBA hours over the life of the warehouse are those seats worth to you? Another piece of advice: don't make a difficult job more difficult. Buy the right tool for the job.

7.1 Parallel Processing

As we discussed in the first chapter, the data warehouse is a strategic system. Its purpose is to transform enormous volumes of data into information. It is imperative in this environment that the business strategist not be satisfied with the passive consumption of static reports from the nether regions of the Information Technology Department. The strategist must interact with huge volumes of data, searching for behaviors within the marketplace. In order to achieve this goal the warehouse must be responsive to requests for information, providing a real-time dialog.

What allows us to achieve this objective—the way in which we are able to rise to the occasion—is parallelism. The data warehouse is a highly parallel environment, both in the way it loads and uses data. Therefore, the data warehouse architect can leverage this inherent parallelism in his or her design to provide the real-time dialog required by the business strategist.

To fully appreciate what parallelism means to data warehousing we will take a *top-down* approach. We will begin at the theoretical level, discussing just what is meant by parallelism. As part of this discussion we will present general rules of thumb for evaluating when parallelism can be of benefit. We will then apply these rules of thumb to data warehousing. Finally, this section will examine the parallelism of the implementation platform.

The implementation platform here refers to the parts of the system that lie beneath the actual application. This includes such software components as the database management system and the operating system. The platform also includes the hardware—from the processors and memory out to the storage subsystems.

7.1.1 The Perils of Parallelism

At the theoretical level parallelism is a very simple concept. Rather than sequentially, a series of tasks are performed concurrently. Unfortunately, this is not always possible; such factors as limited resources or dependencies between tasks limit the degree of parallelism. Imagine a loop where each iteration generates an output which is an input to the next iteration of the loop. Such applications do not lend themselves well to parallel processing, since each iteration of the loop is dependent on previous iterations.

In a parallel application, iterations of the loop are independent of one another. Let's consider an example that would better lend itself to parallel execution. In this instance, a large company is giving all its employees a 15% increase in salary. A loop can be written to retrieve a record from the database, increase the salary by 15%, and then commit the changes. Each iteration of this loop is independent of the others, allowing them theoretically to execute in parallel. If an iteration of the loop took 1 second and we had 3,600 records, the time it would take to change all the records without parallelism would be 1 hour. If, however, we were able to change all the records in parallel—in essence execute all iterations of the loop concurrently—it would take only 1 second to update the entire database.

7.1.2 The Geometry of Parallelism

Parallelism is never as simple as this example. Often a process will have some serial and some parallel components. For this reason we do not expect to get the type of performance improvement described in the example. We understand that there is a limit to the amount of work that can be done in parallel. Some parts of a job have to be done sequentially. If most of a task is limited to serial execution, it is less likely to gain a performance improvement through parallelism.

To demonstrate this point, let's examine two different tasks. In Figure 7–1(a) we show how the processing of these tasks is sometimes parallel and sometimes sequential. In the first graph we get a feeling that the percentage of the task that can be done in parallel is greater for B than for A. To be certain we have grouped the serial processing blocks for both tasks in Figure 7–1(b). We can see that approximately 67% of task A is executed sequentially and about 32% of task B. This tells us something about how well these tasks are able to execute in parallel. Task A would gain much less from running in a parallel environment than task B. Only 33% of task A can run in parallel. If we were able to reduce the execution time of the parallel portion of task A by half, we would have only about a 16.5% reduction in the total execution time. Even if we were able to reduce the parallel portion to the point where it virtually did not exist, we would still reduce the total execution time by only 33%. Compare this to task B. If we were able to reduce the parallel execution time of task B by just half, we would reduce the total execution time by more than 33%. This is better than what we would ever realistically hope to gain with task A.

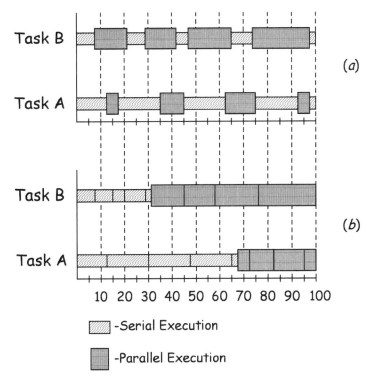

Figure 7–1 Parallel execution of tasks.

Let's replace these percentages with actual numbers. If both task A and task B were each to take about two hours to execute, the total sequential execution time for task A would be about 80 minutes. Task B's sequential execution time would take about 38 minutes. No amount of parallelism could reduce our execution time below this point. We can see that the total serial execution time for our task acts as a limit to the performance improvement we could ever gain from parallelism. It is in essence the floor of our performance.

The second characteristic we need to examine is the depth of our parallelism. Perhaps we could execute a task in parallel, but this parallelism is restricted to two parallel processing streams. This restriction could come from a number of places, the hardware, the operating system or even the application program itself. This means that we could divide the parallel execution time in half. In applying this to task B, the 82 minutes of parallel processing could theoretically be reduced to 41 minutes. If we were able to execute four streams in parallel we would reduce this to 20.5 minutes. If we were to represent this in the form of an equation we would have the following:

$$TET = SET + (PET / NPS)$$

where:

TET = Total Execution Time
SET = Sequential Execution Time
PET = Parallel Execution Time
NPS = Number of Parallel Streams

The problem, of course, is that all these numbers are very theoretical. An increase in the number of parallel streams to 82 would mean a reduction of the parallel execution to 1 minute. Why not do even better than that and increase it by 164? Then the execution time would be reduced to less than a minute. Well, the problem is that there is no free lunch. Every time a parallel stream is added, the system needs to manage another task as well as coordinate the execution of the parallel streams. Each additional stream adds overhead. Since resources within a system are limited, the more time we spend managing work, the less time we spend doing actual work. In other words, increasing the number of execution streams from one to two does not reduce the parallel execution time by half, but by something less than half. Typically one would expect to see something close to but not quite half. We change our parallel equation, then, to allow for this overhead. We end up with the following equation:

$$TET = SET + (PET / (NPS * SP))$$

where:

TET = Total Execution Time

SET = Sequential Execution Time

PET = Parallel Execution Time

NPS = Number of Parallel Streams

SP = Scaling Percentage

We can convert this equation to the following;

$$TET = SET + (PET * (1/ (NPS * SP)))$$

This roughly translates to the equation of a line. SET is the equivalent of the *Y*-intercept and NPS * SP is the slope. The difference, however, between this and the standard equation of a line is that the slope is inverted. This will cause the line to flatten as the product of NPS and SP increases. An increase in the product means that we have an increase in the benefits of parallelism. This results in reducing the total execution time.

To clarify this, refer to Figure 7–2, where we have graphed several examples of a parallel performance line using task B as our example. As we increase the inverted slope, the line flattens, bringing us closer to the theoretical minimum execution time SET. There is another aspect to the flattening of the parallel performance line. As we move to the left on the graph, we experience smaller increases in height than on a steeper parallel performance line. What this means in processing terms is that increases in parallel work will result in less of an increase in total execution time with a flatter parallel performance line than with steeper lines.

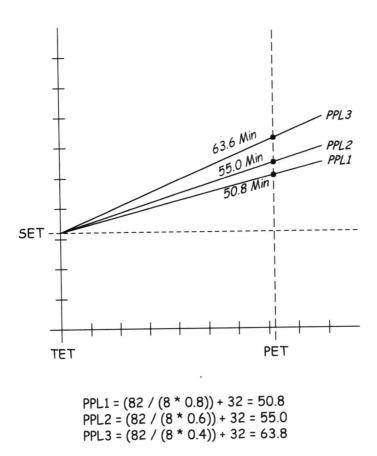

PPL1 = (82 / (8 * 0.8)) + 32 = 50.8
PPL2 = (82 / (8 * 0.6)) + 32 = 55.0
PPL3 = (82 / (8 * 0.4)) + 32 = 63.8

Figure 7–2   Parallel performance line.

This graph points out an important rule of parallelism. When executing a task in parallel, we need to improve the effective parallelism. As we add parallel streams, we want to experience as little overhead as possible in order to improve performance. As we search for applications to run in parallel, then, we need to examine three factors:

1. The percentage of the task that can be run in parallel

2. The number of parallel streams that can be applied to the task

3. The amount of overhead necessary to manage these streams.

In the next two sections we will see how well data warehousing fits into this model. We will first look at the application itself. We will then examine the platform upon which the data warehouse executes. First we look for the characteristics of a database that will facilitate parallelism, and then we look at the hardware architecture.

7.1.3 The Parallel Nature of the Data Warehouse

Now let's turn our attention to the data warehouse. Can it use parallelism to effectively improve performance? To answer this question we must, of course, understand the behavior of the data warehouse itself. We have described the data warehouse as an integrated, nonvolatile, time-variant collection of data. It *integrates* the data from the operational environment into a central repository. That central repository is more than a reflection of the current moment; it is a record of the past, a history of the organization. As with any history, its data is preserved for future analysis. Hence the data within the warehouse is *nonvolatile*. The nonvolatile nature of the data allows us to include a new variable in our analysis: time—that is to say, a *time-variant collection of data*. We are able to change the time frame of our analyses, examining past trends to better predict future conditions.

7.1.3.1   Data Utilization

The transaction-processing system is tactical while the data warehouse is strategic. The operational system is concerned with individual transactions. One could consider each of these transactions to represent a discrete action within the marketplace. Whether it is a sale, a purchase, an inventory reduction, or a shipment, each is an individual action. This is the domain of the tactical operational environment. The concern of the strategic system is not an individual action but behavior within the marketplace. A behavior is a predictable response to a specific set of stimuli. The strategic system does not look at individual actions. The strategic system examines the sum of the individual actions in order to understand a behavior. The data warehouse uses data, therefore, differently than does the transaction-processing system.

First, the warehouse *observes*—it does not interact. One can draw the analogy to a psychologist who observes the behavior of the patient in order to make a diagnosis. This is the job of the warehouse; it must first observe a behavior so that the business strategist can then make a diagnosis. This again leads us back to the subject of nonvolatile data. The data warehouse does not write to the database; that is not its purpose. The warehouse is a reader of data.

Second, the warehouse looks at large volumes of information. Obviously the shift of emphasis from individual actions to behaviors shifts the scope of the data needed to support the diagnosis. The warehouse must examine many actions in order to define a set of actions as a behavior and then understand the characteristics of that behavior. Consider statistical methods: basic statistics tells us that the size of any statistically significant sample is a function of the diversity of the entire population. The very intent of the data warehouse is to understand diverse and complex behaviors. It is implicit that a large volume of data is necessary to properly understand market behaviors. Quite often the volume of data can be described as not just large, but huge!

Observation of behaviors within the marketplace entails one of two basic types of applications: on-line analytical processing (OLAP) or data mining. In each case we are reading large volumes of information. A typical OLAP query would ask for total sales for a product or set of products over a period of time. Further analysis might require the roll-up or drill-down of sales, such as total sales for all products or total sales of a particular product by region. It may be possible to mitigate some of the computational requirements through preaggregation during the data-extraction process, but this would not eliminate the need for real-time analysis of large volumes of data. The data warehouse architect could not possibly anticipate all possible aggregations. Neither could he or she maintain and compute all possible aggregates.

In Chapter 1 we discussed the basic forms of data mining. Keep in mind that, regardless of which of these models is employed, data mining does not necessarily require the entire data set to create an acceptable model. There is no specific answer to the model-size question. Traditional wisdom suggests that models are built on a small subset of the data and then validated against the entire database. We can see, therefore, that data-mining tools will be accessing large volumes of data during either the model construction or validation periods.

The data warehouse user is most often reading large amounts of information. Often these queries entail aggregations and grouping of records. These types of operations actually benefit from two levels of parallelism. The first level can be described as *interquery* parallelism. This is where we concurrently execute multiple queries against the same database. Since these are read operations, we again see a high degree of parallelism. A basic database principle is that readers do not block readers. The data warehouse in this instance is like a billboard; it doesn't matter how many people are reading it. This eliminates the need to lock records, as is done in transaction-processing environments. Record locking often is a hindrance to parallelism.

The second, deeper, level is *intraquery* parallelism, where we divide an individual query into multiple subqueries and run them concurrently. If the user, for example, requested the total sales of a particular product, the query could be divided into some optimum number of subqueries and executed in parallel. These subtotals could then be combined into one grand total.

7.1.3.2 *Data Extraction*

The data warehouse sits outside the operational environment. When we load the data warehouse, we bring in data from the operational world and integrate it into a central repository. This data flow is presented in Figure 7–3. As we can see, the extraction process is composed of three separate subprocesses: Retrieval, Cleansing/Transformation, and Integration.

The retrieval process removes data from the operational environment. This retrieval can be performed in a variety of ways. Data can be *pushed* from the operational environment into the data warehouse or *pulled* by the data warehouse from the operational environment.

The operational environment should not be thought of as a single monolithic transaction system. In fact, it is composed of many and often diverse systems. In the retail world many point-of-sale systems may feed into one data warehouse from many different locations. In a manufacturing environment we may have accounting, production, and inventory systems all feeding into the data warehouse. The two environments vary greatly. The retail system will have many geographically disperse systems, yet the data formats may be consistent. The manufacturing system will most probably have a variety of data formats. The one thing the two environments will have in common is a differing quality of data between each of the systems. This leads us to the second stage of the extraction process: cleansing and transformation.

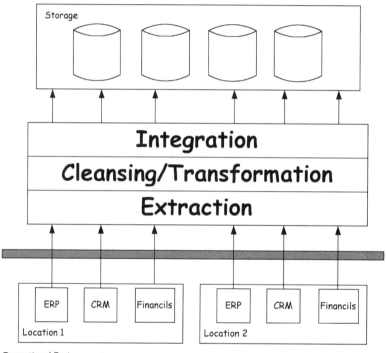

Figure 7–3   Parallel input streams.

The extraction process does not put the data directly into the central repository untreated. The extraction process must first ensure the quality of the data. This is the purpose of data cleansing and transformation. Cleansing attempts to remove and correct erroneous data in the input stream. Data transformation converts the format of the input data into one that is consistent with the central repository.

Once we have data that is clean and in a consistent format, we can then integrate it into the central repository. Integration of the data commits the data to the database. In transaction processing, records are updated to reflect the changing state of the organization. OLTP systems normally have multiple users writing and reading to the database simultaneously. To prevent two users from writing to the same record at the same time or reading from a record that is being modified, the database locks individual records. Some database management systems even lock at the page or block level, preventing users from accessing records that happen to be in the same block or on the same page as another record! This is death to parallelism. As the number of users or as the minimum size of a locking unit increases, so does the probability that two users will collide.

This collision problem is not an issue when loading data into the warehouse. Data within the warehouse is nonvolatile. As data is added to the warehouse, new records are appended to the database. Once a record has been committed to the database, it remains unchanged; it is not updated. Since the addition of data is merely an append process, there is no logical limit on the number of records that can be added in parallel. Any limitation to parallelism will occur within the implementation platform.

7.1.3.3 *Conclusion*

As we can see, the nature of the data warehouse lends itself in several areas to parallelism. The data-extraction process is a highly parallel operation. The actual transformation, cleansing, and integration of the input data streams can be performed in parallel. Similarly, the actual data utilization by the business strategist can be performed in parallel. As shown, data analysis provides even greater opportunity for parallelism than when reading data. When performing data analysis within the data warehouse, huge volumes of information must be examined. The use of interquery and intraquery parallelism expands the data-analysis process into multiple dimensions, reducing the time to solution. Given this level of parallelism within the data warehouse itself, we must now turn our attention to the implementation platform.

7.1.4 Parallel Architectures

Several times in the previous sections we have noted that the nature of the data warehouse will not limit the depth of parallelism. Typically, we will reach the implementation platform's limit long before we reach the limits of the data warehouse itself. Since the bottleneck to parallelism is the implementation platform, we should search out ways to eliminate or at least reduce this potential threat to performance. In the following subsections we will examine four different architectures: Symmetric Multiprocessing, Shared Disk Architectures, Nonuniform Memory Access, and Massively Parallel Processing.

7.1.4.1 Symmetric Multiprocessing (SMP)

The traditional Symmetric Multiprocessing (SMP) environment was designed to allow many processes to run in parallel. If we look at Figure 7–4, we see the basic layout of an SMP system. Each CPU can execute separate tasks independently. This provides us with some parallelism. Looking at this diagram, however, we see a bottleneck in the system: the system bus. Everything communicates over this bus. This significantly limits the number of processors that can be used efficiently. Once the capacity of the system bus has been saturated, additional processors will be starved for data.

Imagine dining at a restaurant. If there is one waiter, he can serve a certain number of customers. As the number of customers increases, the waiter becomes busier and busier. At some point he reaches his limit. Although he is working as fast as he can, the service to the individual customer becomes slower and slower. After a while people start to go hungry.

The system bus in an SMP architecture is similar to the waiter in our restaurant. At first the system bus is making everyone happy. As users require more processing power, more CPUs are added to the system. With each new processor the activity on the system bus increases. That single system resource—that one waiter in our restaurant—becomes busier. At some point the system bus can't keep up with demand: the bus is saturated. Consequently, the data won't be there when the processor needs it. The busier the bus, the longer the processor has to wait for the data it needs. It's like sitting at a table in a busy restaurant waiting for an overworked waiter.

After a while you end up with processors going hungry. This brings us to an important axiom in the world of system design: *A hungry CPU is a bad thing.*

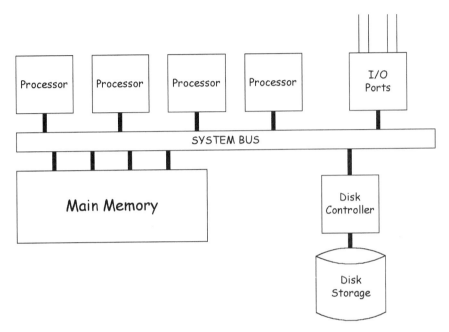

Figure 7–4 SMP architecture.

We can see that a traditional SMP environment, while providing some level of parallelism, does have its limitations. Eventually CPUs can no longer be added to the system. For this reason we see that SMP systems cannot scale to large numbers of processors; typically they are limited to something less than 8 or 16 processors. The possible parallelism that can be distilled from an SMP system is best described in the book *Parallel Systems in the Data Warehouse*. It states that with SMP-type systems "there are architectural features that prevent large numbers of CPUs being used efficiently on a single problem. The most serious issue—the one that most directly limits the ability of the machine to scale to large numbers of CPUs—is memory and bus bandwidth. As we noted earlier, even in a cache-coherent SMP system, the physically shared memory is a bottleneck. Once the available bandwidth has been utilized, additional CPUs will not speed up the problem. To summarize: Bus-based SMP architectures are not scalable to large configurations." [1]

7.1.4.2   *Shared Disk Architectures*

A shared disk architecture (cluster) allows us to overcome the limitation experienced with SMP architectures. A cluster is a group of systems that share disks and behave as one virtual system. The individual systems within the cluster are referred to as nodes. Each node within the cluster has its own local memory and system resources. The nodes share only the disks. Hence, memory within the nodes is private.

Figure 7–5 shows the internals of a typical clustered system. The nodes within a cluster communicate with one another via a redundant LAN. This LAN is private to the nodes in the cluster and is used to report status information. In the event that a node fails, the other nodes take over the services of the failed node. For this reason clustering solutions are often discussed in the context of High Availability (HA), but this is only half the story.

There are two methods of clustering. The first, *symmetric*, is the mirroring of systems. A second node simply stands ready as a hot backup to the first. It does nothing other than wait for the primary node to fail. In *asymmetric* clustering, all nodes in a cluster work independently of one another. When a node fails, a take-over node not only continues to process its own work but takes on the work of the failed node. The take-over node takes the failed node's address and responds to any requests in place of the failed node.

Asymmetric clusters, in addition to providing for greater system availability, also provide a method to scale servers beyond traditional SMP architectures. In a client/server environment asymmetric cluster servers can present to their clients a single system image, a virtual system. Herein lies the power of the cluster. The processing of that virtual system is distributed across multiple nodes, meaning multiple processors accessing multiple memory systems distributed across multiple system buses.

---

1. Stephan Morse and Issace David, *Parallel Systems in the Data Warehouse*, Upper Saddle River, NJ: Prentice Hall PTR, 1998.

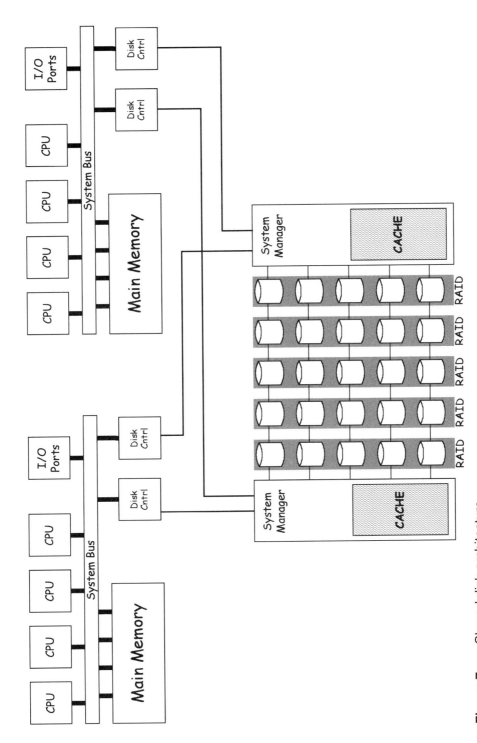

Figure 7 – Shared disk architecture.

Any discussion of saturation of the system bus should apply not only to the movement of data from disks or memory to the processor but also to any component that resides on the bus. The distribution of the processing also distributes the flow of data into the warehouse. This further relieves bottlenecks in the loading of data into the data warehouse. As these parallel streams of data are brought into the warehouse, each node processes its streams completely parallel to the other nodes.

7.1.4.3 *Nonuniform Memory Access (NUMA) Architecture*

Nonuniform Memory Access (NUMA) architectures provide an alternative parallel architecture. NUMA systems are also referred to as Distributed Shared Memory (DSM) architectures. The structure of a typical NUMA implementation is presented in Figure 7–6. We see that a system is composed of multiple nodes, each of which is structured as an SMP system. As shown in the diagram, the nodes contain processors, memory, cache, and an I/O subsystem just like any SMP system. These nodes differ, however, in that they contain some interconnection mechanism. They use this interconnection to share their local memory with one another. All memory becomes global, accessible to all processors within the system, although it is distributed throughout the nodes. Hence the name *distributed shared memory.*

In other architectures memory access is uniform. The distance between a processor and a memory location in an SMP system, for example, is uniform. The time it takes any processor to retrieve data from a particular memory location is not related to the distance between the processor and memory. All processors have equal access to memory. In the NUMA system, memory that is close at hand provides faster data access than memory that is further away. When a particular processor requires data, it first checks to see if the data is present within the cache. If not, it then sees if the data is contained within local memory. Failing to find the data within local memory, it fetches the data from one of the other nodes. This results in nonuniform data retrieval times, or nonuniform memory access.

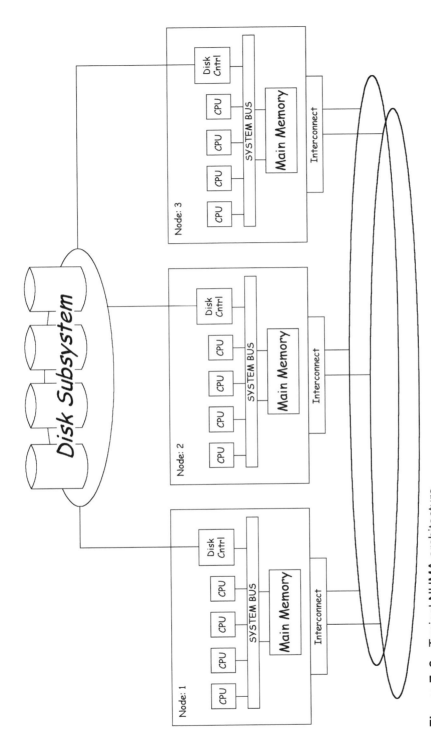

Figure 7-6 Typical NUMA architecture.

The NUMA system attempts to thread the proverbial eye of a needle by providing both the advantages of SMP's global memory and the scalability of MPP systems. The greatest advantage to SMP systems is their simplicity and speed. All memory is global and easily accessible to all components of the system. The drawback to SMP is the limitations of the system bus. The volume and speed of data transfers is limited by the capacity of the system bus. An MPP architecture avoids the bus problem by distributing everything across many nodes and leaving it up to the processes to retrieve the required data from the appropriate nodes. NUMA systems distribute the system components across multiple system buses while maintaining a system-wide global memory.

What makes these systems work well is the locality of data. Typically the next piece of data required by a process is relatively close to the current piece with which it is working. Most memory access becomes local to the node. Once a block of memory is brought into local memory, the process will continue to work with local data. Potentially processes in different nodes may be attempting to access the same data. This is only a problem when these processes are attempting to write to the same location. The NUMA architecture manages these coherency issues within the interconnect.

7.1.4.4 *Massively Parallel Processing*

One proposed solution to the parallel-processing dilemma is the Massively Parallel Processing (MPP) architecture. It comes in basically two flavors: a mesh or a multistage switch network. While this discussion is applicable to both alternatives, the examples will focus on the multistage switch network. Figure 7–7 presents a view of this architecture.

Several characteristics of these architectures are very interesting. First note that memory is distributed across all the nodes. This is why these systems are often referred to as a *Distributed Memory Architecture* (DM). In a DM architecture the only memory that is accessible to the CPU is the memory that is local to that processor. If a CPU needs data that is resident in the memory of another processor, a message must be exchanged requesting the data. This means that the programmer must arrange for a data request to be sent from the node where the data is required to the node where the data resides.

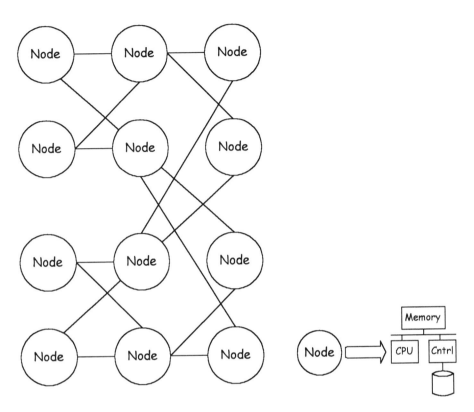

Figure 7–7   Multistage switch network.

Message passing to retrieve data raises another concern. The programmer must address the issue of where the data exists physically. Frequently in a data warehouse there is a need to scan a large table. In the traditional SMP approach this is not a problem, since memory is global; all CPUs have equal access to the data. In the DM approach, partitioning the table among the various nodes is central to the task. In this architecture the rows of the table must be physically partitioned and distributed among the memories associated with the various nodes. The distribution of the data across the various nodes forces a node to access the data from another node via message passing. Instead of addressing one large table, we are addressing many small tables.

As we can see in Figure 7–7, some nodes can be designated to have an I/O capability not provided to others. This further complicates the issue of data distribution. Now only a few nodes within the system have access to the data on disk. In a Banyan network like the one in the diagram, the number of *hops* it takes to get from the input nodes to the output nodes is the power-of-2 exponent, or the degree of the Banyan. In Figure 7–7, we picture a four-by-four network. The degree of this network is four. Four is two raised to the second power, which means that it takes two hops to get to the data. If this were an eight-by-eight, two would be raised to the third power. This gives us a degree of three, which means it takes three hops to get to the data. It is important to note that Banyan assumes that the processing does not begin or end in an interior node. If this were the case, the number of hops would have a major increase.

The distribution of data also inhibits the scalability of the system. As we can see by this discussion, the efficient distribution of the data across the system is contingent on the underlying architecture. As we add nodes to the system—as we scale the system—we must repartition the data to get maximum utilization of the nodes.

All of this communication between nodes places a dramatic emphasis on the interconnection network. As the number of nodes in the system increases, the demands placed on the interconnection network increase significantly as well. Think back to our SMP discussion: the more processors we have and the more system components we have, the more we need to communicate. A major concern in this regard, therefore, is the ability of the interconnection network to smoothly scale to very large configurations. We must be concerned with how the amount of interconnection hardware scales as a function of the number of nodes. We must also be concerned with the performance of the network in relation to the number of nodes.

When addressing these issues, we are concerned with the two dimensions in which we are working—that is, the width and depth of the network. While the width of the multistage network is not usually a concern, the depth of the multistage switching network can have a significant impact on performance. If, for example, we double the number of nodes, we will typically add an additional level of switching. In effect, we increase the depth. This has the very practical implication that doubling the number of nodes will more than double the number of switching elements. This means that the overall overhead of parallelism will increase faster than that of the number of computing nodes.

7.1.5 Parallel Data Storage

Achieving parallelism within the system pays very little dividend if the processors are waiting for data from disk. It is equally important to match the parallelism of server with parallel storage subsystems. The following subsections will address how data can be structured on disk to enhance parallelism.

7.1.5.1 RAID Storage

Redundant Array of Inexpensive Disk (RAID) systems were developed to meet the increasing demands for storage capacity, performance, and reliability. Reliability and performance are just as important as storage volume. RAID systems address each of these concerns. As should be apparent by now, the data warehouse requires storage, lots and lots of storage. While RAID systems are used within the OLTP world, they also resolve many challenges posed by the data warehouse. In this section we will examine how these systems provide increased parallelism.

Just as we distributed processing of data to achieve parallelism within the servers, we distribute the storage of data in a RAID array. RAID levels range from 0 to 5. In addition there is RAID level 0/1. Levels 2 and 4 are rarely implemented, so we will leave them out of our discussion. Figure 7–8 presents the different levels of RAID.

RAID level 0 has the advantage of improving performance by distributing, or striping, the partition across multiple disks. The sequence of blocks goes across the disk partition. So the first block of the partition is on disk one, the second block is on disk two, and so on. The only problem with this scheme is that as the number of disks in the stripe increases, so does the probability of a disk failure. This, of course, is basic statistics. Let us say that there is a one-in-five chance that a component, any component, will fail over a period of time and that you have five of those components.

There is a much higher probability that at least one of those components will fail in the specified time period than if you had just one. So, while RAID level 0 increases performance, it decreases reliability by involving more disks in the storage of the data.

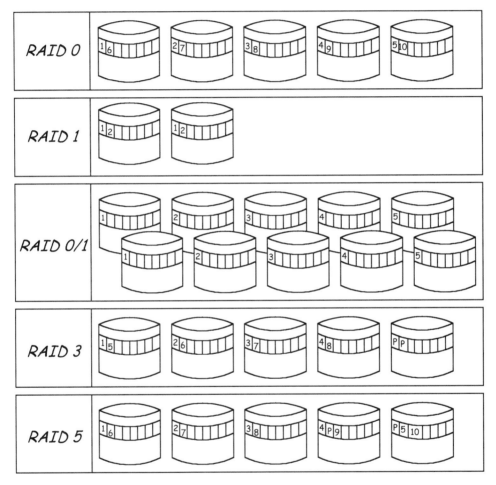

Figure 7–8 RAID levels.

RAID level 1 increases the reliability by mirroring the disks. All the data on one disk is copied to a second. In the event that the first should fail, the second is there as a hot backup. Raid level 1 improves read performance by reducing seek time. Data is read from the disk whose heads are nearest to the requested data. While this reduces read time, it does not improve disk writes. This led to the development of RAID 0/1, which is a combination of RAID levels 0 and 1. RAID 0/1 first stripes the partition across multiple disks, as seen in level 0; then it mirrors the disk, as in level 1. In this way both performance and reliability are increased at the same time. The greatest drawback to level 0/1 is the cost. It requires twice as many disks as does the raw data.

RAID level 3 provides a more cost-effective solution. One disk in the stripe is designated as a parity disk. It contains bit-by-bit parity of the corresponding disk blocks in the stripe. In the example presented in the diagram there is a five-disk stripe. The fifth disk in the stripe is the parity disk. The fifth block is a parity block of the first four blocks—that is, the stripe that precedes it. If one disk fails, the data on it can be interpolated from the data remaining on the other disks.

As a block of data is written to disk, the parity is calculated and written to the parity disk. All data writes to anywhere in the level-3 stripe require at least one write to the parity disk. The parity disk becomes a bottleneck to the entire system. For this reason RAID level 3 is appropriate for large-block writes. RAID level 5 relieves this bottleneck by distributing the parity across the disks along with the data. As shown in the diagram, parity block 1 contains the parity for data blocks one through four; parity block 2 contains the parity for data blocks five through eight. In this way we are able to increase both capacity and performance.

There is still a performance issue. In both RAID 3 and RAID 5 a parity calculation is executed for every write to the partition. The operation cannot complete until the parity has been calculated and written to the parity disk. This causes the write to take longer, which degrades performance. RAID storage subsystems address this issue as well as the pure management of the disks. The architecture of a RAID system is shown in Figure 7–9. We see that a single disk partition is distributed across multiple disk drives. Typically storage subsystems include a storage manager, which is some processor that manages the writing and reading of the data. Also featured within the storage manager is a cache area used for the temporary storage of data as it moves through the storage manager.

Referring to Figure 7–9, the disks in the storage subsystem are distributed across five 40 MB/sec SCSI buses. Creating a file on a similar SCSI disk not on a RAID partition would limit the data-transfer rate to the speed of the bus on which the disk resides. This would mean that a scan of a 200-GB file would take a minimum 1 hour and 23 minutes. We calculate this performance as 200,000 MB divided by 40 MB/sec. By storing this same file on a RAID partition, we distribute the file across multiple SCSI buses. In our example we have a stripe spanning five buses, reducing the minimum scan time of the file to 16.6 minutes.

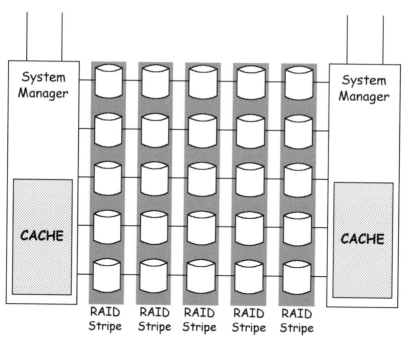

Figure 7–9   RAID storage subsystem.

Of course these numbers are the theoretical minimum transfer rates and do not necessarily demonstrate the effective transfer rates that will be experienced by the application. As the data flows from the disk to the processor, a series of components can act as bottlenecks to performance. For example, once the data is retrieved from the storage subsystem there is a SCSI connection to the server and a single controller interface to that connection. This would again limit the transfer of data to the rate of a single SCSI cable. We can improve this somewhat by providing a second controller.

Even doubling the data-transfer rate does not provide the optimal performance. When performing a full table scan, for example, data will move much more quickly from the disks to the storage manager than from the storage subsystem to the server. Most storage managers can detect operations such as a full table scan and perform a read-ahead. In a read-ahead the storage manager continues to retrieve data from disk while the previously read data is being passed to the server. The read-ahead data is cached in the storage manager and pushed to the server as quickly as it is able to receive the data. A read-ahead will fully load the SCSI controllers. Even with a dual connection, the table described above would take 41 minutes to scan.

7.1.5.2   Fiber Channel Storage

In many data marts and smaller data warehouses the data-transfer rates described in the previous section may be sufficient. Larger data warehouses, however, may require better performance than what is provided with a SCSI connection. *Fiber channel* storage has been developed to address the need for faster data-transfer rates. Not all fiber channel storage is equal. It has three basic flavors: *front-end,* in which the connection between the storage subsystem and server is fiber; *back-end,* in which the connections between the disks and the storage manager are fiber; and *full-fiber,* in which both the front and back ends are fiber based. Some fiber systems also use what is known as *JBOD* (Just a Bunch Of Disks). In these implementations the RAID is software based and incurs approximately a 20% performance penalty. A much more efficient implementation of RAID is hardware based and part of the storage management system. In these systems there is no performance penalty.

A typical fiber storage subsystem supports a transfer rate of up to 1.06 gigabaud; to keep the calculations simple we will assume a 100 MB/sec transfer rate. Since this is a full fiber implementation, data moves from the disks to the storage managers to the hubs at 100 MB/sec. Just as we did with the SCSI storage subsystem, we use multiple disk controllers, doubling the transfer rate of the data from the storage manager to server. Applying this to our previous example, our time to scan the entire table would be only 33 minutes.

7.1.5.3   *Partitioned Tables*

Spreading an individual table or file across multiple disks using a RAID storage subsystem provides one level of parallelism. We could in essence look at this as one-dimensional parallelism. We are distributing the data along one dimension, the RAID stripe. Partition tables allow us to extend parallelism into a second dimension. When a table is partitioned, it breaks into smaller separate objects. Each of these objects is a partition and independent of the others. The individual partitions can be manipulated just as if they were any other table, or they can be used jointly as one complete logical unit. There are database systems that allow this partitioning to be invisible to the application. While much of this discussion focuses on tables, most database objects can be partitioned.

Data warehouses are typically composed of very large tables. Their day-to-day administration is greatly enhanced by table partitioning. The very size of these tables poses many administrative challenges. When a table is partitioned, the individual partitions can be administered separately. A partition can be taken off line and backed up without taking down the entire table. An individual partition can also be restored without touching any of the other partitions for that database object.

There are three basic ways to partition a database object: range, hash, and hybrid. *Range* partitioning is perhaps the most commonly discussed. With range partitioning a column of the table is selected as the partition key. Each partition is given a range of acceptable values, none of which may overlap another. The first partition contains the lowest value in the range and the last partition the highest. The highest acceptable value for any partition must be less than the lowest acceptable value for the next. Let's return to our auto-sales example to demonstrate this point. Suppose we are going to partition our fact table by date. The partitioning scheme for this table will be as follows:

Partition	Range
1	Less than January 1, 1996
2	Greater than or equal to January 1, 1996, AND less than January 1, 1997
3	Greater than or equal to January 1, 1997, AND less than January 1, 1998
4	Greater than or equal to January 1, 1998, AND less than January 1, 1999

Note that the range specified for the last partition still defines an upper limit. This is for future expandability. Simply to establish a lower bound would prevent us from adding on another partition when we started to record sales for the year 2000 without restructuring the partition.

The data warehouse architect knows exactly which partition contains which data with range partitioning. The possibility does exist, however, for data skewing. Rather than selecting date as the method of partitioning, perhaps we use a postal code. Some postal codes will have many more records than others. In our auto-sales example one would expect the rural postal codes to contain fewer records than those in urban areas. The data warehouse architect might attempt to predict the data pattern for these different areas and structure the partitions accordingly. While this might be one solution, it would be simpler to allow the system to balance the partitions.

Hash partitioning is similar to range partitioning in that a column is selected to act as the partition key. Hash partitioning assigns records to the different partitions by a hash algorithm that is applied to the values of the partition key. There is no discernible pattern to how the records are distributed. The main goal of the hashing algorithm is to prevent data skewing within the partitions.

Hybrid partitions actually create a hierarchy of partitions. As one might gather from the name, a hybrid partition combines both hash and range partitioning. The first level of the partitioning uses range partitioning. The second level creates a hashed *subpartition*. While this maintains a logical meaning as to where the data is stored at the highest level of the hierarchy, it prevents data skewing at the lower levels.

As we mentioned earlier, RAID storage provides one type of parallelism. In spreading the data across multiple partitions we are able to achieve yet another type of parallelism. Combining RAID and partitioning creates a multidimensional storage structure. This is shown in Figure 7–10. Returning to our sales example, we have partitioned our fact table by year. This is the first dimension. Each partition is put on a separate RAID stripe; this is the second dimension.

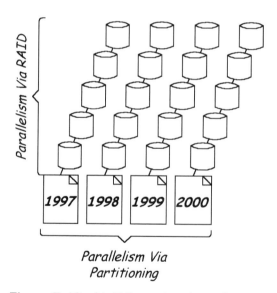

Figure 7–10   Multidimensional parallelism with partitioning and RAID storage.

To create this structure we first create our database partition using the date column of the fact table as the partition key. We then place the files for each of these partitions on a separate RAID stripe. Data is retrieved in parallel from each partition. Data within the partition is retrieved in parallel from the individual disks. When performing a full table scan, data is retrieved from all partitions and across all disks in parallel.

7.1.6 Parallel Databases

The database management system (DBMS) must have parallelism built into the database if it is to take advantage of the underlying hardware. All the hardware parallelism in the world does the architect no good if the DBMS sees only a single monolithic system. To this end the data warehouse architect must look for certain parallel features in the database. We describe here the minimum list of features.

Basically each of the parallel architectures described in this chapter combines multiple SMP nodes to form a single system image. The parallel systems differ in how the nodes are combined. In spite of these differences, the fact that each node is SMP based gives them all some common characteristics. First we see that there are multiple ports to both the outside world, the operational environment, and disks. We also see that each node has its own local memory. At times this memory may be shared, at other times it may be exclusive to the system—so the architect must look at how the DBMS handles multiple ports to operational systems and the disk subsystem. The architect must also be concerned with how well the DBMS handles distributed memory.

First let's look at the memory structure. How does the system manage this environment? As data moves through the system, it must pass through memory. As data is extracted and eventually appended to the database, it must pass through the system's memory. Even as data is read from disk and processed by the system, it must do so via memory. How does the DBMS manage this memory across multiple nodes? Are the structures distributed in such a way that the nodes can operate as complete independent entities while writing to the same database?

The architect should be wary of DBMS that claim parallelism yet structure memory in such a way that a particular node is the sole owner of a systemwide structure. If the DBMS must obtain a key or a block from a single list of available disk blocks, for example, this will create a dependency between nodes, turning the one node into a master. The processing capacity of this master node then becomes a bottleneck to parallelism. This bottleneck will affect parallelism in two areas. First, each node should be able to independently process input streams from the operational environment. A master node would limit this independence. The same is true for reading the data from disk. Interquery parallelism should allow queries to be run in multiple nodes with no single node acting as a master.

The second area of investigation for the architect is how well the DBMS leverages the parallelism of the system when reading data. Interquery parallelism divides the execution of an individual query across multiple processors. With this form of parallelism the DBMS creates a manager process that divides the execution into multiple *segments*. Each segment is then executed as a separate and independent task. The manager process queries the results and delivers them to the calling process. Statements that work on large sets of data at one time run particularly well in a parallel environment.

When evaluating how well a particular DBMS deals with intraquery parallelism, the data warehouse architect should consider the following:

1. **Does the optimizer consider the current system configuration?** System configurations change. The DBMS optimizer should consider the configuration of the system at the time the parallel query is executed every time it is executed. An optimizer that takes a static view of the environment will not take into consideration additional processors or changes in disk partitioning.

2. **Does the parallel query execute across all processors?** The DBMS should allow the distribution of a query to expand across the nodes in the system. Regardless of whether the system is an SMP, NUMA, cluster, or MPP architecture, all processors should be allowed to participate in a the query. Processors that are excluded from the query are wasted capacity. Everyone should be invited to the party!

3. **Is the administrator given the ability to determine the number of parallel streams?** In a multiuser environment it is not always optimal to distribute execution across all available proces-

sors. This should be defined by an initialization parameter that will allow the DBA to define what is optimal for his or her particular environment.

7.2 Bitmapped Indexing

In terms of data warehousing, bitmapped indexing is an enormously important development. It is one of those ideas that is so simple and so obvious that it is brilliant. Figure 7–11 demonstrates bitmapped indexing. The index is composed of nothing more than a series of bits. Each bit in the index corresponds to a record in a table, the first bit to the first physical record, the second bit to the second physical record, and so on for every record in the table up to the last. The bit is set on or off based on a boolean test of a column or columns in the record. In our diagram we created a bitmap index on female clients. Where the gender field of the record indicates female, the corresponding bit is turned on. Note that there is no ordering to the index; it simply indicates that a particular record meets a certain criterion.

Bitmapped Index	Customer Gender	Customer State
0	M	TX
1	F	CA
1	F	TX
0	M	CA
1	F	TX
0	M	CA
0	M	TX
1	F	CA
1	F	TX

Figure 7–11   Bitmapped indexing.

The index allows us to work very quickly with large numbers of records in several ways. First, we are able to perform counts without ever touching the data records. If the business strategist wanted to know the number of female clients, or male clients for that matter, we would simply count the number of bits that are on or off, respectively. This, of course, assumes that a client is either male or female and there is no third choice, such as undefined. Rather than reading 10,000 records, the DBMS simply reads 10,000 bits.

Second, the actual retrieval of records is faster. Let's say in our example that the business strategist is now interested in looking at the detailed records that made up this count. Without a bitmapped index the DBMS has to perform a full table scan. Each record is read and then tested to see if it meets the criteria. The records that do not pass the test are discarded. The time it took to read those records was basically wasted. With a bitmapped index we know exactly which records meet the criterion before they are even read. Every record that is read using the bitmapped index is required. No time is wasted reading records that will eventually be discarded. Neither is any time wasted in testing the value in the record itself.

The example we have used so far has been rather simplistic. It is basically a boolean question, male or female, which of course maps nicely to the bitmapped index. This is rather limited in application. Most fields within the database have a domain of values greater than two. In these instances an index is created for each possible value. This is shown in Figure 7–12. Rather than apply the bitmapped index to gender, we apply it to state. A separate index or bit stream is created for each state. To select all the records for the state of Texas, we simply go to the index for Texas and retrieve the records just as we did for gender. To count the records for the state of California we simply count the bits that are turned on in the California index.

This leads us to the question of when a bitmapped index is appropriate. It is commonly said that bitmapped indices are appropriate for fields with low cardinality. This is only half the story. The number of elements in a field's domain of values must be viewed in relation to the number of records in the database. In even the smallest databases one could gather that gender would be an appropriate candidate for a bitmapped index. At the other end of the spectrum is social security number. A bitmapped index for this field would make no sense. There would have to be a separate index for every record entered in the table. The general rule of thumb is that a column whose domain of values is less than one percent of the total number of records is a good candidate for a bitmapped index. The data warehouse architect should experiment with bitmapped indexing. It has been my own experience that higher percentages than this can at times realize benefits from bitmapped indexing as well.

California Index	Texas Index	Customer Gender	Customer State
0	1	M	TX
0	0	F	HI
0	1	F	TX
0	0	M	MA
0	1	F	TX
1	0	M	CA
0	0	M	HI
1	0	F	CA
0	1	F	TX

Figure 7–12   Bitmapped indexing of states.

Remember that a bitmapped index is a stream of bits and subject to binary operations. Boolean logic can be applied to the stream for more complex select statements. In Figure 7–13 we have combined our two previous examples to form one query. In this example, we are searching for all records where the gender equals female and the state equals California or Texas. As we see in the example, the indices are combined using Boolean operations to form one bitmapped index. First the California index is or'ed with the Texas index to form the California/Texas state index. This index is then anded with the gender index. The resultant index points to all records where the client is a female residing in either California or Texas.

Customer Gender	Customer State
M	TX
F	HI
F	TX
M	MA
F	TX
M	CA
M	HI
F	CA
F	TX

California Index		Texas Index		CA/Texas Index		Gender Index		Final Index
0		1		1		0		0
0		0		0		1		0
0		1		1		1		1
0		0		0		0		0
0	OR	1	=	1	AND	1	=	1
1		0		1		0		0
0		0		0		0		0
1		0		1		1		1
0		1		1		1		1

Figure 7–13   Complex queries with bitmapped indexing.

The index resulting from the query above can be used in the same way that any bitmapped index is used. The records matching the criterion can be used to perform a simple count, or the records can be retrieved from the database for further processing. In either case, there is a significant reduction in I/O for either query.

7.3 Star Query Optimization

As discussed in the introduction to this chapter, most databases have been designed with the OLTP world in mind. The way in which the data is structured in these systems differs drastically from the structure of the data within the data warehouse. Where the data in the OLTP system is normalized, the data warehouse structures its data into a star schema. This change in structure ultimately changes the way the data is accessed and how the DBMS optimizes the queries against the schema. A DBMS will optimize its queries against the database. That is, it will develop what is hoped to be the most efficient strategy for retrieving data. The data warehouse architect must consider the capabilities of the DBMS optimizer and how well it adapts to a star schema when executing a query. There are in fact four basic methods of star schema optimization.

The first method is the simplest. It basically joins the tables in the star schema in the same fashion that it would join tables in a traditional normalized database. The first dimension is joined to the fact table, rendering a set of intermediate records. This intermediate result is then joined to the next dimension, rendering a second intermediate result. This process continues until the final dimension in the query is joined. This requires that the fact table, or at least a subset of fact table records, is manipulated with every step of the optimization process. This could be a very expensive process in terms of time. With each join, tables must be repeatedly scanned. In addition, this method does little to take advantage of the structure we have so carefully built in the previous chapters. It does not recognize the unique nature of the star schema or leverage any of its characteristics. It is basically the same type of optimization that one would expect in any OLTP system.

The second method of query optimization recognizes that the DBMS is working with a star schema and takes advantage of its basic structure. A star-schema-aware optimizer understands that the fact table is usually much larger than the surrounding dimensional tables. When executing the query, the optimizer will first join the dimension tables into one table and then join that table to the fact table. This approach has the advantage that the large fact table is scanned only once. An astute observer, however, will realize that dimension tables have no common fields by which they can be joined. To deal with this problem the optimizer forms a *cartesian-product* join in which every possible combination between the tables is created in an intermediate table. When working with large dimension tables this cartesian product can be huge. Any advantage gained by this approach will quickly disappear.

A third alternative to query optimization is that of an index-join. As the name implies, an index join joins multiple tables via an index. In our auto-sales example we may want to join a dealership with the sales representatives. In this case we would build an index of the dealerships. Each index entry would then list the corresponding sales rep records associated with that dealership. This can be extended to joining multiple tables into one index join. The data warehouse architect could apply this to the fact table, joining the records from each of the dimensions. This is an improvement over the other optimization techniques. Rather than building intermediate results, an index join goes directly from the fact table to the appropriate records in the dimension tables. Consider our auto-sales example. We might create an index-join on the dimension tables (Product, Time, Salesperson, Customer, Promotion, and District).

As one can imagine, the index-join is a rather complex solution and is not necessarily the optimal solution for all environments. A star schema with many dimensions may not be well suited to an index-join. Typically only a subset of dimensions are used to reference the fact table at one time, which means that the query would be working with an index which is much larger than required because of the additional unused dimensions. Using a subset of dimensions has another detrimental affect. The index-join is an ordered set of columns. This means the order of the columns is significant. If the user accesses all of the columns at one time or just the leading columns, then access will be efficient. If, however, we access only a few of the many dimensions and these dimensions are distributed throughout the index-join, performance will be rather poor. Referring to our example, retrieving records by product, time and salesperson will be much faster than accessing records by time and promotion.

The fourth method employs bitmapped indices. A bitmapped index is created for each foreign key in the fact table. These indices are then combined using a bitmap AND operation. The resultant bitmap index will point to the set of records that meet the selection criterion. Remember that none of the actual fact-table records have been read at this point, only the bitmapped index. The records pointed to by the combined indices are then read and this intermediary result is combined with the dimension tables.

Of the four star query-optimization methods presented in this section, no one of them is the best for all possible scenarios. Although some methods may have greater appeal in more situations than others, the data warehouse architect should experiment with different indexing schemes to see which is best for which situations. What is important is that the DBMS selected to implement that data warehouse has access to each of these methods.

7.4 Summation Tables

As we have discussed throughout this text, the business strategist is interested in behaviors within the marketplace. We have defined a behavior as a predictable response to a set of stimuli. To recognize behaviors the strategist must look across the plain of the organization's environment to see which actions are repeated and which stimuli lead to these actions. The strategist does this by looking at summaries or aggregations of data to find patterns. We have seen this in previous chapters. The data warehouse architect attempts to anticipate which aggregations will be used by the business strategist and structures the data accordingly. In this way the architect can improve query performance. Rather than scanning the table with every summary request, the user references the summary table—a smaller table of precomputed results. In our auto-sales example we might have a summary table that contains the total sales by dealership and district. We might also have a summary table for time periods such as fiscal months and quarters.

The problem is that the architect can never truly predict all the possible aggregations required by the business strategists. There will be summaries that the architect just simply didn't expect. There will be other summaries that may seem important to the architect but are not referenced as often as expected. Both of these situations can be detrimental to system performance. Unexpected summaries will take longer to run than those that have been prebuilt, giving the image of poor system performance. Creating unused summaries will put an unnecessary load on the system, again resulting in less than optimal performance. A truly data-warehouse-friendly DBMS will provide the data warehouse architect with built-in summary management.

DBMS summary management creates summary tables containing the precomputed results of expensive aggregations. The difference between DBMS and manual summary management is that of automating the process. This automation occurs at three levels: the recognition of which summaries to create; the updating of these summaries; and the redirection of queries to these summaries. The DBMS should begin with advising the database administrator as to which summaries to create. It should perform this function by tracing the daily use of the warehouse. By understanding which summaries are most often requested by the user community, the DBMS will be able to recommend which summary tables will provide a payoff in performance. The DBMS should also be able to recommend which summary tables are not being used and ultimately dropped.

Once the DBA receives the recommendations from the DBMS, he or she could create the appropriate summary tables. The creation of such a table should be different from that of a standard table. It should signal the DBMS that it is to be maintained by the system and that specific queries should be redirected to it. Summary maintenance should allow either a complete refresh of the data or an incremental refresh. An incremental refresh adds only those records that are new since the last refresh of the summary table. The DBA should also be allowed to select which summary tables are refreshed, selecting either specific summaries, only summaries that use the updated tables, or all summary tables.

An important aspect of summary management is that of query redirection. This is shown in Figure 7–14. Query redirection keeps the implementation of the summary management invisible to the user. True redirection will allow the user to simply execute a standard SQL statement, requiring no special intervention such as hints from the user. The DBMS should recognize the use of a summary based on text matching, summary join-back, or summary roll-up. The DBMS should receive the query from the user, recognize when and which summaries can be used, and rewrite the query in the background to reference those summaries. In the end the only thing the user should notice is improved system performance.

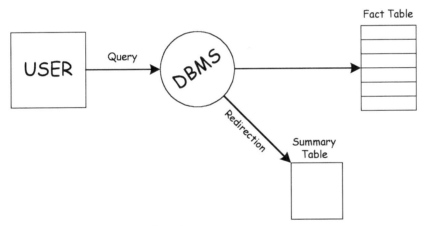

Figure 7–14   Query redirection.

The first form of query redirection is the simplest. This is where the user issues a query asking for a summary that matches a summary table. Earlier in our auto-sales example we created a summary based on the dealership. The following query asks for a summary of sales by dealership;

```
SELECT time.month, dealer.dealer_name,  SUM(sales_fact.sales)
      FROM       time, dealer, sales_fact
      WHERE      sales_fact.date = time.date
```

```
AND          dealer.dealer_num =  sales_fact.dealer_num
GROUP BY     time.month, dealer.dealer_num;
```

The DBMS would redirect this to:

```
SELECT summary.month, summary.dealer_name, summary.sales
    FROM        summary;
```

A summary join-back occurs when there is a reference to a column in the query that is not included in the summary table. The missing column is found by joining the summary table back to the dimension tables. Let's return to our auto-sales example. This time, instead of seeing a summary of sales based on dealership, we want to see a summary based on sales representatives within a particular dealership. The user would submit the following query:

```
SELECT time.month, sales_rep.salesrep,  SUM(sales_fact.sales)
    FROM        time, sales_rep, sales_fact
    WHERE       sales_fact.date = time.date
    AND         sales_fact.rep = sales_rep.rep
    AND         dealer.dealer_num =  14
    GROUP BY    time.month, sales_rep.salesrep;
```

The DBMS would redirect this to:

```
SELECT summary.month, summary.salesrep, summary.sales
    FROM        summary
    WHERE       summary.salesrep in (SELECT salesrep.salesrep
                FROM salesrep
                WHERE Salesrep.deal_num = 14);
```

Summary roll-up aggregates the data at a higher level in the hierarchy than the summary table. Earlier we summarized sales by dealership on a monthly basis. In this example we will take one step up in the time hierarchy and look at this same data on an annual basis. The query for this would be as follows:

```
SELECT time.year, dealer.dealer_name,  SUM(sales_fact.sales)
    FROM       time, dealer, sales_fact
    WHERE      sales_fact.date = time.date
    AND        dealer.dealer_num =  sales_fact.dealer_num
    GROUP BY   time.year, dealer.dealer_num;
```

The DBMS would redirect this to:

```
SELECT sub.year, summary.dealer_name, summary.sales
    FROM summary,
        (SELECT distinct time.month, time.year from time) sub
            WHERE summary.month = sub.month
            GROUP BYsub.year, summary.dealer_name;
```

7.5 Web-Enabled Data Warehousing

To say that the Internet has revolutionized the way in which we do business or to pontificate on how the Internet is a ubiquitous presence in our lives would be simply to repeat trite phrases we have all heard before. So let's try a different tack. Marketing hype has really fuddled the thinking of many in the computer industry. Often you will hear discussions of client/server implementations versus the Internet. The mistake is that client/server is an architecture, not a specific implementation.

A client/server architecture describes two processes. The first is the proactive client that sends requests to the server. The server process is a reactive process that does nothing but process requests from client. It may also run some internal housekeeping processes as well. It is common for people to mistake client/server to mean a desktop workstation communicating over a LAN or phone line to a larger system designated the server. These technicalities, however, are implementation details, not a mandate of the architecture. The focus is not on the hardware but on the processes that run on the hardware. Let's look at an example to demonstrate this point. A company has an application that runs in traditional client/server mode: a desktop client communicates to a server in the back room. A few years later, in light of a more powerful server, the client process is moved from the desktop system to the server in the back room. Isn't it still a client/server application? The hardware is just an implementation detail.

Servers are the reactive portion of the system, and there are many types in the world. There are print servers, files servers, and application servers. There are even, dare I say it, WEB SERVERS! The very terminology of the Internet demonstrates this point. If we were to Web-enable our example described above, we would still have a client/server application! The Internet is just a specific type of client/server implementation.

To demonstrate this point more fully let's look at Figure 7–15. In this diagram we have presented a Web-enabled data warehouse. The browser is the presentation layer of the application. It is the medium through which the user communicates with the Web server. Since the Web server communicates directly with the browser, the client system is invisible to the application. Any client capable of supporting a browser can access any Web-enabled client. Perhaps a district manager would like to see the monthly sales aggregates of all the dealerships in his or her district. The strategist would click on the report icon that causes the browser to send a URL (Universal Resource Locator) to the data warehouse's Web server. The URL contains a CGI (Common Gateway Interface) that points to the application program. This program can be some Decision Support System that will, in response to the request by the Web server, issue a request to the data warehouse. Upon receiving the result, the Decision Support System converts the report into HTML, which is passed to the Web server. The Web server in turn passes this result to the browser on the client.

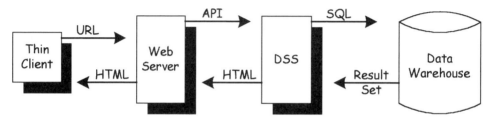

Figure 7–15   The Web-enabled data warehouse.

Compare this to what is traditionally thought of as client/server. In this world the client is a specific type of system; the application is developed for that specific environment. Once developed, the software must be physically installed, maintained, and administered on every user's system. The application runs on that client. Requests are sent directly to the server, where the data is retrieved from the database. The data is then downloaded to the client system and processed on the desktop.

By Web-enabling the data warehouse we shift the processing from the client to the server. The client simply runs the browser. The processing of the data is done back on the server. Also, the client's actual hardware and software are invisible to the application. It doesn't matter if the browser is running on a desktop system, a high-end workstation, or even a mainframe. The hardware and software in an Internet world are commodities. Run whatever operating system you want on whatever hardware you want, just make sure that you have a standard browser.

Shifting the processing from the client to the server has other important benefits. Here are just a few:

1. **Freedom from Client Limitations.** Applications that run on a client are subject to the limitations of that client. If the client is underpowered, the application will run poorly. Upgrading every desktop in an organization may be prohibitively expensive. In an Internet implementation the capabilities of the client are irrelevant to the application. All that matters is that the client can support a browser.

2. **Reduced Administration and Maintenance Costs.** In a traditional client/server environment the application needs to be installed, administered, and maintained on every individual client system. Someone has to deal with every client system that is going to use the application. By shifting the application to the server, the application is maintained in one place—on the server.

3. **Intuitive GUI Interface.** The use of the browser is common to most if not all computer users. The interface design can leverage this commonly known interface.

4. **Easy Distribution of Data.** In a traditional client/server environment many DSS applications download the data and perform processing on the local copy to save on the data transfer time. In an Internet data warehouse the data is all located in one location. Any updates to the data will be immediately accessible to all clients at once.

5. **Almost Universal Presence of the Internet.** The Internet is everywhere. Okay, I gave into a cliché. The fact of the matter is, though, that the Internet *is* everywhere. Access to the central server is as close as the nearest Internet service provider.

7.6 The BBBC Data Warehouse

Now that we have the implementation model complete, we need to figure out how to turn this beast into an actual system. We need to think about some implementation details, such as those discussed in this chapter. In this section we will begin by outlining the hardware requirements for the data warehouse. We will then discuss how we will use which features of the DBMS.

To begin, we have decided on a Web-enabled data warehouse. This will require three servers: the Web server, the application server, and the database server. Although this may sound rather elaborate, the initial iteration of the development spiral will require modestly sized systems. The Web server and application server can begin as mid-sized servers with capacity for further growth.

The database server, the place where the central repository is to reside, will be a bit *beefier,* yet still have significant growth capabilities. To this end we should select a hardware platform that has asymmetric clustering capabilities. Our initial roll-out of the product will be on a two-node cluster. Each of the nodes in the cluster need not be fully loaded, depending on the work load and processor speed. Initially four processors in a eight-processor system may suffice. Since it is the first iteration of our development spiral, one node should be sufficient. The second node is primarily for backup purposes. We will want asymmetric clustering because it would be foolish to spend money on an entire node that simply sat there, especially since we have the ability to take advantage of that excess capacity.

Whichever clustering solution we choose, it should have the ability to expand beyond two nodes. Two nodes may be able to handle the work load of the second and third revisions of the warehouse, but we want to have more than what is necessary for reliability purposes. A single node failure may not be much of an issue if it occurs during the day. Perhaps a strategist will have to wait a little bit longer to receive a report. If a node fails on a cluster with little excess capacity at night during an upload and the extraction windows are tight, the result could be catastrophic.

We will want to partition our fact table. Let's try something a little different, a bit off the wall. We discussed how the fact table of the sale/lease star contains both sale vouchers and lease vouchers. Sometimes it would be nice if we could just work with one of these two sets, while at other times we would like to work with them both as one complete table. Well, that is the point of partitioning. So let's create a range partition where the ranges are the values of our sale/lease flag. That will separate the two nicely, but we're not through yet. To make sure that we get the most out of our partitioning scheme we will create a subpartition that is hashed. This sub-partition will provide for an even distribution of data. Since data will be appended to the data warehouse in bulk loads, we will distribute the partitions across a RAID level-3 stripe.

There are two areas where we would like to investigate the use of a bitmapped index. First, we will want to check the brokers. We will not know definitely if the brokers are an appropriate candidate for a bitmapped index until we do some analysis on the actual data. While intuition may suggest not, we may want to perform an analysis to make sure. Another area that might be an interesting application of the bitmapped index is the profit center. We may want to consider adding a profit center key to the fact table and then creating a bitmapped index off the profit center. The number of profit centers in comparison to the number of deals would probably make this modification beneficial. Again, we would want to perform an analysis on the actual data before attempting any changes.

As far as summary tables are concerned, we will allow the database to recommend where we should and should not have a summary table. Initially we would want the DBMS to create and maintain summary tables on the following:

- Profit Center
- Business Unit
- Each Fiscal Period
- Client Type
- Property Type

These summaries are to be created for both the sales/lease and the listing fact tables. Having the DBMS do this will eliminate the need to manually maintain a Profit Center summary table. Figure 7–16 reflects the changes this and the other suggestions will make on the schema presented in the preceding chapter.

7.7 Summary

In this chapter we discussed some of the implementation issues facing the data warehouse architect. The following features should be present in any DBMS that is to be used for the construction of the data warehouse:

- Asymmetric Clustering
- Bitmapped Index-Joins
- Bitmapped Indexing
- Cost-based Optimization
- Index-Joins
- Interquery Parallelism
- Intraquery Parallelism (*Note:* Queries should expand across all processors in all system nodes.)
- Range Partitioning
- Rules-Based Optimization
- Shared Disk Architecture Support
- SMP Support
- Star Query Optimization
- Summary Redirection
- Summary Table Recommendation
- Web Enablement

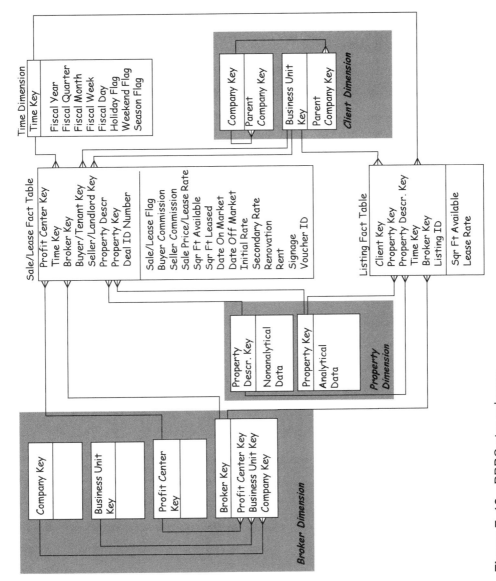

Figure 7-16 BBBC star schema.

The following features are not necessary but are helpful:

- Hash Partitioning
- Hybred Partitioning
- MPP Architecture Support
- NUMA Architecture Support

7.8 Glossary

Asymmetric Clustering   A clustering scheme in which each node in the cluster is involved in performing meaningful work.

Bitmapped Index-Joins   A method of joining tables where a bit-mapped index is created for each foreign key in the fact table. These indices are then combined using a bitmap AND operation. The resultant bitmap index will point to the records that meet the selection criteria.

Bitmapped Indexing   A method of indexing in which a stream of bits is created. Each bit in the stream corresponds to the physical record in the database. The first bit represents the first physical record. The second bit represents the second physical record. The bit is turned on or off based on whether the record passes or fails some boolean test.

Clustering   Also known as *shared disk architectures*. Nodes in this architecture have exclusive ownership of local memory but share disks with one another.

Hash Partitioning   A partitioning scheme in which records are distributed across the database partitions based on a hashing algorithm. Data is distributed evenly across the partitions, preventing data skewing.

Hybrid Partitioning   A two-level partitioning scheme that combines hash and range partitioning.

Index-Joins A technique that joins tables via their indices by creating an ordered set of columns.

Interquery Parallelism The concurrent execution of multiple queries against a single database.

Intraquery Parallelism The division of a single query into multiple subqueries that are executed concurrently.

Massively Parallel Processing Architecture Also known as *shared nothing architectures*, where each node in the system has exclusive ownership of local resources.

NUMA Architecture Nonuniform Memory Access architectures which are composed of multiple nodes sharing memory and disks. Memory in each of the nodes is combined into a single global memory.

Range Partitioning Partitioning of the database where records are placed into each of the separate partitions based on a range of values.

Shared Disk Architecture Also known as clustering. Nodes in this architecture have exclusive ownership of local memory but share disks with one another.

SMP See *Symmetric Multiprocessing*.

Summary Redirection An optimization technique in which queries are rewritten by the DBMS to query against aggregate tables. Queries redirection is invisible to the user.

Symmetric Clustering A clustering scheme in which one node in a cluster stands by as a hot backup waiting for the primary node in the cluster to fail.

Symmetric Multiprocessing Architectures Architectures in which all local resources are equally shared by all processors in the system. All system components reside on a single system bus.

The Spacially Enabled
Data Warehouse

Consider the definition of a data warehouse; "a subject-oriented, time-variant, nonvolatile collection of data in support of management decisions." The data within a data warehouse is time encoded, allowing the business strategist to manipulate time as a variable in the analysis. We described the activity of the business strategist as looking across time to understand behaviors. It becomes a dimension of the analysis space. Time, however, is related to space. It is just as reasonable to study the effects of space as it is the effects of time. The behavior of objects in our organization's environment can be studied according to their spatial relationships. To understand the effects space has on objects related to our business, to make it a variable within our analysis, we must dimension the analysis space by the object's geographic properties. This added dimension to the analysis space provides a number of benefits to the data warehouse architect that are not available otherwise. The spatially enabled warehouse has:

- A more organized data structure
- Better integration of disparate data
- Spatially enabled analysis
- Reduced decision cycle time
- Improved decision making

Spatially enabled analysis allows completely new types of inquiries. The strategist can provide informed answers for the following types of situations:

- Service Scheduling—The delivery of service to customers can be planned in a more efficient and cost-effective manner. Analysis can be made of transportation factors and street patterns. Service managers can now answer such questions as, "Where are my service areas and how should I define them?"

- Marketing—Customer demographics can be spatially encoded to profile responses to various marketing campaigns. Future campaigns can then be refocused to deliver a more effective message to specific market areas. Marketing managers can now answer such questions as, "Where do my most profitable customers live?"

- Site Selection—Locations of new outlets and service centers can be analyzed based on existing conditions in the area and projected future demand. Site planners can answer such questions as, "Where are facilities in relation to my customers, how close are they to my locations, and which areas have the least amount of coverage?"

- Competitive Tracking—Spatial data will enable marketing to view the location of competitors and their penetration into different market segments. Marketing managers can define not only where competitors are, but where they aren't, and which geographic areas are the least covered.

To achieve these ends, to be able to answer these types of queries, the data within the warehouse must be spatially encoded. This is no simple task. A map is a two-dimensional representation of a three-dimensional object. At this point we should be pretty well versed in the study of different dimensions. A map is a projection. When creating a map we take a three-dimensional object, the earth or some portion of it, and project it onto a two-dimensional plane. We have shown this in Figure A–1. It has been described as taking an orange peel and flattening it out on a table. If you try to flatten an orange peel, you quickly notice that as the pieces get flatter, the more curved pieces start to tear to accommodate for the lost dimension. This is what happens when we make a map. We must stretch it at certain points and contract it at others. A variety of different projections address this problem. The most common is a Mercator projection, where the space between the latitudinal lines increases as we approach the equator. There are also a variety of conic projections. These are maps that view the earth from a perspective above the poles. Without going into great detail about the many types of projections, the point is that spatial encoding of data captures the location of an object on the surface of a significantly less than perfect sphere, the earth.

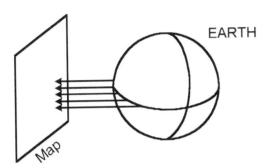

Figure A–1 Map projections.

There are three different types of map objects. These are shown in Figure A–2. The simplest is a point, a specific location. In the data warehousing environment we will probably encounter points as representations of addresses. A line, the next object, is a series of points. In a purely geometric sense a line is a series of points that goes on to infinity in both directions. What we draw on paper is technically a line segment. (There, I have made my high school geometry teacher happy.) Map lines are used to represent streets, rivers, rail lines, and other such objects.

Actually, a line on a map is a bit different from the lines we all discussed in high school geometry. Lines on a map are rarely simple straight lines; often there are bends and turns. We therefore store a series of line segments in our database. If we look at Figure A–2, we see it as a series of line segments. The end point for the previous segment is the starting point for the next. We can store these points in one of two ways. The first is as absolute points—the absolute latitude and longitude of the beginning and ending points of the line segment. We can also store the points as offsets of the previous point. The first point would be stored as an absolute latitude and longitude. Subsequent points would be so many degrees, minutes, and seconds plus or minus the previous point.

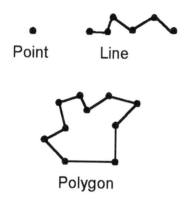

Figure A–2 Spatial data objects.

The final spatial object is a polygon. This is used to represent an area such as a postal code area, city boundaries, or census block. The polygon is composed of a series of line segments that are defined as either absolute points or offsets of previous points.

Spatially encoding the data begins with some spatial data element. This could be an address, postal code, or even telephone area code. This data is then mapped into some spatial coordinates. This is only part of the story, however. Simply having the data in the database does not make it meaningful. The data must be presented to the business strategist in such a way that the spatial relationships between the different objects become clear. Consider the following list of customers:

Gertrude Strode
2232 Hawthorne Blvd.
Torrance CA 90303

Gunther Agnew
400 W. 190th St.
Torrance CA 90303

Ravi Seery
2525 Crenshaw Blvd.
Lomita CA 90293

Luisa Martinez
2800 Plaza Del Amo
Torrance CA 90303

Peter Pearly
300 Rosecrans
El Segundo CA 90319

If the analyst is not familiar with the Los Angeles area, she may know nothing about how these addresses are related to one another. In fact, she may not even know they are in the Los Angeles area. In examining the behavior of some these clients we may notice that Getrude, Peter, and Gunther all shop at the same camping supply store. Ravi and Luisa may shop at a totally different store. What is the difference between these clients? Perhaps Ravi and Luisa shop at a store in Torrance and the others shop at a store in Manhattan Beach or Manchester. What this data doesn't show is that these clients live at different ends of Torrance. Luisa and Ravi are actually physically close to one another. The others live near a major freeway and have easy access to the Manhattan Beach store. This is all hidden when we depend on simple addresses.

The possibilities for the use of spatial data within a decision support environment are virtually endless. In a retail environment we can apply spatial data in a number of ways. Many retail chains consist not necessarily of one type of store but of many store types that appeal to different market segments. Perhaps a grocery store chain has stores that appeal to upper-income homes, other stores that appeal to a particular ethnic group, and yet a third set for more economically minded shoppers. First, management may want to define which geographic areas are the least covered. Perhaps certain areas are heavily saturated with high-end grocery chains while others remain pretty much unclaimed. By combining how far a shopper is willing to travel with street and demographic information, a retailer can determine which areas are the best candidates for new locations.

The example given above is external to the store. It is the type of big decision that is not typically made on a daily basis and certainly not by business strategists close to the lines of production. Those decisions are primarily external to the actual retail outlet. We can apply spatial data at a deeper, much more interesting level. We can apply spatial data to everyday management decisions.

Let's look at our retail example, but this time let's look inside the store. Business intelligence experts are always talking about market-basket analysis. What about applying spatial data to market-basket analysis? What someone puts on that conveyer belt at the register gives us a pretty good idea where they have been in the store. It can also tell us something else: it can tell us what path they took through the store. We won't be able to know for certain, but we can come pretty close. We know something else when someone checks out. We know what time it is. Put these things together and we can define the different hot spots in our store at different times during the day. We can also track this over a period of months and see if it changes seasonally. We can then stock our shelves accordingly.

There is the old story about beer and diapers. A large retail chain discovered that on weekends the sales of beer and disposable diapers were heavily correlated. As diaper sales rose, so did that of beer. As the story goes, the business strategists discovered that on the weekends mom would leave the kids with dad so she could have a little bit of a break from the little ones. Dad, after being home with the little darlings, would discover that he was out of diapers and run to the store to get some. While at the store he would think, "Heck, while I am here let me pick up some beer for the game this afternoon." Why is this important to the retailer? Simple—Friday night you move the high-margin beer to the end of the diaper aisle. The stuff you don't make anything on you put as far away from the diapers as you can. End result: greater profitability for the store.

The point of the lesson is simple. If we know the customers' buying patterns in conjunction with where they go and when they go there, we can be there first. We can be there to deliver the goods and services we know they will want when they get there.

A.1 Analyzing Patient Needs

To see how this works in real life, let's look at an example of how one health care provider, St. Peter Hospital in Olympia, Washington, took advantage of spatially enabling its data. This case study has been provided courtesy of Environmental Systems Research Institute Inc. and is featured in *GIS Means Business* by Chris Harder.

As we have all become aware from watching the news, health care organizations are challenged with defining ways of practicing good medicine while staying financially healthy. Meanwhile, America is aging. As the *baby boomers* age, greater demands are placed on health care providers. One model that has been implemented to meet this challenge is managed care. In this environment doctors, hospitals, and other providers join cooperative groups to deliver health services. In such an environment spatial analysis allows business strategists to define demand in relation to resources according to their location. St. Peter Hospital in Olympia, Washington, used ArcView GIS to perform just such an analysis.

St. Peter Hospital is composed of over 200 physician offices, a major HMO, a large multispecialty clinic, a radiation therapy facility, nursing homes, and a variety of other businesses. St. Peter serves over half a million people in a five-county area. St. Peter faces the same competitive pressures as other organizations. In light of the changing face of health care, St. Peter established a Decision Support Group to provide strategic information to management. As part of its mission that group has used ESRI's ArcView GIS for spatial analysis of geographic relationships between patients and facilities.

Earlier we discussed understanding patients and the spatial relationship to health care service. This is just what St. Peter Hospital did. The hospital provides 95% of all dialysis treatment to patients living in the five-county area it serves. People with kidney disease require regular hemodialysis treatment. This treatment basically does the work of the kidney, which is to clean the toxins from the blood. The hospital wanted a detailed analysis of current and long-term demand for this treatment.

The Decision Support Group of St. Peter Hospital used Arcview GIS to perform their spatial analysis. This was basically a two-step process. First the group mapped the current demand to determine how well it was being satisfied. It then went on to study population growth and the effect it would have on demand. In this way management would be better able to predict the best placement for future dialysis treatment centers.

The group made two basic assumptions. First, it is reasonable to expect a drive of 20 minutes to reach a dialysis treatment center. Second, most people would travel to these centers over major roads. Rather then defining a simple circle with a 20-mile radius, the group went one step better. Using ArcView Network Analyst, they generated service areas along major roads. The resulting polygons are shown in Figure A–3. In the center of each polygon is the dialysis treatment center, represented by a white cross.

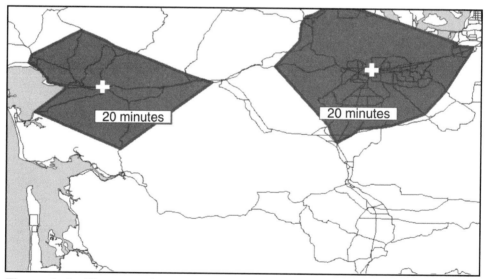

Figure A–3   The two polygons cover areas within a 20-minute drive of St. Peter.

The next step was to identify the patients' locations. This was done by taking the patients' postal codes and color-coding each area according to the number of patients. These areas were mapped with the service-area polygons laid over them, as shown in Figure A–4. In the figure, the darkest grey areas have the most patients. Although some large dark grey areas extend beyond the service areas, subsequent investigation showed that these are mostly rural areas whose populations largely live within the service area.

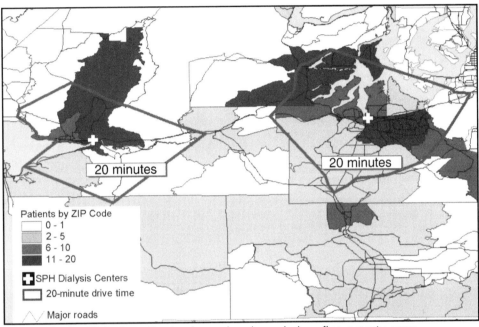

Figure A–4   Dialysis patients shown by zip code in a five-county area.

While the map in Figure A–4 demonstrates how well the current sites meet current demand, the Decision Support Group also needed to consider future demand. The next step was to determine which areas were expected to grow the most over the next decade. Here external data was brought into the decision support process. Aggregating data to the census-block-group level, the Decision Support Group was able to generate the map presented in Figure A–5. The group visually coded the data and used ArcView GIS to generate a map that included both the projected areas of growth and the service-area polygons. Looking at this map, management was able to identify four census blocks of projected growth at over 20% that were outside the 20-minute service area. This map, with the areas highlighted in black, is presented in Figure A–6.

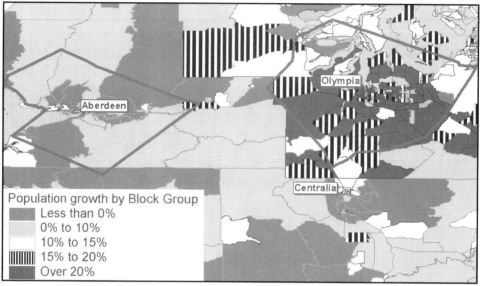

Figure A–5   Projected areas of growth.

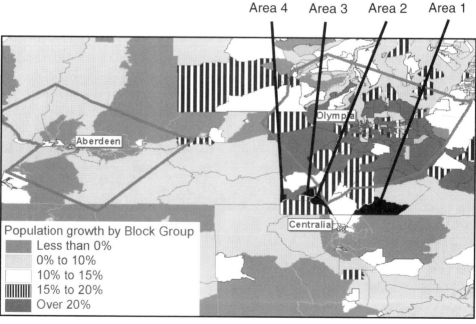

Figure A–6   The four fastest-growing areas outside the dialysis service areas.

Extraction, Transformation, and Loading

The data warehouse, as described in previous chapters, sits outside the operational environment. Data is *extracted* from these systems, *transformed* into a format consistent with the data warehouse, and *loaded* into the central data repository. The data warehouse is perhaps the first system to combine the data from the many disparate systems in the operational environment. Typically these systems are developed independently of one another. The warehouse is the first system to come along and attempt to combine all of their data into a single cohesive view of the organization. While the first chapter discussed extraction, transformation, and loading (ETL) in principle, its implementation was not really addressed. The importance of this topic requires that we take a few moments and look at the implementation of ETL.

This appendix discusses an ETL strategy and an ETL process. The ETL strategy is the overall plan of attack. It deals with such issues as how to extract the data and how to deal with errors in the data. The ETL process carries out the strategy. It defines which data is extracted and how it is transformed into a consistent format.

B.1 The ETL Strategy

The development of any ETL strategy must take into account the challenges of integrating data from independently developed systems. These systems are not static entities sitting in some back room, unused and unattended. Any discussion with the teams responsible for their development and maintenance will quickly reveal that these environments are just as dynamic and demanding as any data warehouse. Given these realities, the ETL strategy should take the following into consideration:

- **Differing Data Formats**—Independently developed systems format the same data elements differently from one another. This is covered in detail in Chapter 1. The ETL strategy must define a single format acceptable to the user community. In addition, transformations must be defined to convert the differing formats to that one single format.
- **Bad Data**—As data is brought from the operational environment to the data warehouse, it must be cleansed and verified. Data cleansing is a significant issue when transforming data. Not only must the ETL strategy deal with missing or invalid data items, it must also concern itself with data that may pass all edit checks yet is incorrect.
- **Incompatible Source Systems**—The larger the organization, the greater the number of information systems. The greater the number of information systems, the more likely it is that these systems will be incompatible with one another. While the data warehouse may be implemented with a particular relational database, the source systems may be large legacy mainframe systems using hierarchical databases. Some source systems may feed the data warehouse via a direct connection or through flat files. In any event, as the number of source systems increases, the complexity of just getting the data to the warehouse for transformation will increase as well.
- **Changes in Source Systems**—Often in data warehousing circles we forget that the operational environment can be just as dynamic as the data warehouse. The format and structure of the data within these sources are subject to change; the ETL strategy should plan on it. The data administrator should review the data loaded into the warehouse

as well as the extraction log to detect changes in the source system. Metadata changes to the source systems must also be reflected in the transformation process.

- **Extraction and Load Windows**—The additional load put on the source systems by the extraction process may exceed their processing capacity. As a result, the extraction of data from the source systems may be limited to the night shift, or to a few off-peak hours. Loading the data into the warehouse may also put undue burden on the warehouse, restricting the loading of data to a limited time window. The ETL strategy must take this into consideration.

As we can see from the list above, the data warehouse construction crew must work within certain limitations. Many of these limitations are based on the source and target systems. Another source of limitations is the business strategist. Strategists being served by the data warehouse will have certain expectations that will have a direct impact on the ETL strategy. What level of detail does the user expect? The granularity of the data affects the volume of the data to be updated. Strategists expecting individual detailed transactions will require larger volumes of data than those expecting aggregations of those transactions. Currency of the data is another issue. In some environments weekly or even monthly updates are acceptable. In other environments data that does not include information that is only minutes old may be useless. In either case the expectation of the business strategist who is served by the data warehouse will determine the volume and frequency of the ETL strategy.

One of the first issues to be addressed is how the data is going to be extracted. This really involves answering two questions. First, what will determine when to execute the extraction process? Second, how will the process determine which data to extract? There are actually five basic methods that answer these questions: database comparison, application logs, database logs, time stamps, and bitmapped indexing. The following paragraphs discuss these methods.

The first method, database comparison, is perhaps the simplest to understand. The extraction process takes a snapshot of the entire database.

The duration of this interval is determined by the needs of the user. Each snapshot is compared to the one immediately preceding it. The differences between the two snapshots are recorded in a delta file, which is then transported to the data warehouse. The data within the delta file is then transformed and integrated into the central data repository. The problem with this methodology is that it is expensive in terms of both time and resources. The time is takes to compare two entire databases can be substantial. In addition, the comparison will place heavy loads on the processors and the I/O subsystem. In some instances, however, this may be the best solution, especially where it is the only viable solution.

The second methodology, application logs, has a much lower resource requirement. As part of the normal operation, the application on the source system records changes to the data as they are made. The application logs contain the same data that was in the delta file in method one. The log file is then transported to the data warehouse for integration. How often it is transported depends on the needs of the user. This method differs from the first one in that the extraction process does not have to go through the tedious task of comparing two entire databases to arrive at the delta file. Its weakness lies in the volume of work required on the source application side. This will require significant coding within the operational environment. Like all code, this new extension to the application will also require maintenance. Will the application team want to take on this additional burden? If not, will they allow the warehouse construction crew to touch their application? Regardless of who may support this software, it is an extension to the operational application that may not be a welcome one.

An alternative to application logs is the use of database logs. Database management systems maintain logs in an OLTP environment for data recovery and integrity purposes. The extraction process can examine these logs to determine which records have been modified since the last extraction. This strategy does not require any coding on the part of application programmers. The maintenance of the database logs is performed automatically by the database management system. The drawback to the method is that it requires a knowledge of the internals of the database system. Any changes in the structure of the content of these logs will also mean changes to the extraction process.

Time stamping is the fourth method of identifying data that is to be extracted from the operational environment. In this method records are time stamped when they are changed. The extraction process then retrieves those records having a time stamp later than the last retrieval. This method is less invasive than the application log, but it still requires some coding within the application environment. It also requires the extraction process to scan the entire database supporting the operational system in order to find the records that have changed since the last update. The alternative to a full table scan is to create a time index on the operational system. Such an index, however, may cause performance problems with the application.

Bitmapped indexing, the final method of extraction, attempts to minimize both the volume of code that must be maintained and the resources used to extract the data. First, an update field is added to each record within the transaction-processing application. This field will have a domain of three values: unchanged, modified, and pending. A bitmapped index is created for this field for each value in the domain. When a record is added to the database, or a record is modified, the field is set to modified. When an extraction occurs, the extraction process uses the bitmapped index to read the records that are flagged as modified. If records are changed or modified within the transaction-processing system while the data is being extracted, their update values are set to pending. Once the data has been extracted, the modified records are set to unchanged, and the pending records are set to modified.

The data-extraction methods discussed above deal with how the data to be extracted is to be identified. We still need to know how the extraction process determines when the data is to be extracted. There are two basic methods: time based or event based. Time-based extraction starts the process on some regular interval. This interval could be a number of hours, days, weeks, or even months. It could be based on the calendar or some fiscal time period, such a fiscal month or quarters. The frequency of the interval is really dependent on the needs of the user, as we have stated above. Event-based extraction triggers the execution of the extraction process based on the occurrence of some event. The concern here is whether the event occurs at a time when extraction is inconvenient. Note that any of the methods described above can be triggered on the basis of either time or events.

The final question in the ETL strategy is where to run the extraction process. As noted in previous chapters, data can be moved into the warehouse by two different methods. In one method the operational system pushes the data into the data warehouse. In this environment the extraction process runs on the operational system. In some cases the data warehouse architect will have no choice other than to push. If the operational system's database is incompatible with that of the data warehouse, the data transfer may have to occur via a flat file. In such a case the extraction process would have to run on the operational system. The second method is for the data warehouse to pull the data from the operational system. In these environments the two databases are typically compatible and the extraction process can run on the data warehouse. Generally, data warehouse sages prefer to run the extraction process on the operational system whenever possible. While there are some benefits to running the extraction on the operational system, the best solution is really dependent on the individual needs of the user.

B.1.1 ETL Process

Once the ETL strategy has been defined, the ETL process must be designed. This is perhaps one of the greatest challenges for the data warehouse construction crew. It has been projected that 80% of the effort in constructing a data warehouse is expended on the ETL process. When one considers the nature of the data warehouse, it is easy to see why this may be so. Once the data has been loaded into the data warehouse, the primary work is reporting the data to the business strategist. Much of this data delivery is done on an ad hoc basis. The retrieval and transformation of the data, however, is a very lengthy and tedious process.

Figure B–1 shows how an extraction process is developed. At the center is the *data archeologist*. The archeologist searches through the legacy operational systems in search of data, both meta and actual. The search, however, does not begin on the operational side. The data archeologist works backward. The first question we ask isn't "What do we have?" but rather "What do we need?" The answer lies with the business strategists. We begin with: what questions do the strategists need to ask of the data warehouse? This was shown as part of the methodology. We then define the data that will support the requested analysis. This definition is documented within the data warehouse's metadata. Here is where the data archeologist begins.

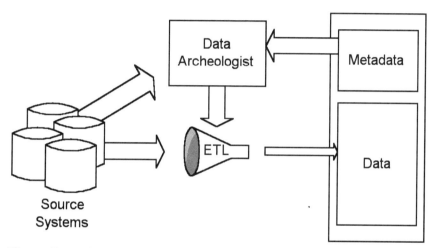

Figure B–1   Data extraction.

Based on the warehouse's metadata the archeologist starts to search for source systems. Source systems are not necessarily within the organization. Perhaps the data warehouse requires demographic data; in many instances this would come from an external source. Data may also originate, as we have seen throughout this text, from several systems. In either case the data archeologist finds the source data and documents its format. The data warehouse construction crew now knows the required data and its format as well as the source of the data and its format. The construction crew now has enough data to proceed to the next step: defining the transformations.

The data transformation process, in this context, involves more than just changing the format of the data. It means preparing the operational data, transforming its structure and content, to be acceptable for integration into the data warehouse. It also means cleansing the data and preparing the records to be included within the warehouse. There are six basic types of transformations:

1. **Type Conversion**—Source data may be converted from one data type to another. The source system may, for example, store boolean values as zeros and ones, and the data warehouse may store the data as boolean trues and falses. The transformation would perform this conversion.

2. **String Manipulation**—Operations may be performed on character fields, such as concatenations and trims. Perhaps the source system stores the first name and the last name in separate fields. The data warehouse may specify that these fields be combined into one. The source system may allow fewer characters for a name than a source system. In such a case the transformation would trim the field to the appropriate number of characters.

3. **Arithmetic Functions**—The data warehouse may require data that can only be derived through some computation. The transformation in this case would compute the value based on the input from the source systems.

4. **Referential Integrity**—As data is brought over from the operational environment into the data warehouse, it is checked to verify that any data upon which it is dependent is already in existence within the warehouse or that it is part of the data being extracted. For example, when a car is sold to a customer, the transformation needs to make sure that the customer data exists within the data warehouse or that the required customer data is being brought over into the warehouse.

5. **Keys Translation**—Keys in the operational system are translated into the surrogate keys created by the data warehouse. This transformation will also take into consideration the method by which

the data warehouse architect has decided to handle slowly changing dimensions. The surrogate key does not overwrite the operational system's keys. Instead, it is brought over to the data warehouse. This is useful in handling slowly changing dimensions. It is also useful in determining whether a record represents new data or data that is being updated.

6. **Aggregations**—An optimum time to compute aggregates is while the data is being loaded into the data warehouse. Where it makes sense, aggregates can be computed in parts.

A number of ETL tools are available on the market. There are also a number of texts that describe a methodology for choosing the best ETL tool for your environment. Regardless of which tool you may choose, they all basically are trying to achieve the same goal—to map the source data to the target data. While I would not necessarily recommend that a data archeologist attempt to manage the extraction process manually, especially a large system, Figure B–2 provides a basic form for documenting a transformation process.

SOURCE		TRANSFORMATION	DESTINATION	
SYSTEM OR FILE	FIELD		TABLE	FIELD

Figure B–2 Transformation form.

The form is composed of a three columns: source, transformation, and destination. The source column identifies the system and field from which the data originates. The destination column describes table and field within that table. Note that the source column can have either the system name or the file name. The file name can be used when doing a flat file transfer. The transformation column describes in detail the transformation that must be performed on the data before it is brought into the data warehouse.

Metadata Standards

We have described business intelligence as a loop. Data extracted from the operational environment is cleansed and transformed prior to integration into a central repository. This is the data warehouse portion of the business intelligence loop. Decision support systems retrieve data from the warehouse for analysis by the business strategist. Based on this analysis, the strategist develops a strategic plan. The business intelligence loop is closed when the changes resulting from this new strategy are reflected in the operational system. This new data is extracted and the process begins again.

We review this structure to demonstrate a point. Business intelligence requires that many systems exchange data. In Figure C–1 we have presented the business intelligence loop, where each of the arrows represents an integration point. There are basically six points of data exchange:

1. The operational environment to extraction, transformation, and cleansing
2. Extraction, transformation, and cleansing to the central repository
3. The central repository to the decision support tools
4. Between the decision support tools
5. The decision support tool to the business strategist
6. The business strategist to the operational system

In reviewing this list, it may seem that the business strategist should not be included as a data exchange point. Actually, the strategist is the most significant point of data exchange.

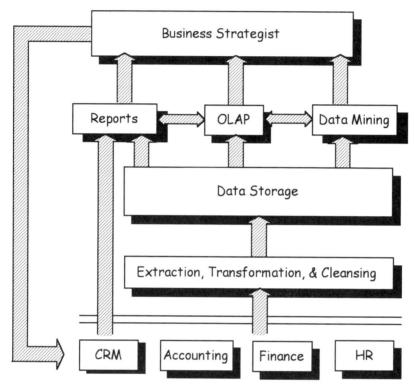

Figure C-1   Business Intelligence loop data exchange points.

At each point two types of data are exchanged. The first is the raw data—the actual pieces of information desired by the requesting system. The second is the metadata—the data that provides the context for the raw data. The metadata is critical to communication. It conveys the meaning of the data being transferred.

We have described metadata as data that transcends normal data. It is data that goes beyond the individual data items and provides the context in which the data exists. This context extends from the static or structural characteristics of the data to the dynamic or operational characteristics. These different types of metadata are described in Figure C–2. What is critical to the exchange of data is the static or structural data elements. As data moves from one process to the other, the process receiving the data must fully understand the format of the data, the domain of possible values, and the relationship between data elements. Critical to the business strategist's analysis are the business rules that govern the data. The business rules tell the strategist just what he or she is analyzing.

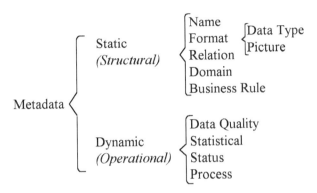

Figure C–2 Types of metadata.

Despite the importance of metadata to successful systems, we have seen many problems in compiling it throughout the construction of the warehouse. At times the metadata was incomplete or out of date. Invariably the metadata conflicted between the disparate operational systems. At other times the different departments within the organization would develop their own metadata which was inconsistent with that of other departments. All of these ailments, however, are symptoms of a much larger problem, which is the way in which we view metadata.

In the past, metadata was seen as some static entity buried in a catalog, virtually inaccessible to anyone outside the Information Technology department. This may have been sufficient; after all, most users didn't care about the metadata. System designers and engineers got all the metadata they needed by simply looking at the code. Forget the expense of the learning curve for any new programmer. Well, that was the past, when systems were information prisons and there was no exchange of data.

Today, the truly intelligent business sees information differently. We have discussed how the information infrastructure of an organization is like the central nervous system of an organism. It provides a medium of information exchange from one part of the organization to another. This dynamic integrated environment changes the way in which users interact with not just the data but the metadata as well. Users need to do more than simply browse static text, they must be able to collaborate across the organization to provide true knowledge and insight. This requires that the metadata be as integrated as the actual data. In addition to establishing a central repository, the information infrastructure must also include the interfaces to this repository.

A number of groups have proposed strategies for the exchange of metadata. These different proposals fall within two categories: integration or interchange. The interchange approach describes a standard by which different processes can exchange or share metadata. It establishes a standard format for the exchange of metadata but does not define the data to be contained within that format. The integration approach goes to a deeper level of detail and establishes a standard for both the structure and the content of the metadata.

The interchange technique has several difficulties. While establishing a syntax by which different processes may communicate is certainly a step in the right direction, it does not deal with the concepts represented in that syntax structure. When applications are independently developed, either within a single organization or as the result of purchases from separate companies, there will be basic differences. These differences will include variations in data types, calculations, or the presence or absence of certain structures. The democratic nature of the interchange technique is one of its greatest failings. As we have noted, each application and department will have its own version of metadata. The interchange method does nothing to remedy this problem. The specification of an exchange methodology does nothing to define who holds the ultimate version of the truth. The Metadata Coalition, founded in 1995, established a common standard for metadata interchange. This was delivered in 1996 as the Metadata Interchange Specification (MDIS). It failed, however, to gain much strength in the market.

An integration technique combines the concept of metadata interchange with that of a central metadata repository. It establishes common objects, object interpretations, APIs, and transactions by which processes access the central repository. Standard database operations provide metadata coherency, allowing the different processes to update the metadata at the same time. The Common Warehouse Metadata standard is currently being reviewed by the Object Management Group and employs an integration approach to metadata management.

The following subsections discuss two different standards that are competing to gain market attention. The first, the Open Information Model, was first promoted by Microsoft. This standard focuses on providing a common format for tools to share metadata. The second, the Common Warehouse Metadata (CWM) standard, tackles the issue of metadata integration.

C.1 The Open Information Model

The Open Information Model (OIM) has its origins in Microsoft and the Microsoft repository. The rights to maintain and evolve OIM were turned over to the Meta Data Coalition (MDC) in December of 1998. The MDC was founded in 1995 to establish a standard for the exchange of metadata. It is comprised of different vendors of enterprise and data management tools as well as producers of data warehousing products. In July 1999 the MDC accepted the OIM standard and integrated it with the Metadata Interchange Specification 1.0. The objective of MDC is to develop the OIM standard as an independent, vendor-neutral standard.

The focus of OIM is the exchange of metadata. The specification is composed of specifications for over 200 types and 100 relationships. These types and relationships are divided into different subject areas or models. Each model identifies a set of objects as well as the interface by which they are manipulated. Tools wishing to exchange data via the Open Information Model do so by manipulating the objects within each model. Object manipulation is carried out via the object's interfaces. Figure C–3 shows the inheritance structure of the OIM architecture. Note that Cde and Dbm inherit their structure from both the Gen and Dtm models.

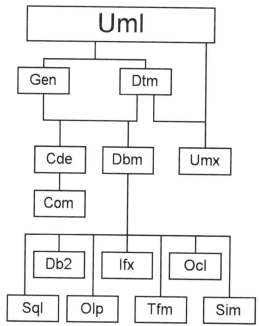

Figure C–3 Open Information Model architecture.

The following is a more detailed description of each model:

- **Uml—The Unified Modeling Language Model**

  The Uml is the parent model from which all others descend. From it, the base structure and properties of all models within this hierarchy are derived. Uml defines the metadata and how it will be displayed. Unification modeling does not address data exchange. Since tools will still make use of their own specific formats, the exchanged data will have to be converted. Rather than developing conversion utilities between each of the tools, a standard data exchange format is used.

- **Umx—Uml Extension Model**

  This model provides a set of generic extensions to the Uml model. It provides for stereotypes established in the conceptual level of the Unified Modeling Language.

- **Dtm—Data Type Model**

  The model specifies the interfaces for describing the data types. It also includes the implementation languages and databases.

- **Cde—Component Description Model**

  The Cde model establishes the interfaces and classes for the run-time components and their specifications.

- **Com—Component Object Model**

  The Com model provides a set of extensions specific to itself.

- **Gen—Generic Model**

  The generic model provides a set of general-purpose, or generic, interfaces for use across a variety of information models.

- **Dbm—Database Model**

  This model describes the enterprise's database schema information.

- **Sql—SQL Server Model**

  SQL-Server-specific extensions to the database model.

- **Ocl—Oracle Model**

  Oracle-specific extensions to the database model.

- **Db2—DB2 Model**

  Db2-specific extensions to the database model.

- **Ifx—Informix Model**

  Informix-specific extensions to the database model.

- **Tfm—Database Transformation Model**

  This model describes the movement of information between databases.

- **Olp—OLAP model**

  A extension to the database model that describes a multidimensional view of the data.

- **Sim—Semantic Information Model**

  Allows the user to interact with the data in the database without learning a language to query the database.

C.2 Common Warehouse Metadata

The Common Warehouse Metadata architecture takes a much different approach—an integrated approach. As we have discussed, the integration of the different information systems into one infrastructure places new demands on the management of metadata. Any new standard that attempts to establish an integrated approach to metadata management must allow users across the organization to collaborate on the creation and mainte- nance of the metadata. In addition to establishing a way to communicate metadata between the different tools within a BI infrastructure, CWM defines a central repository for the data. The Common Warehouse Metadata standard was initially proposed by IBM and Oracle. It is currently under review by the Object Management Group.

CWM keeps the metadata in a central repository that maintains the sin- gle authoritative version of the metadata. The repository controls access to the data and the coherency of the metadata between users. Users wishing to access the central data repository do so via a layered protocol. Each layer provides a different level of functionality. The following is a description of the layers shown in Figure C–4:

- **Value Added Services**

  The value added services layer allows users to extend the functionality of the CWM central metadata repository. Vendors wishing to leverage the CWM yet develop some differentiation can do so by extending CWM with value added services. Some services that can be included in this layer are query generation, configuration management, and/or ver- sion control.

- **Basic Services API**

  The basic services API provides tools and application developers with high-level object services such as object verification and archiving. This level also provides macros for functions such as the creation of default versions of dependent objects.

- **Persistence Layer**

  This layer acts as a firewall between the upper layers and the actual storage structures. It is through this layer that the objects within the central repository are accessed and manipulated. The methods found in the persistence layers are used to create, destroy, set, and get objects.

- **Object Model**

    This is the lowest layer of the model and is used to define the objects defined in the central metadata repository. The object model includes mappings of the objects to the relational data store.

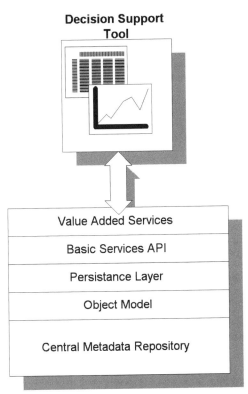

Figure C–4 CWM architecture.

The CWM data model is actually a set of integrated submodels, each having a specific focus. The base model is the data submodel, which is divided again to provide for the following areas of support:

- **Concrete Relational Model**

    The elements within the concrete relational model extend the data dictionaries of the underlying database to include information needed by the BI tools. The objects in this model, such as schemas, tables, columns, and keys, map directly to objects in the database.

- **Abstract Relational Model**

  The abstract relational model does just that: it abstracts the implementation details of the concrete relational model. The model is the point at which application developers can create simpler *views* into the concrete model.

- **Multidimensional Model**

  The purpose of the multidimensional model is to provide support for on-line analytical processing. OLAP tools, as we know, work in a multidimensional environment. The multidimensional model provides the mechanisms to support this view of the data. It creates a mapping between the multidimensional tool and the relational database to allow for the analysis of the relational data in multidimensional terms.

- **Application Model**

  The application model is used in the operation of the data warehouse. It can be used in such instances as the verification of transformation, ensuring that the transformation is not performed until all the dependent information is made available. This model also is used for the scheduling of feeds from external batch systems. This is useful when loading or refreshing the data warehouse.

As can be seen, the CWM addresses both issues facing the integration of metadata. CWM first provides the models by which users can access the data in the central repository. Second, it establishes a central metadata repository where there resides an ultimate single view of the truth.

Conventional Wisdom, Tips, Hints, and General Advice

Each step along the road to a successful business intelligence implementation can spring open the trap doors to pits from which your project may never emerge. One can imagine an Indiana Jones character carefully moving down some dusty, web-draped cavern littered with the carcasses and skeletons of those who had preceded him—a treacherous course where every step could be his last. This, with perhaps a touch of hyperbole, is the course upon which you—the data warehouse architect—are about to embark. It may be helpful to end with a road map, a bit of advice on how to avoid the obvious and at times not so obvious pitfalls.

1. **Find a Sponsorship Within the User Community**

   The selection of a project sponsor is critical to the success of the data warehouse. The sponsor is the medium through which the development team communicates with the user community. The sponsor is the user community's representative within the development group. The sponsor also serves as the data warehouse champion to the rest of the organization. He or she continually sells the project to management, assisting the development team in overcoming political and organizational obstacles. There are several important keys in finding the correct project sponsor:

- **Belief**—The project sponsor must have a strong belief in the data warehouse. Remember, the sponsor is the warehouse champion. A champion must believe in the cause for which he or she fights. A champion must be willing to take a position in the face of opposition. If the champion does not believe in the cause, he or she will be unable to take such a stance.

- **Respect**—The project sponsor must have respect within the organization. When the sponsor endorses the data warehouse, it should mean something. It should tell the rest of the organization that this is something important. The warehouse will become known as the sponsor's project. If the sponsor is respected, some of that respect will rub off on the warehouse. If the sponsor is seen as someone who chases every wild idea that comes up, the warehouse will be seen as another wild idea.

- **Cynical**—The sponsor should, to some extent, be cynical. In the heat of selling a project to management, development teams tend to paint grandiose scenes of idyllic environments. Often turning this vision into a reality is more daunting a task than they anticipate. The sponsor should be able to sort reality from *enthusiasm*. When something doesn't sound right, the sponsor should be ready to probe further.

- **Decisive**—The sponsor should have the authority and ability to make decisions. Design by committee will result in long and needless delays. Every time a decision has to be rubber-stamped by upper management because the sponsor is concerned with CYA, precious time is lost.

- **Communicative**—The sponsor is the principal medium of communication between the development team and the user community. He or she must have the skills to deliver the message.

2. **Set Your Users' Expectations**

   Users want what they think they were sold. In the heat of trying to sell the system the development team can promise more than they can deliver. It is far better to promise less and deliver more than to do the reverse. Speaking from actual experience, it is difficult not to promise more functionality. Often, in trying to help sell the system, a project manager will toss in some functionality that at first does not seem too difficult to implement. After all, it will only take a week or two of additional work. In the end that week or two turns into months.

The other challenge is that users are buying what they *think* they were sold. The development team may say one thing and the users may hear another. To whatever extent is practically possible, therefore, it is critical to document exactly what is being promised. In one system implementation the development team went so far as to create the individual screens for the user interface. The user was then able, before any code was written, to click each button and see exactly what functionality was going to be delivered. Today, many tools allow the developer to build and test the interface prior to actually developing the application.

3. **Think BEFORE You Speak**
   While this may seem obvious, it isn't. In trying to sell a project or defend the allocation of funds one could get carried away in the heat of the moment. I have been witness to some pretty ludicrous statements. How about: "With information systems like this it is a testimony to the IT department that anything is getting done." Another favorite: "No wonder management can't make informed decisions, look at the data they are given!" I like this one better than the first. The first statement only insults IT. The second takes a shot at both.

   It would be too personally embarrassing to mention who made such statements, but they do serve as an object lesson. It is far too easy to get caught up in the heat of the moment and make ridiculous statements. Think before you speak. If there is any way for anyone to take the statement in the wrong way, think of another way to say it.

4. **Be *User-Centric***
   The point of the data warehouse is to solve a user's problem, not to get your hands on some neat new technology. We have already

talked about not alienating the user, but we need to go further. We need to be the user's ally. Developing a system that is technically advanced, yet does little to solve the user's problem, does no one any good. The data warehouse is not like a general ledger system or a payroll system. Once one of these systems is implemented, the people in Accounting are stuck with it. They may complain, but they cannot choose to simply not use it. The decision support system, however, can be avoided. There is nothing that requires business strategists to use it. If the users are not incorporated into the team, if they feel that the system was not designed to meet their needs, that it was shoved down their throats, they will simply not use it. Even if the system is a technological masterpiece, it is a waste of resources if business strategists refuse to use it.

The shame of development teams that are not user-centric is that they are failing to make use of one of their greatest resources—the business strategist. Incorporating strategists into the process will tap into their creativity. No one understands their needs and desires better than they. Rather than resist their "mucking" with the system, embrace it. Ask them to provide input; ask them to be involved. The resulting system may not be the system you envisioned; in fact, it will NOT be the system you envisioned. It will, however, be the system they envisioned.

5. **Plan on Battles over Metadata**

The data warehouse is probably the first system in the organization to bring all the data from the different operational systems into one place. The data warehouse project, therefore, has the pleasure of resolving all the conflicting metadata. One department will define a deal as being completed when one event occurs, and another department will define it completely differently. In the context of their individual lines of business each will be correct. This is a job for the project sponsor. When a problem occurs, the sponsor needs to find a resolution. If an agreement between the parties cannot be reached, it may be appropriate to get a higher level of management involved to resolve the issue.

6. **Embrace Change**

   Nothing is static. Live with it. Even in a three- to four-month development cycle there will be change within the organization. Some of this change will affect the data warehouse in a minor way. Some will affect it in a major way. In either case, resistance is futile. When waves start to pound against you, you can do one of two things. If you stand firm and the waves are big enough, you will get thrown down. You'll end up with sand in your hair and starfish in your swimsuit. If you try to surf the waves, you'll probably get a pretty nice ride out of the deal. You might wipe out the first time or two, but eventually you'll get better at surfing. Sooner or later you'll spend more time riding the waves than being thrown around by them. Embrace change. Learn to use it as a force that will help you achieve your goals.

7. **Always Be Aware of the Differences with the Data Warehouse**

   In the first chapter of this book we discussed the differences between the data warehouse and the operational environment. As a data warehouse architect you must continually be aware of these differences. Everything from the user, who is the business strategist, down to the actual data stored within the system is different. This means that the approach in building the system is different. Users are not employees involved in the daily lines of production. The decision support system is a highly visible system. If developed properly, it will be a strategic tool for the highest levels of the organization. Keep the differences outlined in Chapter 1 in mind when building the data warehouse. More importantly, keep the ultimate objective in mind—building a system that will support management in making strategic decisions.

8. **Build for the Future**

   The development-spiral methodology outlined in this book is based on the concept that the data warehouse will grow. When building the data warehouse, keep an eye on the future. Remember, you are laying down a foundation upon which future iterations are going to build. This has a far-reaching effect on all aspects of the process. When defining a data structure consider how the structure will accommodate future needs. Decide how to manage the metadata. How well will the metadata management tool handle revisions of the metadata? What about the implementation platform? How will you grow capacity? The time horizon for your design has to extend beyond the delivery of the product. It has to look three or four revisions down the road.

9. **Resist Scope Creep**

Scope creep is a nefarious villain that will get you every time unless the project manager stringently guards against it. Scope creep is closely related to overselling the data warehouse. In the heat of selling the system the development team agrees to seemingly minor increases in the scope of the project. This problem does not end once the system is sold. It is easy during the development process to add a function here or a data element there, but beware. Agreeing to add just one little data element can have profound effects on the team's ability to deliver a product. That one little data element could open an entire debate on metadata or require the extraction of data from an entirely new data element.

While it is important to be user-centric, it is also important to maintain scope. It is difficult to refuse a user some functionality, especially when it seems to be something minor. The added functionality, however, once promised, becomes just as important as any other requirement, and failure to deliver that functionality is just as much a negative as not delivering on one of the original requirements. It is best to leave these additional requests to future iterations of the development spiral. First, deliver something, then worry about the optional requests.

10. **Think of New, More Efficient Ways to Deliver Information**

Don't be satisfied with delivering electronic versions of hardcopy reports. The proliferation of the Internet and a flood of tools to leverage it provides the development team with other avenues of information delivery. Take advantage of these. Rather than presenting rows and columns of numbers, think of ways to develop dashboards with graphic representations of data. Part of the user interface could include alerts to draw the user's attention to critical areas.

Be creative. Try to develop new ways for the business strategist to interact with the data. The more interesting the delivery of information, and the easier it is for users to interact with the system, the more likely they are to want to use it.

11. **Plan on ETL Consuming Most of Your Time**

It has been projected that ETL takes up the majority of the project—some have said as much as 80%. The challenge with ETL is metadata discovery. A team member (sometimes more than one), euphemistically referred to as the data archeologist, must search out the sources of the data along with the business rules around that data. The search for the metadata in and of itself is a daunting task. Often legacy systems lack documentation, or the documentation is out of date. Defining the correct metadata is a tedious and difficult process. Metadata conflicts also become known during this process, and the political battles around the data definition must be resolved.

12. **Expect Problems with the Source Data**

Source data is never clean. Don't expect it to be, regardless of how vehemently the IT department may vouch for it. The quality of data for the data warehouse is far higher than what is required for the operational environment. It is common for users to use dummy information to get past edit checks in the user interface. Test the quality of the source data.

13. **Expect to Find Holes in the Operational Systems**

The definition of the extraction process, as described earlier, works backward. The data warehouse architect first determines what data is needed by the business strategist and then maps the data back to the source systems. At times the architect may find that no operational system contains the data. In such cases the architect must find a source for the data. Perhaps data from an external source can provided the desired information, or the data warehouse itself can generate the new information. Sometimes data is simply not available, or the cost is too high to make it worthwhile; in such cases the data warehouse architect will have to do something that no system architect wants to do—say no.

14. **All Things Will Take the Time Allotted to Do Them**

As schedules are put in place, realize one cold hard fact of management. No matter how much time you leave to perform a task, it will always take at least that amount of time. If you allow two months for a task that really could be done in one, you are guaranteeing the task will take two. It is not uncommon for an architect to have three schedules. The first is shown to the development team; this is the most optimistic. The second is shown to management; this is the most pessimistic. The third is kept private; this is the most probable.

15. **Develop a New Security Philosophy**

Remember that when working with the data warehouse we are looking at aggregate data. Traditional security walls should be reconsidered. In a recent medical application doctors were concerned when a hospital developed a decision support system. The system analyzed the treatments and results of the different doctors. Naturally the physicians did not want their performance reviewed by their peers or anyone else who had access to the system. The problem was resolved when two different sets of reports were generated. One set was for the individual doctor and was accessible only by that doctor; the other consisted of only aggregate data. While management was able to view data at the detail level, average users were restricted to aggregate data. The result was an overall improvement in patient care. When physicians were able to review practices in terms of their efficacy, they were able to improve their practices.

16. **Don't Trade a Practical Solution for a Theoretical Stance**

In the end remember that this is not a holy war. There is what is theoretically correct and then there is what works. At times during the construction process you face conflicts between the *right* way of doing things and the way that will work. Doing things the right way is important. There are standards to which the data warehouse architect must ascribe, but in the face of practical realities the architect must deliver a working system. If, out of necessity, your design slightly violates a design principle, live with it and move on. I managed a development team back in the days of FORTRAN'77. Being a good structured software engineer, I forbade my crew to use GOTOs. I was very proud of the fact that I made no exceptions to this rule. While a good percentage of the time this was fine, I now realize the time I wasted making my team contort their code to meet some standard.

17. **Be Judicious in Selecting Data to Include within the Warehouse**

    One of the largest data warehouses I ever designed was large not out of necessity, but out of my own lack of experience. The first thing I did was to send out a list of all the data elements, asking the users to rate the data on a scale of one to ten. Anything above a seven would definitely be included in the system. Guess what? Everything was rated as a ten. Some thoughtful users rated a few items as nines and eights, but everything was considered by them as necessary.

    As described in the development spiral, find out what the business strategist is trying to discover. Include only the data needed to support those types of analysis. More data is more work and more risk. If the user requests that data be added to the warehouse to support new types of analysis, it can be added during future iterations of the development spiral. Include only the data necessary to support the currently required analyses.

18. **Leverage All Sources of Data**

    Once you have determined the data necessary to support an analysis, get data from whichever sources are available to support that analysis. Don't limit your vision of data sources to the transaction-oriented operational systems. Look for outside sources such as demographic data or spatial data that is hidden within the normal operational data. Think of linking document-imaging systems to the warehouse through degenerate dimensions.

19. **Create Clear and Concise Metadata**

It is imperative that the business strategist be able to interact with the data. To do this the strategist must understand what the data means, where it comes from, and what business rules govern it. The strategist cannot have this understanding without having metadata that is easy to understand. Metadata that is littered with technical jargon or provides conflicting definitions will be of little use. To create useful metadata:

- Be concise in your metadata.
- Use terminology familiar to the strategist rather than to the engineer.
- Reach consensus within the organization on the meaning of the data.

If strategists don't understand the data because of the metadata, they will not use the data warehouse. Worse yet, if strategists rely on the warehouse and misuse the data because of the metadata, they will be openly hostile to the data warehouse. In either case, the warehouse will not be used by the very people it was designed to help. The best tools, the cleanest data, the fastest database, and the greatest data structure will be wasted if strategists don't understand what all that data means.

20. **Benchmark, Benchmark, Benchmark**

The first question you have to ask is, what is good performance? When designing one decision support system, my development team was concerned that certain reports took anywhere from ten to fifteen minutes. The project sponsor, however, was ecstatic. "Right now it takes me three days to get that same data," he told me. "Do you really think that I would find fifteen minutes unacceptable?" It goes back to what we have said before: let your user needs drive the project. It was the engineers who were concerned with the performance, not the business strategist. What really matters is not what an engineer thinks of the data warehouse, but what the business strategist thinks.

Once you understand the performance requirements, benchmark. Don't trust standard benchmarks. No generic benchmark will give you a true reading of performance in your environment. The only way to understand how a certain implementation platform will behave in your environment is to test it.

21. **Watch the Amount of Supporting Data That Will Be Required**
    Your data warehouse will be much larger than the amount of data stored within it. There is also support data to be considered. This data will include indices and aggregate tables. If you are using RAID storage, you will have to deal with parity data. If you are using a multidimensional database, you will have to deal with sparsity issues. When sizing your system, consider all the disk space you will need—not just the raw data. Once you have this number, increase it; you will need the extra space.

22. **Clean the Data as It Goes into the Warehouse, Not on the Way Out**
    Make sure that the data within the data warehouse meets the standards of the data warehouse. Don't try to make up for poor data within the central repository by tweaking it as it is being delivered to the user.

23. **Leverage the Internet**
    The Internet is a massive shift in the compilation and delivery of information, not just within the information systems industry, but within all of society. Take advantage of this infrastructure. Develop ways to deliver data to the strategist via the Web. More than just the delivery of information, the Web also provides the data warehouse architect with ways of attaching to remote systems. Earlier we discussed how to leverage new sources of information. The Internet gives us access to those sources.

Glossary

Additive Facts   Facts that can be combined to form aggregates.

Analysis   A detailed methodological examination of the current user environment as well as the user needs expressed in the definition phase of the development spiral.

Analysis Model   Preliminary model in the design process. Identifies the objects within the analysis and their interaction with one another.

Analysis Space   Space defined by the dimensions of an analysis.

Analytical Data   Object attributes used to select objects or groups of objects for analysis. The domain of values for an analytical data element is finite.

Asymmetric Clustering   A clustering scheme in which each node in the cluster is involved in performing meaningful work.

Behaviors   The predictable response of an object in response to stimuli. Behaviors as they relate to software objects are the object's permitted actions.

BI   Business Intelligence.

Bitmapped Index-Joins A method of joining tables where a bit-mapped index is created for each foreign key in the fact table. These indices are then combined using a bitmap AND operation. The resultant bitmap index will point to the records that meet the selection criteria.

Bitmapped Indexing A method of indexing in which a stream of bits is created. Each bit in the stream corresponds to the physical record in the database. The bit is turned on or off based on whether the record passes or fails some boolean test.

Business Intelligence Thinking abstractly about an organization, reasoning about the business, organizing large quantities of information about the business in order to define and execute a strategy.

Business Strategist The primary data warehouse user. Responsible for defining strategy for the organization or some subset of the organization.

Central Metadata Repository Contains the EDM. The central metadata repository is accessible to the entire organization and contains all the metadata for the organization.

Central Repository Storage for the data, metadata, and master data within the warehouse.

Clustering Also known as a *shared disk architecture*. Nodes in this architecture have exclusive ownership of local memory but share disks with one another.

Conforming Dimensions A dimension that is common to two or more analysis spaces. The values of the dimension are sufficient to bind both spaces. In a star schema a conforming dimension is joined to multiple fact tables, allowing the business strategist to traverse the structure from one fact table to another.

Constellation A schema containing multiple stars joined together by conforming dimensions.

Coordinate System   The set of related dimensions emanating from a point of origin.

Counts   A type of measure employed in the data warehouse. Counts provide a count of a particular object.

Data Administrator   Team member responsible for the quality of the data in the data warehouse. The data administrator reviews the extraction log for metadata changes, inaccurate data, or data errors.

Data Cleansing   The portion of the data integration process that removes errors from the data being loaded into the data warehouse from the operational environment.

Data Cube   Three-dimensional object composed of columns and rows of cells. The edges of the cube are the dimensions of the analysis space.

Data Extraction   The process of extracting data from the operational environment and loading it into the data warehouse. Data can be pulled from the operational environment where the warehouse proactively retrieves the required data, or pushed from the operational system, where the warehouse passively receives data.

Data Integration   The process of taking data from the operational environment and consolidating it into the central data repository. The three-step data integration process consists of data extraction, data transformation, and data cleansing.

Data Mart   A data warehouse whose scope is limited to a single subject area, such as a department. Data marts come in two flavors. Dependent data marts receive their data from the enterprise data warehouse. Independent data marts receive data directly from the operational environment.

Data Mining   The discovery of the information hidden within the data.

Data Transformation   The process of converting data from many disparate systems into one standard format.

Data Warehouse "A subject oriented, integrated, nonvolatile, time variant collection of data in support of management's decisions."[1]

Decision Support Systems The presentation of data to support management in making decisions.

Definition The phase of the development spiral in which the objective of the project is established. The output of this phase is the mission statement which is a collaboration between the project sponsor and the data warehouse architect.

Degenerate Dimensions Dimensions whose single attribute is stored within the fact table.

Degenerate Facts Measures stored within the intersection table of dimensions that have a many-to-many relationship with the fact table.

Design The process of developing a detailed implementation model from which databases may be constructed and software written. The design phase is an iterative process that begins with a high-level conceptual design and is refined with each iteration.

Detailed Design Model The last model to be developed by the system architect prior to system development. The detailed design model provides all the information necessary for the system engineers to begin work. It takes into consideration all aspects of the actual implementation requirements.

Development The phase of the development spiral that transforms the detailed design model into an actual system. In this phase that database is constructed and software is written and tested.

---

1.   W. H. Inmon, *op. cit.*

Development Spiral   An iterative object-oriented software engineering methodology. Each iteration of the development spiral expands the scope of the functionality of the system. Initial iterations provide limited business functions to the end user in order to lay the infrastructure upon which future iterations will be based.

Dicing   A constriction of the analysis space across multiple dimensions. Dicing selects a subset of the data to form another, smaller space.

Dimension   The axes of a coordinate system that bind the space defined by that coordinate system. In an analysis space the dimensions are the objects of the analysis.

Drill-Across   Traversal of a constellation from one fact table to another via a conforming dimension.

Drill-Down   Presentation of the data at a deeper level of detail.

DSS   Decision Support System.

Dynamic Metadata   Metadata that primarily reflects the overall state of the system. Dynamic metadata is in a constant state of change. Dynamic metadata describes the data quality, usage, and status.

Enterprise Data Model (EDM)   A data model whose scope encompasses the entire organization. The Enterprise Data Model receives metadata from all systems within all departments in the organization, combining it into one cohesive model.

Evaluation   The final phase of the development spiral, in which the delivered product is examined and assessed as to how well it meets user requirements. The evaluation phase also takes into consideration the development process. The result of the evaluation phase is most critical to the development team. It provides them with a means to improve future iterations of the development spiral.

Extraction Log A record of the status of the extraction process. The extraction log records any exceptions to the extraction process. This log serves as input to the data administrator to verify the quality of the data loaded into the warehouse.

Extraction Store Temporary storage of operational data as it undergoes transformation and cleansing.

Factless Fact Table Fact tables that do not contain any measures. The existence of a relationship between the dimensions is significant in and of itself.

Granularity The level of detailed captured by the data warehouse. Granularity can be at the transaction level or rolled-up to a higher level.

Hash Partitioning A partitioning scheme in which records are distributed across the database partitions based on a hashing algorithm. Data is distributed evenly across the partitions, preventing data skewing.

Hybrid Partitioning A two-level partitioning scheme that combines hash and range partitioning.

Hypercube An object of four dimensions or more composed of columns and rows of cells. The edges of the cube are the dimensions of the analysis space.

Implementation The phase of the development spiral in which the product is delivered to the users. This phase is also referred to as roll-out.

Index-Joins A technique that joins tables via their indices by creating an ordered set of columns.

Interquery Parallelism The concurrent execution of multiple queries against a single database.

Intersection Table An intermediate table used to link two tables in a many-to-many relationship. Each record in the intersection table has a unique combination of the foreign keys of the tables it is linking, creating a many-to-one relationship between the intersection table and each of the linked tables.

Interval Scale A scale with equal distance between ordered units. The origin of an interval scale is non-zero.

Intraquery Parallelism The division of a single query into multiple subqueries that are executed concurrently.

Maintenance This phase corrects any problems that are encountered in the use of the product. It continues for the life of the system.

Massively Parallel Processing Architecture Also known as *shared nothing architectures*, where each node in the system has exclusive ownership of local resources.

Measure The facts of the fact table. Measures describe some attribute of the relationship or action between the dimensions of the analysis space.

Metadata Metadata describes, or provides a context for, the data. Metadata transcends data in the sense that it goes beyond it and provides a description of what exists around the data. Metadata also describes the business rules of the data, in essence the use of it within the organization.

Mission Statement Defines the overall objective, or mission, to be achieved by the project in a simple single statement. The mission statement provides the foundation for establishing the scope of the project.

Model An abstraction of reality. A model of an object is something with which an analyst works when the actual object cannot easily be manipulated or modified.

Multidimensional A space or database that exists in more than one dimension.

Nominal Scale Labels of objects within a set. A nominal scale does not provide an ordering between the labels.

Nonanalytical Data   Data elements included in the dimension for reporting purposes but contain little analytical value. Their domain of values is not necessarily finite and they cannot be used to create groups of objects.

Nonadditive Facts   Facts that cannot be added together into aggregates.

Nonvolatile Data   Data that remains unchanged. Once the data is written into the data warehouse it is not updated as long as it is within the warehouse.

NUMA Architecture   Nonuniform Memory Access architectures which are composed of multiple nodes sharing memory and disks. Memory in each of the nodes is combined into a single global memory.

Object   Discrete entities that are either tangible or intangible. Objects can be atomic entities that cannot be decomposed into lesser objects. Objects are also aggregations, which are combinations of other objects to form a new object.

Object Aggregation   Object aggregation should not be confused with aggregation of data. Object aggregation combines objects to form a new object. For example; a disk drive, memory, terminal, motherboard, CPU, and keyboard are combined to make a computer. The computer is an aggregation.

Object Class   A grouping of objects based on a set of common attributes and behaviors.

Object Superclass   An object classification that contains classes of objects.

Object-Oriented Analysis   A methodology that views the environment in terms of objects and their associated behaviors.

Object-Oriented Design   The expression of a system design in terms of objects and their behaviors.

OLAP   On-Line Analytical Processing.

On-Line Analytical Processing   The interactive access and display of data in multiple dimensions.

Operational Environment   The systems that support day-to-day functions. These are typically transaction-oriented tactical systems. The functioning of these systems usually entails the automation of some manual process.

Ordinal Scale   The ordering of objects based on some criterion.

Point of Origin   The point at which all axes of a coordinate system meet. The value of all dimensions in the coordinate system at this point is 0.

Precision   The number of significant digits within a measure.

Range Partitioning   Partitioning of the database where records are placed into each of the separate partitions based on a range of values.

Rank   The placing of objects in a hierarchical structure such as an organization chart.

Ratio   A scale with equal distance between ordered units and having an origin of zero.

Roll-up   The presentation of data at a higher level of detail.

Semiadditive Facts   Facts that must be broken down to their additive components to form aggregates.

Shadow Dimension   A separate table of nonanalytical data linked to a dimension table in a one-to-one relationship.

Shared Disk Architecture   Also known as clustering. Nodes in this architecture have exclusive ownership of local memory but share disks with one another.

Slicing   A constriction of the analysis space to include only a subset of the data. Slicing can occur along any of the dimensions.

Slowly Changing Dimension   A dimension whose object attributes change infrequently over time.

SMP   See *Symmetric Multiprocessing*.

Snowflake   A star schema whose dimension tables have been normalized.

Static Metadata   Data that describes data elements. Static data changes less frequently than dynamic metadata and is relatively stable. In addition to describing the format and domain of the data, static metadata also describes the business rules that govern the data elements.

Subject Orientation   The structure of the data that groups the information pertaining to a specific subject. Subjects include such things as products, customers, competitors, or employees.

Summary Redirection   An optimization technique in which queries are rewritten by the DBMS to query against aggregate tables. Query redirection should be invisible to the user.

Surrogate Keys   Keys generated by the data warehouse, used in place of keys from the operational environment. Also known as synthetic keys.

Symmetric Clustering   A clustering scheme in which one node in a cluster stands by as a hot backup waiting for the primary node in the cluster to fail.

Symmetric Multiprocessing Architectures   Architectures in which all local resources are equally shared by all processors in the system. All system components reside on a single system bus.

Synthetic Keys   Keys generated by the data warehouse. Also known as surrogate keys.

Time Variant   Allowing the time variable to be manipulated by the business strategist.

Waterfall Development   A methodology that focuses on establishing a set of formally accepted system requirements which are frozen during the development process. The waterfall development methodology is composed of the requirements-specification, analysis, design, implementation, unit-test, acceptance-test, and roll-out phases.

Index

A

abstract class, 102
abstract relational model, 314
acceptance testing, 36
acceptance-test phase, 59
additive facts, 215, 231, 232
    definition of, 231, 232, 327, 334
aggregates, 147, 221, 322
    calculating, 173
aggregating data, 293
aggregation, 51, 58, 140, 141, 143, 190, 196,
    234, 243, 271, 272, 297, 303
    between objects, 51
    operator, 101
    performed in a multidimensional data-
      base, 142
analysis, definition of, 56
analysis model, 61, 62, 92, 94, 98, 107, 124,
    127
    case study of, 98
    creating a narrative describing one, 94
    definition of, 124, 327
    demonstration of, 93
    documenting findings in, 67
    used by data warehouse architect, 100
analysis phase, 56, 59, 124
    details of, 67
    output of analysis model, 62
analysis space, 130, 143, 145, 146, 155, 158,
    167, 227, 285
    and geographic properties, 285

    and shadow dimension, 177
    and time, 179
    definition of, 155, 327
    incorrect, 227
    measuring interactions between objects
      in, 209
    objects outside of, 166
    points within, 158
analysis space coordinates, 159
analytical data,
    definition of, 203, 327
    in a property table, 196
analytical data elements, 159
    used to group objects, 159
    values of, 159
anonymous keys, 148
application logs, 298
application model, 314
    and verification of transformation, 314
ArcView GIS, 291–292
ArcView Network Analyst, 292
asymmetric clustering, 248, 278, 280, 282
    definition of, 282, 327
    in data warehouse construction, 280
attribute, 52, 105, 112, 146, 150, 177
    analytical,182
    difference from fact, 209
    nonanalytical, 182
    normalizing, 151
    of an object, 159
    represented graphically, 101

B

Banyan network, 254
base model, 313
basic services API, 312
beer and diapers, 290
behaviors, 5, 12, 30, 51– 52, 54, 56, 100, 105, 271, 285
    and stimuli, 241
    attributes of, 205
    between objects, 51
    definition of, 56, 327
    of objects, 205, 285
    passed down to each subclass, 103
    predicting, 181
    represented graphically, 101
BI, 1, 2, 30–31
    definition of, 31, 327
bitmapped index, 266, 271, 279
    when appropriate, 266
bitmapped indexing, 209, 265–268, 280, 282, 299
    definition of, 282, 328
    in data warehouse construction, 280
bitmapped index-joins,
    definition of, 282, 328
    in data warehouse construction, 280
broker dimension, 182
browser, 276, 277
bus bandwidth, 247
Business Intelligence, 1, 2, 5, 30, 31, 305, 327
    definition of, 30, 328
    sustainable competitive advantage, 2
Business Intelligence loop, 1, 8, 305
business nouns, examples of, 5
business strategist, 4, 31
    definition of, 31, 328
business unit, 185

C

cache-coherent SMP system, 247
cartesian-product, 270

Cde, 309, 311
census block, 288, 293
central data repository, 298
central metadata repository, 45, 56, 309
    and the object model, 313
    definition of, 56, 328
central nervous system, of an organization, 6
central repository, 1, 8, 11, 19, 31, 241, 243, 278, 305, 309
    and CWM, 314
    definition of, 31, 328
    role in the flow of data, 11
cerebral cortex, in organizational evolution, 6, 7
CGI, 276
classification, of objects, 51
cleansing, 14–16, 243–244, 305
    definition of, 10
    of data, 1
client, 275, 277
    dimension, 185
    system, 276
client/server, 275, 277
cluster, 278
    and parallel queries, 264
clustered system, 248
clustering, 280, 282, 283, 327, 336
    definition of, 282, 328
collision problem, when loading data, 245
Com, 311
Common Gateway Interface, 276
common objects, 309
Common Warehouse Metadata, 309, 312
Common Warehouse Metadata architecture, 311
Component Description Model, 311
Component Object Model, 311
conceptual design, 57
concrete relational model, 313
conforming dimensions, 166–169, 203, 225
    consistent between two stars, 169
    definition of, 203, 328

conic projection, 287
constellation, 168, 203, 216, 222, 228
    and conforming dimensions, 166
    concept of, 228
    definition of, 203, 328
    with conforming dimensions, 168
coordinate system, 128, 158, 205
    definition of, 155, 329
cost-based optimization, in data warehouse
    construction, 280
count measure, and additive values, 215
counts, definition of, 231, 329
CPUs, 246, 247, 252
currency, of the data, 297
CWM, 309, 313, 314
    and central repository, 312
CWM architecture, represented graphically,
    313

D

dashboard, 140
data,
    cleansed, 1
    demographic, 10
    distribution, 254
    skewing, 261
    transformed, 1
data administrator, 10,11, 15, 16, 31–32, 47
    definition of, 31, 329
    interaction with metadata repository, 47
data archeologist, 300, 301, 303, 321
data cleansing, 14, 15, 31, 296, 329
    definition of, 31, 329
data cube, 134, 136, 137, 140, 142, 209
    definition of, 155, 329
    sparse, 145
data dictionaries, 313
data exchange, 305
data exchange point, 306
data extraction, 242, 245
    definition of, 31, 329
data integration process, 10, 14, 31

data cleansing, 31
data extraction, 31
data transformation, 31
    definition of, 31, 329
data mart, 1, 2, 9, 11, 31, 38, 41, 169–170,
    233, 329
    definition of, 31, 329
    independent, 9
    role in the flow of data, 9
data mining, 1, 21, 25–28, 31, 242
    classification, 26
    classification vs. estimation process, 26
    definition of, 31, 329
    estimation, 26
data model, 95
data skewing, 262, 282
data submodel, 313
data summaries, 25
data transformation, 10, 14, 16, 31, 302, 329
    definition of, 31, 329
    role in the flow of data, 10
Data Type Model, 311
data warehouse, 1, 2, 3, 5, 7, 8, 9, 10, 11, 12,
    14, 15, 16, 17, 18, 19, 20, 21, 22, 23,
    26, 30, 31, 32, 328, 329
    and types of data mining, 26
    definition of, 32, 330
    difference from a data mart, 9
    Web-enabled, 275, 277
data warehouse architect, 56
database, multidimensional, 1, 11
database administrator, 10
database comparison, 297
database logs, 298
Database Model, 311
database partition, 262
Database Transformation Model, 311
Db2, 311
DB2 Model, 311
Dbm, 309, 311
decision support system, 1, 21, 32, 35, 68,
    276, 305

decision support system (*cont'd*)
    definition of, 32, 330
    objective of, 205
    requirements, 37
decision tree, 27
definition, definition of, 56, 330
definition phase, 157
    case study of, 64
    details of, 62
degenerate dimension, 218, 222, 231
    definition of, 231, 330
degenerate facts, 218, 231
    definition of, 231, 330
delta file, 298
demographic, 286, 290, 323
demographic data, 10, 301
demographics, 26
denormalization, of attributes, 151
denormalization process, 109
denormalized, 177
    subject-oriented decision support
        system, 108
dependent data mart, 31
    and conforming dimensions, 169
    role in the flow of data, 11
design,
    definition of, 57, 330
    of a system, 36
design model, 61, 127
design phase, 57, 59, 124, 220
    creates implementation model, 99
    creates object model, 99
    details of, 99
    output of the object model, 62
detailed design model, 57
    definition of, 57, 330
development, definition of, 57, 330
development spiral, 319, 323, 35, 36, 38, 53,
      97
    advantages of, 41
    analysis phase, 40, 61

and implementation considerations, 233
definition of, 57, 331
definition phase, 40, 61, 62
design phase, 40
development phase, 40
evaluation phase, 40
first three phases of, 61, 124
graphic of, 39
implementation phase, 40
maintenance phase, 40
using to modify the model, 104
dicing, 208, 156, 209
    definition of, 156, 331
dimension, definition of, 156, 331
dimension tables, 157–204
    single-dimensioned, 205
dimensionality, 128
    and information systems, 131
Distributed Memory Architecture, 252
Distributed Shared Memory, 250
DM, 252, 253
document-imaging system, 218
drill-across, 168, 232
    definition of, 204, 232, 331
drill-down, 25, 142, 173, 177, 213, 242
    definition of, 156, 331
DSM, 250
DSS, 1, 2, 3, 7, 21, 22, 32, 88, 222, 278, 331
    definition of, 32, 331
    reports-based, 22
    See also Decision Support System
DSS tools, finding patterns with, 7
DSS-type tools, 80
Dtm, 309, 311
dynamic metadata, 331
    definition of, 57, 331

E

EDM, 47, 48, 49, 56, 57
    definition of, 57, 331
enterprise data model, 47, 48, 57

and the central metadata repository, 47

    definition of, 57, 331

    graphic representation of, 48

Environmental Systems Research Institute
        Inc., 291

ESRI, 291

ETL, 295, 321

ETL process, 295

ETL strategy, 295, 296, 297, 300

ETL tools, 303

evaluation, definition of, 57, 331

Excel, 82

exchange methodology, 308

external source data, role in the flow of data,
    10

extracted data, 295

extraction, 21, 32, 297, 305

    of data, 1

    role in the flow of data, 10

extraction log, 10, 11, 15, 31, 32, 44, 47, 297,
    329

    definition of, 32, 332

    role in the flow of data, 10

extraction process, 298, 299, 300, 303, 321

extraction store, 10, 32

    definition of, 32, 332

    role in the flow of data, 10

F

fact tables, 150, 206–216

factless fact records, 216

factless fact table, 216, 217, 232

    definition of, 232, 332

facts,

    additive, 215

    nonadditive, 215

    semiadditive, 215

fiber channel storage, 259

fiber systems, 259

fiscal periods, 179

foreign key, 150, 186, 218, 229

format, 296

    of data, 18, 296

full-fiber, 259

G

Gen, 309, 311

Generic Model, 311

genetic modeling, 29

geographic areas, 289

geographic properties, 285

geographic relationship, 291

Gestalt, 8

grain, 213

granularity, 213, 232, 297

    affecting star schema, 214

    definition of, 232, 332

    level of, 213

grouping, of records, 243

H

HA, 248

hash algorithm, 261

hash partitioning, 261, 282

    definition of, 282, 332

    in data warehouse construction, 282

hashed, subpartition, 279

health care, 291

hemodialysis, 291

heterogeneous fact tables, 219

hierarchical databases, 296

hierarchies, 185, 190

    changes in, 176

    within organizations, 175

    within the star schema, 173

hierarchy keys, 173

high availability, 248

HTML, 276

hybrid partitioning, 262

    definition of, 332

    in data warehouse construction, 282

hypercube, 134, 136, 147, 150, 209

    and possible views, 138

hypercube (*cont'd*)
   definition of, 156, 332
   determining size, 143

I

Ifx, 311
implementation, definition of, 58, 332
implementation considerations, 233–283
implementation model, 56, 62, 124, 127, 157,
   167, 182, 278
   and time dimension, 182
   creates dimension tables, 153
   multidimensional structure, 127
   varying from the object model, 181
implementation phase, 59
independent data mart, 31
index-joins, 270
   definition of, 283, 332
   in data warehouse construction, 280
information infrastructure, 30, 308
Informix Model, 311
instances,
   difference from objects, 53
   that compose the analysis, 159
integrated, 32, 241
integrated collection of data, 30
integration, 16, 243, 305
integration point, 305
integration process, 15
Internet, 275, 325
   and delivering data, 320
   data warehouse, 278
interquery parallelism, 243, 264
   definition of, 283, 332
   in data warehouse construction, 280
interrupt driven, 3
intersection table, 172, 182, 204, 217
   and degenerate facts, 218
   attributes of, 185
   definition of, 204, 332
interval scale, 210, 232

   definition of, 232, 333
interval scale encoding, 17
intraquery parallelism, 243
   definition of, 283, 333
   in data warehouse construction, 280

J

JBOD, 259

K

Keys Translation, 302

L

LAN, 248
   redundant, 248
limbic system, in organizational evolution, 7
line, 287
line segment, 287
locality of data, 252
Lotus 1-2-3, 82

M

maintenance, definition of, 58, 333
many-to-many relationships, 172, 218, 221
map, 286, 287
market-basket analysis, 290
Massively Parallel Processing, 246, 252
   definition of, 283
Massively Parallel Processing Architecture,
   definition of, 333
MDC, 309
MDIS, 308
measure, 209, 232
   definition of, 232, 333
Mercator projection, 287
metadata, 10, 11, 15, 31, 32, 42–46, 55–58, 297,
   306, 307, 308, 320, 321, 324, 328
   definition of, 32, 58, 333
   dynamic, 44
   impact on design of data warehouse, 36
   integration, 308

interchange, 308, 309

management, 309

static, 43

types of, 43

what is, 42

Metadata Coalition, 308–309

Metadata Interchange Specification, 308, 309

metadata repository, 11, 45

interactions with, 46

Microsoft, 309

mission statement, 4, 58, 62, 66, 68, 70, 104, 124, 125

defining objects in the data warehouse, 66

definition of, 58, 125, 333

describing project's scope, 157

in definition phase, 63

samples of, 63

model, definition of, 125, 333

MOLAP, 23

MPP, 252

and parallel queries, 264

MPP architecture support, in data warehouse construction, 282

multidimensional, 109, 205, 227

database issues, 133, 143

definition of, 156, 333

star schema, 127

storage structure, 262

multidimensional analysis, 56

multidimensional database, 23, 128, 325

benefit of, 138

multidimensional model, 314

Multidimensional On-Line Analytical Processing, 23

multidimensional tools, spreadsheet, 132

multidimensionality, 128

multiple dimensions, working in, 137

multiprocessing system, 29

multistage network, 254

N

neural network, 28

axons, 28

dendrite, 29

dendritic tree, 28

neuron, 28

nominal, 196

nominal scale, 210, 232

definition of, 232, 333

encoding, 17

nonadditive facts, 215

nonanalytical attributes, 164

nonanalytical data, 176, 177, 178

changes in, 185

definition of, 204, 334

in a property table, 196

nonanalytical data elements, 160

nonanalytical data space, 160

Nonuniform Memory Access, 246, 250

nonvolatile collection of data, 30

nonvolatile data, 12, 18, 32, 160, 241, 285

definition of, 32, 334

nonvolatility, of the data warehouse, 19

normalization, 12, 134, 174, 269

normalized, transaction processing database, 108

NUMA, 250, 252

and parallel queries, 264

NUMA architecture, definition of, 283, 334

NUMA architecture support, in data warehouse construction, 282

O

object, 54, 56

and maps, 286

and the persistence layer, 312

classes and superclasses, 50

definition of, 58, 334

difference from an instance, 53

in a concrete relational model, 313

object (*cont'd*)

 in an analysis model, 93

 in the development spiral, 35

 inherit behaviors from a superclass, 103

 must relate to an instance, 102

 objective of, 49

 relationships between, 104, 208

 using a model to represent, 61

 using to organize design, 62

 within a dimension table, 177

object aggregation, definition of, 58, 334

object class, 50, 58

 defining a dimension, 158

 definition of, 58, 334

object interpretations, 309

Object Management Group, 309

object model, 52, 53, 55, 99, 102, 103–109, 157, 226, 313

 as basis for implementation model, 62

 as influenced by the business strategist's requirements, 107

 complete, 100

 lists the object attributes, 105

object modeling, 51

 advantages of, 53

object orientation, 35, 53

object superclass, 58

 definition of, 334

object-oriented analysis, 55, 133

 definition of, 58, 334

object-oriented approach, 53, 100, 233

object-oriented design, definition of, 58, 334

object-oriented methodology, 56

Ocl, 311

OIM, 309

OLAP, 1, 21, 23, 24, 25, 32, 242

 and the rotation of data, 25

 definition of, 32, 334

 See also On-Line Analytical Processing

OLAP model, 311

Olp, 311

OLTP, 255, 269, 298

On-Line Analytical Processing, 1, 21, 23, 32, 242, 334

 definition of, 32, 335

one-to-many relationship, 172

Open Information Model, 309

operational environment, 1, 2, 8–9, 15, 30–32, 35, 222, 243, 295, 296, 299

 and parallelism, 264

 changes in keys in, 206

 cleansing and transforming of, 305

 definition of, 32, 335

operational keys, 206

operational system, 300

Oracle Model, 311

ordinal scale, 210

 definition of, 232, 335

ordinal scale encoding, 17

P

parallel, databases, 263

parallel performance line, 239

parallel processing, 235

parallel processing system, 29

parallelepiped, 136

parallelism, 235, 245, 246, 255

 and data storage, 255

 and RAID, 255

 and second dimension, 260

 bottlenecks to, 264

 depth of, 238

 limit in degree of, 236

 perils of, 235

 rules of, 240

partition, 260

 hash, 260

 hybrid, 260

 multiple, 262

 range, 260

partition key, 262

 and hashing algorithm, 261

partitioning, a fact table, 279
Pentium, 80, 81
persistence layer, 312
pivoting, a data cube, 137
point, 287
    absolute, 288
point of origin, definition of, 156, 335
point-of-sale systems, 243
polygon, 288, 292, 293
PowerPoint, 82
preaggregated, elements, 234
preaggregation, 242
precision,
    definition of, 232, 335
    difference from correctness, 212
    in digits, 211
precisions, working with different ones, 212
primary keys, 148, 150, 163, 196, 206–207,
        221, 229
primary node, 248
product sponsor, 77
project, scope of, 157
project sponsor, 56
    and belief in the data, 316
    and respect within the organization, 316
    dialog with data warehouse, 68
    finding one, 315
    lacking support within the user
        community, 69
    objective of interviewing, 70
    questions to ask, 70
    role of, 63
projections, 287
property dimension, 196

Q

query redirection, 273

R

RAID, 255, 256, 259, 260, 325
    combining with partitioning, 262
    storage, 255
RAID 0/1, 257
RAID 3, 257, 279
RAID 5, 257
range partitioning, 260, 279, 280, 283
    definition of, 283, 335
    in data warehouse construction, 280
rank, definition of, 232, 335
ratio, 211, 232
    definition of, 232, 335
ratio scale, 211
ratio scale encoding, 17
read-ahead, 259
record versioning, 190
    to track changes, 190
recursive table, 176
Redundant Array of Inexpensive Disk, 255
relational data store, 313
Relational On-Line Analytical Processing, 23
reporting, 22
reptilian brain, in organizational evolution, 6
requirements specification, 36
requirements-specification phase, 59
retail, 289
retrieval, 243
ROLAP, 23
roll-out phase, 59
roll-up, 25, 142, 242
    definition of, 156, 335
rotating, a data cube, 137
rotation, 25
rules-based optimization, in data warehouse
        construction, 280

S

scales, 210
    count, 211
    interval, 210
    nominal, 210
    ordinal, 210
    rankings, 211
    ratio, 210

schemas, 56
scope, of project, 157
scrubbing, 10
SCSI, 259
SCSI buses, 258
Semantic Information Model, 311
semiadditive facts, 215
    definition of, 232, 335
sequential, vs. parallel processing, 236
server process, 275
shadow dimension, 177, 178, 182, 204, 218
    definition of, 204, 335
shared disk architecture, 246, 248, 282
    definition of, 283, 335
shared disk architecture support, in data
    warehouse construction, 280
Sim, 311
slice, 208
    of space, 139
slicing, 138–140, 142, 156, 208
    data, 139, 153
    definition of, 156, 335
slowly changing dimension, 160, 163, 164,
    185, 207, 303
    definition of, 204, 336
SMP, 246, 247, 248, 253, 254, 263
    advantages, 252
    and parallel queries, 264
    definition of, 283, 336
SMP support, in data warehouse
    construction, 280
snapshot, 297, 298
snowflake, 170–171
    approach, 185
    appropriateness of, 172
    definition of, 204, 336
snowflaking, the warehouse schema, 170
source system, 297, 298, 302
sparcity, 145, 152
sparse data, 145
spatial, 285, 286, 288, 323
spatial data, 286, 290

within a decision support environment,
    289
spatial data element, 288
Sql, 311
SQL Server Model, 311
St. Peter Hospital, 291–292
star query optimization, 269, 271
    in data warehouse construction, 280
star schema, 99, 109, 124, 127, 128, 148, 157,
    171, 178, 225
    affected by granularity, 214
    and index-join, 270
    and snowflakes, 170
    and the fact table, 150
    as related to the data cube, 206
    creating from an object model, 181
    dimensionality, 149
    methods of optimization, 269
    nucleus of, 205, 206, 207
    slicing and dicing, 209
    standard in, 177
    structure of, 147
    using to slice or dice information, 208
    working with, 152
static metadata, 44, 58, 336
    definition of, 58, 336
storage subsystem, 259
structured analysis, 53
subclasses, 52, 93, 146, 219
    represented graphically, 101
subject, 54
subject orientation, 12, 33
    definition of, 33, 336
subject-oriented, 32
subject-oriented collection of data, 30
subject-oriented data, 285
subject-oriented database, 54, 56
subpartition, hashed, 262
summary, 271
    join-back, 273, 274
    maintenance, 272

management, 272
roll-up, 273, 274
unexpected, 272
summary redirection, 234, 280, 283
definition of, 283, 336
in data warehouse construction, 280
summary table, 271, 272, 273, 274, 279
summary table recommendation, in data
warehouse construction, 280
superclasses, 51–52, 93, 102, 146, 219
as dimensions of an implementation
model, 181
difference from classes, 101
represented graphically, 101
surrogate keys, 156, 206, 302
definition of, 156, 336
symmetric clustering, 283, 248
definition of, 283, 336
symmetric multiprocessing, 246
symmetric multiprocessing architectures,
definition of, 283, 336
synthetic keys, 156
definition of, 156, 336
system bus, saturation of, 250
system requirements, 37
system-generated keys, 148

T

table partitioning, 260
Tfm, 311
thin client, 80
time, 179
as an interval scale, 210
as an object, 179
time coordinate, 208
time dimension, 196
time stamping, 299
time-based extraction, 299
time-variant, 19, 23, 32–33, 179, 196, 241

collection of data, 30
definition of, 33, 336
time-variant data, 285
top-down, 235
transformation, 14, 16, 17, 18, 206, 243, 296,
297, 305
of data, 1
transformation process, 303
transformation/cleansing, 10
transformed data, 295

U

Uml, 310
Uml Extension Model, 310
Umx, 310
Unified Modeling Language Model, 310
unit-test phase, 59
units of measure, 18
UNIX, 80
URL, 276
user-centric, 317, 318, 320

V

value added service, 312

W

waterfall, graphic of software development
cycle, 37
waterfall approach, 35, 36, 53
shortcoming of, 37
waterfall development methodology, versus
software development spiral, 55
definition of, 59, 337
Web, 325
See also Internet
Web servers, 276, 278
Web-enabled data warehouse, 278, 280
Windows, 80
Word, 82